A
GAMEKEEPER'S
NOTE-BOOK

A PIPE OF PEACE

A GAMEKEEPER'S NOTE-BOOK

by
OWEN JONES
&
MARCUS WOODWARD

with an Introduction by
JOHN HUMPHREYS

EXCELLENT PRESS
LUDLOW

EXCELLENT PRESS
9 Lower Raven Lane
Ludlow
Shropshire
SY8 1BW

ISBN 13: 978 1 900318 167
ISBN 10: 1 900318 164

First published by Edward Arnold in 1910.

This edition published in 2002.
Introduction © 2002 by John Humphreys

Reprinted 2007

Printed in Great Britain

A GAMEKEEPER'S NOTE-BOOK

FOREWORD
BY JOHN HUMPHREYS

Of all the characters woven into the rich tapestry of rural life the gamekeeper is one of the most significant. He was a fearful ogre to small boys, trespassers and anyone he suspected had designs on his precious birds. A man apart, he did not visit the pub nor become too friendly with his fellow villagers. A loving shepherd to his feathered flock he was ruthless with hawks, crows and ground predators that might threaten his charges. A fustian figure in the gloaming, standing as motionless as an old stump and watching for weary hours, often the whole night long, his bible was the woods, streams and fields and there was little he did not know about the birds, beasts and fishes that lived and died there. A patch of undisturbed earth unnoticed by you and me told him what creature of the night had passed that way. The chatter of a blackbird warned him that a stoat was prowling, a pinch of grey rabbit belly fur on the grass told him that the first kits of the year had been born.

Not for nothing did Lady Chatterley find this icon of rusticity so compelling while Richard Jefferies immortalised him in one of the finest books about English country life, '*The Gamekeeper at Home*'. Secretive by nature 'old velveteens' took with him to a green mound in the village churchyard a wealth of knowledge that few normal mortals might accumulate in five lifetimes. Like many countrymen who dealt with life and death he accepted with resignation his own mortality. The pages that follow contain a treasure trove of secrets from the accumulated wisdom of the gamekeeper, prised from him by two authors almost a century ago. Books from the first decade of the last millennium are often creakingly wordy and riddled with olde-worlde notions. Remember that the Great War that took many keepers before their time lay but four years after publication.

This book is an exception, ahead of its time for it is written with a lightness of touch that belies the year in which it was published. It is jam full of little tips, fragments of countrymen's lore and scraps of wisdom, some of them dated, all of them fascinating. The ancients believed, for example, that the harmless nightjar was responsible for giving calves a disease they called puckeridge. The birds were seen wheeling round herds at night to catch the insects they disturbed and so received the blame. To make a reluctant dog retrieve a strong scented woodcock train him with an old baccy pouch. We learn the secret habits of, among a host of others, rats, sparrow hawks and broody hens, for those were the days of the pre-electric, open field rearing system. There is much that remains current for many of the great truths of the countryside are eternal. The predatory cat was vilified and this very day is again in the news for its fearful depredations. The friction between gamekeeper and fox preserver is as acerbic now as then. As now they spared hen pheasants after the Christmas shoot and debated long and earnestly about the mysterious habits of woodcock. In 1910 they had problems with their retrieving dogs and worried about impeding shooting parties; they watched the skies with an anxious eye for changes in the weather. Little has changed. The old keeper grew vegetables and supplemented his income as best he could for then as now he was not over generously paid.

Divided into four sections, one for each season of the year, this is a wonderful and fascinating book that will bring much pleasure to countryfolk of the 21st century who at heart still yearn for older and gentler times. Divided into bite-sized snippets, temptingly easy to dip into at the bedside, this rare and delightful collection of fascinating facts has for too long been unobtainable for to find a first edition would indeed be fortunate. I read my copy avidly and wish this re-publication the success it so richly deserves.

John Humphreys
June 2002

PREAMBLE

A gamekeeper's notes are written for the most part on the tablets of his mind. He is a man of silence; yet he is ever ready to unlock the casket of his memories if old friends, and sympathetic, are about him. We have known keepers who could talk, when so minded, as well as they could shoot, making their points as certainly as they would bowl over any straying cat that crossed their paths. But few keepers can handle a pen with the same confidence as a gun. Some keepers, it is true, carry note-books, and therein make certain brief notes—simple records and plain statements of fact, interesting enough to glance over, but nothing to read.

The vermin bag has an honourable place in these notes—year by year the keeper may set down precisely how many malefactors (and others) have fallen to his gun and traps. It is a record in which he takes almost as much pride as in his daily and yearly list of game; the grand total of a good season for game or vermin lingers for ever on his lips. The date of a shoot, the beat, the number and names of the guns, and what luck befell them, all may be noted with scrupulous care, with a word about the weather, perhaps, and possibly also on the benefits in cash received by the keeper at the day's end. Many carry little pocket note-books wherein they keep an account of dates and places—the date of all dates in the year being, of course, that on which the first wild pheasant's egg was found among the primroses. A page of the book may be filled with the names and nicknames of poachers caught, and a record of their transgressions and penalties. For the rest, for all the details that should clothe the nakedness of these briefly written words, one must go to the keeper's mind. And the best of all a keeper's notes are the ones he never jots down.

In this book the notes set out are culled chiefly from a series of genuine note-books, covering a certain keeper's ten years' experience of game-keeping and life-long experience in woodcraft: we have taken the rough jottings of his pocket books, and done our best with thoughts and memories to sketch in the foreground and background of his facts. Where he has merely noted, "April —, first wild pheasant's egg seen," we have tried to picture him as he set out hopefully expectant, and to describe his feelings as he found that egg, to him more precious than all others of the year. Where, again, he only says, "Saw cubs at play," we have sympathised with him as he noted what wings of partridges and pheasants, what legs of hares and bones of rabbits, littered the play-ground.

An abundant source of incident and story we have found in our dealings with many good gamekeeper friends, old men and young, some of them locally renowned as "characters," and all good sportsmen. We have elaborated many a note on gamekeepers themselves, about their wives and children, their cottages, their dreams, their ways of speech and their philosophic sayings, matters which no gamekeeper would trouble to record.

Should we be pressed to name the original author of the note-books from which our memories have been mainly refreshed, we should have to name one of our-selves: we would be excused. Together, we share the recollection of glad companionship through many a long night; and, above all, that magic interest in the countless phases of a gamekeeper's life and work covered by that wide word, Woodcraft.

O.J. and M.W.
September 1910

LIST OF CONTENTS

SPRING

SUMMER

AUTUMN

WINTER

SPRING

THE position of a gamekeeper in England is a curious one. Admittedly he is among the most skilled and highly trained workers of the country-side. His intimate knowledge of wild life commands respect. Often he is much more than a careful and successful preserver of game—a thoroughly good sportsman, a fine shot. His work carries heavy responsibility; as whether a large expenditure on a shooting property brings good returns—and on him depends the pleasure of many a sporting party. On large estates he is an important personage—important to the estate owner, to the hunt, to the farm bailiff, and to a host of satellites. His value is proved by the many important side-issues of his work—dog-breeding and dog-breaking, or the breaking of young gentlemen to gun work. Yet, in spite of the honourable and onerous nature of his calling, he is paid in cash about the same wage as a ploughman.

The Keeper's Lot

The actual wages of a first-class gamekeeper may be no more than a pound a week. A system has sprung

A

up by which he receives, in addition to wages, many recompenses in kind, while his slender pay is

Per-quisites

fortified by the tips of the sportsman to whom he ministers. This system has bred in him a kind of obsequiousness—he is dependent to a great extent on charity. With a liberal employer he may be well off, and all manner of good things may come his way ; but with a mean employer the perquisites of his position may be few and far between.

At the best, he may live in a comfortable cottage, rent free. His coal is supplied to him without cost, and wood from the estate. Milk is drawn freely from the farm—or he may have free pasturage for a cow of his own. A new suit of clothes is presented to him each year. He may keep pigs for his own use, usually at his own expense, but this is a small item, and even here he may be helped out by a surplus of pig-food from the kitchen of the house or from the farms. He has a fair chance to make money by dog-breeding and exhibiting. Then there is vermin and rabbit money which he earns as extra pay, and useful sums may flow into his pocket from the hunt funds. He may keep fowls at his employer's expense, and if not solely for his own use, he has the privilege of a proportion of the eggs, and a reasonable number of the chickens may be roasted or boiled for his own table. The estate gardeners aid him with his gardening operations, and many surplus plants and seeds find their way into his plot. To rabbits he may help himself freely, also to rooks and pigeons. After each shooting party his employer—if a generous master—invites him to take home a brace of pheasants and a hare ; and there may be other ways in which game comes to his larder. Commissions and fees of various indeterminate sorts may swell his coffers. All kinds of supplies he secures, if not freely, at reduced prices. And always there is the harvest of tips. Clearly there is every chance for a gamekeeper to receive charity of some form or another, if it is not always offered ; and this must tend to weaken that independence which is found by the man who is paid for his labour fairly and squarely in cash.

One usually sees a pretty assortment of pets about the keeper's cottage, where there are children. The keeper himself is not above a pet animal, **Pets at the Cottage** though he may not confess it—and, strange to say, the keeper's favourite is often a cat. But you may be sure it is a cat among cats, and without sin—an expert among rats, mice, and sparrows, yet able to sit for hours on the hole of a rabbit, or alone with a canary, and not yield to temptation. At one keeper's cottage a dormouse is to be seen—at this season he is broader than he is long. Here lives " Billy," a buff bantam cock, who will sit on your knee and take a mouthful of bread from your lips ; here also is " Tommy," a game-cock, who takes lunch and tea on the inside of the kitchen window-

ledge ; and here is " Sally," a goose that will lay
more than threescore eggs in the spring, lives on grass,
likes to explore the cottage's interior, and puts all
the dogs to shame as a guard, loudly proclaiming the
arrival of strangers.   In a coop on a lawn lives a white
rabbit, whose mission in life is to keep the grass short ;
this rabbit will not look at a carrot, but rejoices in
bread and milk, and above all in cold chicken.   In
the yard is a retriever, who is always careful to offer
you her right paw in greeting, loves blackberries, and
is the special friend of a little terrier.   Once there
was a pet lamb.   On many a little rough grassy
grave the keeper's child places wreaths of wild flowers.

❧   ❧   ❧

The shooting of pigeons is the keeper's special feather-
sport—he is always on the spot to take advantage
of favourable circumstances.   It goes on
**Wood-
Pigeons** in summer as in winter, and remembering the tremendous amount of damage done
to pea-fields, corn crops and roots by pigeons, there
is a justification for this shooting which cannot be
urged in favour of pheasant-shooting.   The keeper
understands the sport.   He knows the pigeons' habits
and feeding times, and that concealment is the secret
of success.   Lying at ease on the ground, with his
back to a tree-trunk, he waits in all patience for the
pigeons to come to their favourite trees.   Or, having
noted the part of the feeding-field where the birds
alight, he conceals himself in a hedge, or behind bushes

arranged by himself, so that from his butt he can shoot comfortably at any bird within range. As birds are shot he sets them up as decoys. A stick about nine inches long is put in the ground, and one pointed end inserted in the pigeon's throat, the bird being set up in a life-like way. Knowing that they are thirsty birds, especially when feeding on the ripe, hard grain, he builds a hut near the pond where the pigeons drink, and if he cannot see them on the ground or in the trees, creeps out to stalk them, and the shots they give as they rise, diving and turning in all directions, are such that no one need despise.

☙ ☙ ☙

Wood-pigeons are among the gamekeeper's perquisites. Apart from a very occasional request from "the house" for the wherewithal **The Keeper's Larder** for pigeon-pie, the pigeons shot are for the benefit of the keeper and his family, and when he shoots more than he requires there are always labourers and others glad of a pigeon or two "to make a pudden." Rabbits, also, are perquisites, but to be sold no more than pigeons. The popular idea is that keepers may help themselves to any game they please—true, they could if so minded. But no matter what a keeper's ethics in other directions, as a rule he deals honourably with the game in his charge. The keeper has no more right to take a brace of birds or a hare without permission than has an ironmonger's assistant to take a coal-scuttle.

There is little to be said against the keeper making use of game killed, but not eaten, by foxes or vermin, or of chance-killed game unsuitable for his employer's table.   One old keeper was so anxious to make every available pheasant figure in the game-book that he would never keep the brace given him at the end of a day's shooting.   Instead, he would include the birds with the bag on the following day, and this he would do day after day.

Free though they are to kill and cook rabbits, few keepers care for them, or eat them often.   Most keepers, indeed, would be as pleased to go to penal servitude, or to live in London, as to eat rabbits more often than once a month.   This is not because they have eaten too many, but because the smell of rabbits has become distasteful.   However, rabbits prove a great help to the keeper with children to feed.   Usually his larder is well stocked, and his good-wife has a store of all kinds of dainties in her cupboards—from home-made pickles to home-brewed wine.   Often your keeper is a clever gardener; he takes prizes for his vegetables, and he will grow fine cucumbers and even melons under fragments of glass.   Something of a cook himself, well accustomed to preparing luxurious meals for his sacred birds, he is a judge of cooks and cooking, as many a keeper's wife has discovered.   If she does not know, he can tell her how to prepare a savoury dish which shall have the special advantages of not spoiling through being kept warm or from being warmed up—for the keeper's dinner is a movable feast, and must be ready at any time between noon and night. The sheet-anchor of one such dish is proper home-cured bacon, in winter baked in a pie-dish with alternate layers of parboiled potatoes, for which in summer the contents of eggs beaten just enough to blend the yolks and whites are substituted. Served with new potatoes, it is the very dish to put heart in a man.

☙ ❧ ☙

The gamekeeper is among the few people left in the country who have any knowledge of herb-lore, and

Homely Medicines faith in home-brewed herbal remedies. His medicine-chest contains a varied assortment. From rose-pink centaury he boils an appetising tonic for his pheasants, which he is not above drinking himself. The roots of couch-grass provide him with a powerful emetic for dogs in the first stages of distemper. He bakes acorns, grinds them to powder, and with its aid quells a rebellious stomach. His good-wife has the secret of cowslip and nettle tea. From the pounded leaves of dock blended with lard, he prepares a salve for cuts. Rheumatism, from which all keepers suffer in their old age, is treated with the fat of hedgehogs, well rubbed in—not that this is a herbal remedy. Cramp in pheasants calls for cayenne pepper boiled in their food; chopped onions are for gape-worms; a little saffron with drinking water—as much as will lie on a threepenny-bit in the water for a thousand birds—

assists young birds through the troubles of feather-growing; while the first moult is aided by a few crystals of sulphate of iron in water. But oil is the sovereign remedy : castor-oil for dogs out of sorts, oil of almonds for the glued eyelids of blind birds, linseed-oil and laudanum for gapes—oil of every kind for every purpose. With corn scented with oil of rhodium-wood the keeper lays a trail which every pheasant must follow.

☙   ☙   ☙

The reward paid to keepers from the funds of fox-hunts is a sovereign for a litter of cubs when hounds come cub-hunting. Ten shillings is paid **The Earth-Stoppers' Feast** for each fox found by hounds. And a florin is the keeper's usual reward for stopping earths when the meet is within a distance of four miles. These moneys are paid in round sums on a great occasion in the keeper's year —the earth-stoppers' dinner. In olden days keepers were full of resources for benefiting themselves from the hunt funds, while saving their pheasants' skins from foxes at the same time. The cunning keeper would induce a huntsman to pay a stealthy unofficial visit to the home of a litter, and after his departure, when a reward had been made sure, would quietly take steps to rid himself of fox troubles. Visiting the earth with a supply of sulphur matches and bags of grass, he would light the matches within, block the holes with the bags, and leave the deadly fumes to do their work. Or two keepers would combine to defraud the hunt. One would show a litter and pocket his sovereign, then shift the litter to the preserves of his friend, who in turn would call in the huntsman and pocket his reward, then return the cubs whence they came ; and so the game would go on. Luck plays a great part in this matter of fox-rewards. It often happens that foxes which have been harboured honestly by one keeper are found in the preserves of another who is a vulpicide, yet is not above accepting the reward which really is the due of his scrupulous friend in the next parish. How to show foxes to the hunt and pheasants to a shooting party is the prickliest of all the manifold problems of the gamekeeper's life.

❧   ❧   ❧

The gamekeeper, like many a countryman, would be at a loss without his garden. His little plot of land means much to him : green food for his table, tonic foods for his pheasants, and a place where, by digging, he may bury some of his cares. He knows no such exercise as digging for keeping away ill-humours. He believes that the more a man sows the more he will reap—it is a lesson daily brought home to him. So he puts his best work into his garden, which is often the model plot of a rural community. In March he divides his time between spade work and his never-ending war on vermin. If he has a pen of stock

The
Keeper's
Garden

pheasants he spends a good many minutes a day in admiration of the birds, besides tending to their wants ; and he will defy you to prove that you ever saw a finer lot of birds. " Look at that old cock up agen yon corner—ain't 'e got some 'orns ? Bless ye, them birds is worth a pound apiece."

So many a March afternoon finds the keeper hard at work at home with spade, fork, trowel or dibbler. His great object is to finish the more laborious work before the time of pheasants' eggs. A feature of the garden is the neat and spacious onion-bed, smoothed with the polished back of a favourite spade, which has dug out countless rabbits. There must be plenty of onions for the young pheasants to come. In time of need a keeper may sacrifice the whole of his onion-bed to his birds, gladly buying such onions as his wife demands for the table. Then there are two or three long rows of peas. Before sowing, the seed is sprinkled with red lead against the ravages of long-tailed field-mice, and after sowing strands of black thread are carried up and down the surface against the attacks of sparrows, while above, as a terrible warning, swings the body of a sparrow-hawk. The site of an old pheasant pen is devoted to Brussels sprouts. A dilapidated dog-kennel will serve to coax rhubarb to be ready for Easter Sunday's dinner.

Flower seeds are not forgotten : in shallow cartridge-boxes, protected by a small home-made frame, seeds are sown for making the little patch of flower-garden gay with stocks and asters, sweet peas, sun-

flowers, tobacco-plants, and zinnias. The keeper
puzzles over zinnia seed, which is like the fragment
of a dead leaf, yet will come up and grow with the
speed of mustard and cress, producing a wealth of
bloom.

But the planting of the potato patch is the chief
work. The neat little furrows which mark each row
of potatoes, allowing the hoe to be plied fearlessly
before the potatoes show above ground, give a neat-
ness to the cottage garden all the time while the soil
is brown and bare.

Gamekeepers, though their work for wages is
never done, yet have a few legitimate ways of adding
to their incomes. Of course they have the opportunity
of making a good deal of money if they trespass on
their employers' time; but your keeper is an honest
man, and his work is the object of his life. Most
keepers are skilled vegetable gardeners, and may
make a few shillings from peas and beans. Often
enough they have a cunning way with flowers, though
envious amateurs are free with their hints about the
advantages to be gained from burying foxes to enrich
the soil. We know one who will put in a fair day's
work with spade and wheelbarrow before even the
waggoners have stirred to give their horses breakfast.
Going his rounds, the keeper marks good briers for
budding; if he does not sell them, he will beg choice
buds from rose-growers, and a year or two later the
passer-by may be tempted to offer half-a-crown for
the fine roses of his little plot. Possibly by this time

his roses mean so much to him that he will make some such excuse as, " The missus, she thinks a mortal sight of they."

☙   ☙   ☙

In February a few lucky gamekeepers may take a voluntary holiday, many must take an involuntary one—restful, perhaps, but not beneficial to pocket, health, and spirits. Keepers come and keepers go in these days when so many shoots are let for short terms. Resting between berths has one advantage—there can be no haunting worry as to the welfare of game. It would be interesting to collect cases of keepers and other country workers who have held the same berth for long periods, and have never been for a holiday right away from the scenes of their labours. Many and many old keepers would be found to have lived their whole lives on the estates where they were born. The best holiday for keepers would be a change to a bustling town ; or they should be sent to a country where game is different to the game at home, the partridge man going to the home of grouse, the moorland keeper to the South.

Keepers' Holidays

Most keepers would be the first to say it is impossible that they should take holiday. Their work is peculiarly personal ; and even when it is essential to arrange for somebody else to " give an eye to things," they can never feel happy and confident that all is going on in the accustomed way. The

work, too, is cumulative—each item must be considered in its relation to several others.   Even where
there are several keepers, each on his own beat of a
shoot, there is a jealous rivalry between them ; and
any one who went for a holiday would suspect advantage to be taken of his stock of breeding game in his
absence.   If there is one thing a keeper can endure
less than being scored off by a poacher, it is to be scored
off by a brother keeper.

☙   ☙   ☙

For the first time in many a long year a gamekeeper may find himself taking a holiday in the early
days of February—either because he has
An Advant- left his place of his own free will, or has been
age of
Marriage dismissed.   " Left owing to shoot being
given up "—that is the usual reason for a
keeper's enforced holiday.   Married keepers seldom
leave berths of their own accord except to better
themselves ; but a young bachelor keeper with a light
heart may be fond of change, and scores of places are
open to him from which married men are barred.
Often he can afford to take a holiday while he looks
about for a new berth ; he can find lodgings anywhere, and what with odd jobs and the money he has
saved he can exist comfortably until he finds an
employer to suit him.   The married keeper is not so
light-hearted, and perhaps on this account the best
permanent berths go to the married men.   The
chance of such a berth gives the country maiden her

best chance of bagging an elusive bachelor. Sometimes she captures the heart of a bachelor before he has found a berth that will support a wife ; then he will advertise for a place, making the ambiguous statement : " Married when suited." No doubt some keepers who have issued this form of advertisement could tell strange stories of the applications received.

❦   ❦   ❦

When going out to look at a place where the chance of a berth has offered itself, the keeper always takes

The Keeper seeks a New Berth good stock of the game in the country through which he passes. You may meet him, at the end of the season, setting out by road or by rail ; he is clad in his best, you will see ; bright new gaiters encase his legs, his boots glitter with polish. However great his hurry, as he goes along through park-lands or woods, he is looking out for everything to be seen ; not a sign of game escapes him. And there lives a keeper who, passing through an estate on his way to a personal interview with the owner, chanced to be led out of the direct path by certain suspicious sounds which he heard, and caught a poacher redhanded. It is hardly necessary to add that he stepped forthwith into the vacant berth.

❦   ❦   ❦

Many long leagues separate the moor-keeper of the North from the keeper of South-country preserves ;

their eyes look out upon different worlds; the two
men are as different in type, in ideas, and in methods
as the North is different to the South, the
In North and South open, rolling moor to the jungle-like
covert. There are certain matters on which
they agree—as in their mutual hatred
of foxes; the moor-keeper, when the season is
out, has no hesitation in killing all foxes and vermin
within his power. He has an advantage over his
brother in some things; as in nesting-sites. The
heather affords an unlimited number of well-concealed
places for grouse nests, whereas in Hampshire or
Sussex a nesting hedgerow after the heart of pheasant
or partridge is likely to be overcrowded, and to
attract every sort of egg-thief. Again, he has an
advantage in his natural and abundant food-supplies;
though much of his success in raising a stock of
healthy birds will depend on his judgment in burning old heather, and insuring a plentiful growth
of young shoots. When heather is late in starting to
grow, and birds are forced to feed on old, dry shoots,
digestive troubles may prove fatal to many.

Poachers on the moor differ in many habits and
tricks from South-country poachers. They know
how to trap grouse with gins, setting up little
Poachers— piles of gravel, which the birds eagerly seek
for digestive reasons, and besetting the gravel with
traps. They know how to trap grouse in winter

without causing them injury ; this they do by pressing a bottle into hard snow, thus shaping a hole-trap (to be baited with oats) from which the grouse cannot escape, having fallen into it head first. But on the whole the sneaking type of poacher has fewer chances on the moor than in the pheasant coverts.

❦   ❦   ❦

A poacher owns to a dog, so marvellously trained that his master can send it for anything—but at the least sign of anybody watching its movements, or at the approach of a gamekeeper or a policeman, the dog drops whatever it may be carrying, makes off for cover, and hides itself.   The dog has many rivals to fame of this sort.   We knew a poacher whose plan it was to dawdle along the road in his pony-cart while his lurcher foraged in the fields.   But at a certain signal the dog would come instantly to heel ; on suspecting danger, all the master did was to lift his cap, and scratch his head in the most unconcerned manner in the world.   When once a dog grasps the meaning of a signal, he will obey it faithfully in all circumstances if he is kept in practice.   In the olden days, in the Netherlands, dogs were trained to smuggle, and without attendants.   They were sent off on a journey at night, loaded with goods, the keenest-nosed dog leading, and at the moment when he sighted or scented a custom-house official, he would turn back as a signal to the whole pack to rush off to cover, and hide

And their Dogs

until the danger passed. This is vouched for in an old work, " Brown on Dogs."

❦   ❦   ❦

Probably there would be no great difficulty in training a dog to drop a hare, or anything else, at the approach of somebody other than its master. Dogs are sometimes trained to lie down, without receiving any signal or order, when their owners meet friends and stop to talk. One old gamekeeper would consider his dogs to be very ill-mannered if they did not lie down of their own accord when he stopped walking. Another keeper has trained his dog to quite an out-of-the-way trick, which is to the keeper's personal advantage, if highly detrimental to his duties. The trick is for the dog, on command, to spit from his mouth any food he may be eating. The keeper will take his dog to a public-house, and set the example of throwing him biscuits, which he will eat greedily. He will then make a boast about the dog's obedience (in the shooting field, by the way, we have never known a more disobedient animal, though he is exceedingly clever). Eventually the keeper wagers a pint of beer to a quart that the dog not only will cease eating biscuits on command, but will eject any crumbs from his mouth, and not touch them again until so ordered. Many a pot of beer has the dog won for his master by this trick. When the two go home, it is the dog that finds the way.

B

In February the gamekeeper's thoughts and energies are turned mostly in the way of vermin and trapping.

And where vermin is really plentiful it is **The Black List** a wonderful wild sport that he enjoys in tracking and trapping the creatures of his black list. In the North the vermin bag is more mixed than in the South, and in the olden days contained such a great variety of creatures as to suggest that the keepers enjoyed better sport than their masters. They were ruthless in their war on all that they held to be enemies to game ; how ruthless may be judged from the following list of vermin, bagged in three years by a famous keeper on Glengarry, Inverness-shire. It indicates the proportion of the different sorts of animals classed as vermin found in the Highlands in the middle days of the last century : 11 foxes, 198 wild cats, 246 martens, 106 polecats, 301 stoats and weasels, 67 badgers, 48 otters, 78 house cats going wild, 27 white-tailed sea eagles, 15 golden eagles, 18 ospreys, 98 blue hawks or peregrine falcons, 7 orange-legged falcons, 211 hobby hawks, 75 kites, 5 marsh harriers, 63 goshawks, 285 common buzzards, 371 rough-legged buzzards, 3 honey buzzards, 462 kestrels, 78 merlin hawks, 83 hen harriers, 6 gerfalcons, 9 ash-coloured or long blue-tailed hawks, 1431 carrion crows, 475 ravens, 35 horned owls, 71 common fern owls (nightjars), 3 golden owls, 8 magpies. A total of nearly 5000 head, giving an average of more than 1500 head a year, or about five head a day. The list, strangely enough, does not contain a single jay, rat, or hedge-hog.

⚘ ⚘ ⚘

A Southern keeper's list of about the same period—from 1869 to 1878—shows a total of just over 8000 head. In the year that saw the greatest destruction of hawks—nearly all sparrow-hawks and kestrels—46 were killed. The greatest number of magpies killed in a year was 205. Probably cats were not very carefully counted—their numbers in different years rise from 47 to 122. Usually more than 100 squirrels were killed each year. And over 100 carrion crows were killed yearly. But jays headed all lists in numbers sacrificed ; the largest bag of 346 was made in '78, evidently when the influence of the breach-loader was beginning to make itself felt. Hedgehogs suffered least persecution among the keeper's sup-posed enemies, only 6 going into the bag in one year —45 was the highest hedgehog loss. Exclusive of rats, this keeper, a Hampshire man, waged war on nine species only, whereas the Inverness-shire keeper destroyed as vermin thirty-one different kinds of birds and beasts. The lists make no mention of rooks. To-day, on the Southern estate to which the list of thirty years ago refers, not a crow or a magpie is left, and the persecution has told heavily on the sparrow-hawks, and many another kind. The present keeper's sport with vermin is as different to his predecessors' as

A South-Country Record

the sport of his master to his master's ancestors—to-day about 300 pheasants are bagged on this estate in the course of a big day's shooting, instead of the 30 birds that would have been a good bag in the olden times.

❦   ❦   ❦

In olden days the gamekeeper set up his vermin gallows in each of his big woods. It was to his credit to show that he had killed a large amount of vermin ; on his gallows he wrote his own testimonial. Nearly all the vermin he killed was duly displayed. But now the day of the gallows is passing. Keepers have little time to give to the display ; nor do employers always encourage it. The gallows foster a growing feeling against the destruction of wild life involved by the preservation of game, and lead to bitter, if often mis-judged attacks. Keepers are contenting themselves with modified forms of gallows, as the trunk of a tree, to which the heads, tails or claws of the male-factors are nailed. These small gallows do not speak of the keeper's successful war-waging in the bold manner of the old-fashioned, full-measure pattern. But there is much in their favour. As one old keeper remarked of his tree-trunk gallows, the faint odour was only enough to set-off the scent of the flowers.

Woodland Gallows

To the gallows comes a varied bag of robbers. The vermin list of a typical North-country estate included in a recent season 133 stoats, 36 weasels, 62 cats, 98 rats, 115 hedgehogs, 10 hawks, 381 jack-

daws, 82 rooks, 23 carrion crows, and 52 magpies—
a total of nearly a thousand head.   The rats included
would probably only be those caught incidentally
in the vermin traps, not the far greater number killed
during special campaigns by ferret, gun and dog.
Hedgehogs are usually spared the indignity of the
gallows.   Though a keeper cheerfully carries a stoat
in the pockets of his Sunday coat—and we have
known him in an emergency to put a fox into his
pocket—he knows that to pocket hedgehogs means
the entertainment of their numerous and active de-
pendants.   Of cats only the tails are exhibited, and
they are discreetly chosen, the keeper avoiding very
striking tails that might be recognised.   It would
be bad policy on his part to advertise dead cats too
freely.   He has no desire to make enemies.

⚘   ⚘   ⚘

Though kestrels, unhappily, are still brought to
the gallows, with the barn-owl and other creatures
innocent of injury to game, keepers grow
more discriminating in the matter of vermin.
The Gallows Martyrs Education has had its effect—it has taught
the men to think, and to act according to
reason rather than convention.   The old men remain
obstinate, and we remember how vainly we wasted
an hour's good argument on one old fellow who
seemed to hold badgers chiefly responsible for his
ruined game-nests.   It was at a keepers' dinner, an
annual entertainment given by the Hunt.   Only one

badger remained out of a colony that formerly had inhabited our friend's preserves ; and he expressed a firm intention of " fetching her hout on it." In a rash moment he went so far as to declare that he would prefer three litters of fox cubs to one of badgers. Overhearing this, the Hunt secretary made a good point by saying : " Very well, my friend ; if you kill this badger, next time hounds come your way we shall expect to find at least three litters of cubs." It was notorious that every fox seen on this keeper's ground was, according to him, a mangy one and therefore " best put out of the way."

❦ ❦ ❦

Some creatures, after they have been trapped and have escaped, learn the lesson of their lives, and are never trapped again, while others find no **Once** moral at the end of their adventure, and live **Trapped,** to adorn the gallows. It is very seldom that **Twice** **Shy** a rat is trapped twice. Scores escape from traps at the expense of a leg ; this is a common matter, but a man may trap vermin for a lifetime and yet never catch a three-legged rat. Stoats, on the other hand, far less cunning than rats, are often trapped again after escaping with the loss of a foot. We have known a stoat trapped by its last remaining leg, after having been about for a long time on one leg and three stumps. A keeper who was at special pains to preserve the foxes on his ground was much upset by the way in which his neighbours killed them.

One year his anxiety for his cubs was so great that he caught them all in weak gins—and released them. He knew that after this experience the cubs would never allow themselves to be again caught in a gin. On the same principle, keepers sometimes net and release their own partridges, hares and rabbits, to save them from falling into the meshes of poachers. In the ordinary way, the fox is never caught in a trap set for other vermin—or foxes would have been extinct years ago. If they could be trapped as easily as the ordinary cat, twenty-four hours would be enough for catching every fox in the country.

❦　❦　❦

The skilled trapper, setting a baited trap for vermin, places it at such a distance from the bait that the creature he wishes to catch cannot reach the **Cunning Trappers** food without treading on the pan. Just when it can reach the prize is the moment when it is most likely to overstep the safety-line : desire overcomes suspicion. A fox, if so minded, can reach over the pan, and take the bait of a trap properly set for vermin, without risking a pad. Yet he seldom takes a bait : he detects the scent of man for a longer time than a trap is likely to remain unvisited. A keeper with an experience of more than twelve years vouches for it that though he used a hundred traps for vermin he never lost a bait through a fox, nor the Hunt a fox through a bait. But one keeper surpassed the cunning of the fox. A certain fox had troubled him greatly by too frequent visits to his poultry-run. He decided to attempt to trap it at the bottom of a chalk-pit near by, where the fox went to eat his suppers. Before setting his trap he sacrificed some half-dozen chickens on different days, with a two-fold object : in order to practise throwing a chicken from the top of the chalk-pit so that it should fall exactly where he desired, and in order to cause the fox to expect to find a meal in the pit. One fine day he set his trap. Then he bided his time until his scent should have passed away : and after four or five days he killed another chicken. Making his way to the top of the chalk-pit, he threw the chicken into a bush at the bottom, where the fox could reach it only by treading on the pan of the trap, which it did that night, at the cost of its life.

February is the month when it is fashionable for stoats and weasels to begin courting. The keeper finds the trapping of stoats or weasels **The Time to Catch a Weasel** less difficult work than usual in conse-quence. He maintains that all is fair in love, war, and gamekeeping. He relies chiefly on tunnel-traps. The old way was to fix a long, low, narrow box in a likely run—a box open at each end, but with shutters which dropped when a pan in the middle of the floor was touched by a weasel's feet ; so the weasel would be caught alive, without injury—only, however, to be executed.

Another old-time trap was the figure 4 trap, set with a heavy stone or slate, which fell upon and instantly killed its victim.   These cumbersome and not always reliable traps have passed from the woodlands, and now the keeper merely slips a gin into the entrance of a tunnel.   This is made sometimes of earth and sticks, or is a drain-pipe, or is made of three lengths of plank, about a yard long and six inches wide.   A hole in a hedge-bank is a favourite place for the gin.   These tunnel traps are commonly set a few yards from the end of a hedge, because stoats and weasels have a weakness for cutting corners.

We have heard the suggestion many times that there are two varieties of the common weasel, but think this

Changes of Coats

is not the case.   The mistake no doubt arises from the marked difference in size between the males and females;   the dog weasel is twice or sometimes three times the size of its sister, and is nearly as big as a small female stoat, while the dog weasel's sister may be hardly larger than a big mouse.   Then the changes in the weasel's coat are deceptive.   In spring a rusty red fur takes the place of the soft winter brown of the upper parts, while the white under-parts turn to a yellow tone.   The ordinary brown of rats also changes to a striking rusty red shade in spring.   This is most obvious in the case of rats living in burrows in soil, and often going short of food, and the rusty fur is specially marked on rats that have been feeding on carrion sheep and lambs. Shortness of food has the effect of prolonging the business of coat-changing, as is well seen in the case of a ferret kept on short commons. A white ferret is deep yellow in the spring before it has changed its coat. Stoats, too, show yellow on parts which will be white in the new coat.

❧   ❧   ❧

We met, by chance, an old keeper who, on first acquaintance, seemed a remarkable specimen—for he informed us that his orders were to set not a single trap anywhere on his ten thousand acres. Thinking that we saw a movement of his eyelid, we put the blunt question to him : How many traps did he usually set ? And he replied unblushingly, " Forty dozen." He kept no record of his bag of vermin ; but as he trapped on such a whole-sale scale (remembering that the estate is supposed to be trapless), no doubt his employer would be startled if he knew the numbers of vermin killed ; his vermin bag must be exceptional. The old-fashioned keeper is stubborn ; the kestrel, as we have said before, is seen too often on his gibbet, and he has no respect for the useful wood-owl, which he ruthlessly exter-minates. A record of a year's bag of vermin on one big estate reads thus : Jays, 350 ; magpies, 160 ; crows, 150 ; squirrels, 140 ; weasels, 80 ; cats, 70 ; stoats, 60 ; hedgehogs, 40 ; hawks, 30 ; total, 1080. This record says nothing of rats, rooks or owls,

The Vermin Bag

though no doubt numbers of rats and rooks were
sacrificed.

♀   ♀   ♀

The gamekeeper whose bag of vermin in a year included 140 squirrels is, we may hope, exceptional.

The Ways of Squirrels Squirrels are not always treated by keepers
as vermin.   Now and again a squirrel has
been proved guilty of meddling with the eggs
and young of pheasants—but so rarely that
even keepers speak of these misdeeds as " not worth
mentioning."   The traditional crime of squirrels is
that they damage various sorts of coniferous trees by
nipping their shoots when young.   Even if they gave
this work all their time and attention, their numbers
in the woods to-day are so small that the whole
damage done would not amount to a very great injury
to the country.

Squirrels are the most innocent creatures in the
woods, so far as any harm to game preserving goes.
It is their misfortune that many keepers look upon
them as a convenient form of ferret-food.   We have
found a freshly killed squirrel, apparently the victim
of a bird of prey, beneath a spruce fir, from which a
barn owl flew as we examined the body ; no doubt
owls would take a chance to attack a squirrel.   As to
what squirrels kill there is little evidence.   We have
known a squirrel to do away with part of a brood of
tits in an apple-tree, and one which visited a pheasant's
nest, carrying away an egg, and once we saw a young

pheasant in a squirrel's mouth ; but we have no doubt that the bird was picked up dead. The squirrel's alarm-cry reminds us of the sound produced from the hole in the body of a rubber doll ; it is amusing to see how he stamps his fore-feet while uttering this cry, as if doing his best to frighten away his human intruder by a show of force and fury.

Squirrels always seem to be among the happiest of wild animals. They have few foes, and none to equal their agility and speed in the tree branches. The stoat is a good climber, and if he were to attack the squirrel's nest there would be small chance for the young ones ; but stoats rarely climb so high. In the bitterest weather the squirrel is secure in his drey ; he dreams away the hard days, while around him birds and animals die of cold and hunger. His only trouble seems to be that hazel-nuts are sometimes blighted.

We know an old keeper who believes that squirrels eat everything eatable in a wood, and that nothing does more damage to his interests. He **The Squirrel's Appetite** reviles squirrels bitterly, saying that they steal as many of his precious eggs as rats ; the eggs of small birds too, and, on occasion, nestlings. There seems no end to his accusations. He declares squirrels will take strawberries and apricots if they have the chance, and that they eat mushrooms and dig up truffles. A favourite

food is supplied by the Scotch pine ; though in hot
weather larch, silver fir, and spruce are added in liberal
quantities to the dietary.   While he rejoices in hazel-
nuts, beech-mast, acorns, and spruce-seeds, he is
sometimes tempted by berries, walnuts, and apples.
He eats freely off buds and young shoots, and peels the
bark off trees—digging a spiral course with his teeth
near the top of the tree, so that the first strong
gale blows over the tree-top.   It is the sweet stuff between bark and tree, rather than the bark itself, that
attracts his fancy.   In the spring he plays havoc with
the tender shoots of the horse-chestnut, showering
them on the ground ; while he is so fond of acorns
that he is accused even of pulling up young oak plants
to devour the remains of the acorns below.   But we
doubt that one squirrel in ten inflicts serious injury on
anybody.

We suppose that more cats disappear from the
domestic hearth in February than in any other month.
The Departure of Cats   The gamekeeper may or may not know
more about this than he will admit—it is
certain that the cats go, and it is true that
many of them turn up again.   Whatever
the February fate of the cat, the nearest keeper to its
home bears the blame of having spirited it away.   He
may deny all—that he knows anything about the cat
or its colour or its fate—but the more he denies the
more strongly will he be suspected, the more furiously

accused.   One old keeper met all inquiries about the departure of cats with this sound piece of wisdom : " If ye makes 'em bide at 'ome, there won't be no need for wantin' 'em to come back."

☙ ☙ ☙

New times give the keeper new excuses.   Taxed with a cat's disappearance, he blames the motor-car ; some day he will blame the flying-ship ; where a
Skeletons railway is at hand he always has a ready
and
Cobwebs excuse.   We would be the last to suggest that when the mortal remains of a cat are found on a road frequented by motor-cars the presumption is always justified that the cat was slain by a keeper who endeavoured to put the blame on an innocent driver.   We are confident that many cats in game-preserved places live to die from old age.   Ten years is a ripe age for a cat, but some die from accidents more natural than execution or murder.   Like the birds, when they know their hours to be numbered, cats creep away to some quiet hiding-place to await death—perhaps beneath the floor of an old barn, or among the rafters of a familiar roof, where they hunted rats and mice in youthful days.

Now and again, in old buildings, death-chambers are discovered where the skeletons of cats have been hidden among cobwebs and dust, perhaps for hundreds of years.

☙ ☙ ☙

Magpies will soon be exterminated in many parts of the country unless they receive special protection.

Like sparrow-hawks, the tribe suffers collectively for the sins of the individual. The ordinary magpie is no more harmful to the interests of game than the ordinary rook. His beauty, certainly, is far more striking. But he has been given a bad name; and magpies are destroyed on every possible occasion. The keeper finds the magpie only too easy to destroy, in spite of the bird's wonderful keenness of eye and his wary ways.

Magpies go year after year to the same huge, domed nest. The birds may be trapped a hundred times more easily than sparrow-hawks; and they may be shot without any difficulty, so slow, laboured and straight is their flight. An imitation of their call lures them unsuspiciously to their doom. Add that the plumage is showy, and it is clear that the thoughtless keeper finds magpies easy targets.

They are in demand as cage-birds, and even if a keeper should reprieve a few lingering pairs, he is likely to complain of " they bird fanciers," who " won't let the birds bide."

Like all of its tribe, the magpie attacks the eye of its victims, whether alive or dead. His taste is for carrion, and this accounts for the ease with which he may be trapped. Here the magpies differ from the hawks, which are seldom to be caught by a dead bait, unless killed by themselves—as when they have been disturbed after a kill and return to an unfinished feast. In trapping for magpies, the keeper ties a rabbit's eye to the pan of his trap, which he covers carefully with moss so that only the eye is visible; then the magpie swoops down; unerringly, and with great force, he drives his bill into the eye, and the trap holds him fast.

While usually building in high trees, some descend to thick bushes, and from this has arisen a popular idea that there are two sorts of magpies—bush and tree. The idea is hard to shake; and it is argued that the bush magpie is the smaller of the two. The nest is always fortified with strong and ugly thorns; marauding crows or rooks would attack it at their peril. Careful as they are to protect their own nests, magpies have small respect for the sanctity of other bird homes; but though they are inveterate egg-stealers, a good word is sometimes heard for their usefulness in destroying slugs, rats, and field-mice.

No solution has been found to the problem of a substitute for the steel trap for rabbits and vermin.

The Merciful Trap So the steel trap remains a painful necessity, as those know who have tried to keep great numbers of rabbits within bounds. But steel traps are sometimes used where more merciful ways of catching rabbits might serve as well. Rabbit catchers who never think for themselves, but do things only because they have always

done them, will use steel traps where they could save
themselves much labour, and the rabbits a good deal
of suffering, if they were to use snares. Several
hundred snares can be set in the time it would take
to set a hundred traps, and the snares cost little,
and weigh next to nothing—a consideration when
traps or snares have to be carried a long way. A
few traps make a heavy load.

❦   ❦   ❦

Snares themselves are far from ideal. If they
are properly set a good many rabbits may run into
them at speed and kill themselves almost
The　　　instantly ; but the majority of the rabbits
Rabbit in　caught will not be thus neatly despatched.
a Snare
Half a night's catch may be found dead
in the morning, some having been hanged out-
right, others strangled more or less slowly ; but half
will be found still living, if nearly dead. This slow
strangulation is prevented when a knot is made in
the snare, or some sort of ring or washer is attached,
so that the wire cannot be drawn tight enough to
prevent the rabbit breathing ; but no rabbit then is
killed swiftly and mercifully by the wire, and on
other accounts the plan could not prove a real solution to the problem. There is still another way of
setting a snare which prevents a slow death : a
bender—a springy stick of hazel or ash about four
feet long—is fixed firmly in the ground : the snare
is made fast to the thin top of it, the stick is bent

c

down, and the top lightly inserted at the edge of the rabbit's run.   When a rabbit then rushes into the snare, the bender flies up, swinging him off his feet, so that he is killed quickly.   This is a poacher's dodge to prevent rabbits from squealing when caught : it can be practised only in an open place.   There are many situations where the steel trap is the only means of dealing with the rabbit pest, and must be used perforce until a substitute is found—unless man is to give way to rabbits.   We do not think that any gamekeeper uses steel traps for rabbits unnecessarily.

❦   ❦   ❦

The gamekeeper perhaps sees more of sleeping birds than most people; and makes many interesting mental notes of the resting habits of creatures in his woods.   He observes that perch-roosting birds always rest with their heads to the wind.   If when a high wind is blowing a rook alights on the home-tree, he swings his head into the wind before settling.   So when the wood-pigeons come home with the wind behind them they pass over their roosting trees, then beat up into the wind.   This is done to defeat the force of the wind, which might prevent the bird alighting where desired, or might blow him from his perch.   At rest, the bird doubles the knees, as it were, which causes the toes to contract, the weight of the body resting chiefly on the breast and on the out-spread wings—not on the eggs, if in a nest.   The birds' legs and feet have sinews which work an auto-

The Sleep of Birds

matic locking action of the claws, so that, roosting
with knees doubled up, the feet grip the branch
unfailingly. On rough nights, the pheasants take
the precaution of roosting in lower branches than
usual. If a strong gale springs up after a bird has gone
to roost on an exposed tree, it may be driven to seek
a berth on the ground—and to the wind that does no
good to the pheasant the passing fox owes his supper.

Some birds seem always half-awake. Wild-fowlers
will strike a match at night to test the question of the
presence or absence of wild duck in the distant creek ;
if present, an instant quacking will betray them.
Pheasants seem ever vigilant, and on the darkest
night it is difficult to stalk them unawares, however
quietly you move. If you come within a hundred
yards of guinea-fowl at night they will raise the
alarm. They excel at talking in their sleep. Sparrow
catchers know that directly their nets touch one part of
an ivy-covered wall birds fly out from another. But
some birds, such as the wrens when cuddling in a
hole in the thatch, seem to sleep soundly. And while
we have found that on striking a match beneath a
tree where wild pigeons were roosting they have
flown out at once with a clatter of wings, a pigeon-
lover in London informs us that his city birds, roosting
on his window-ledge, lose their wariness by night,
and will hold their own in face of a candle, while a
hand is outstretched to touch their necks.

As the day closes in, the partridges seek some sheltered, dry-lying hollow in the fields, and a covey of

twenty birds will huddle on a spot a yard in diameter. The colder the weather the closer they roost. The birds on the edge of the ring have their breasts outwards. Sometimes, by the way, it is unfortunate for partridges and pheasants that the positions of their nests prevent them from flying to and fro. Having to force their way through tangled undergrowth, a trail is left for the fox to follow home. The barn-door fowl, in captivity, may walk from her nest ; but when in possession of a stolen nest abroad, she resumes the flying habit. Fowls suffer frequently from deformed breast-bones, perhaps from roosting when their bones are young and soft. That they and their cocks are not heavy sleepers most people have cause to know.

☙   ☙   ☙

Wild animals asleep fall into graceful attitudes. The fox curls himself up with all the luxurious air of a cat ; he rests his head in the lap of the two front pads, then twines his brush neatly round over his long, pointed nose. He is a light sleeper ; but hares and rabbits are still more easily roused. We believe hares sleep with their eyes wide open ; the uncapped lenses of the eyes remain active through sleep, so that any vision of danger conveys an automatic alarm to the brain. People are sometimes puzzled when, in open fields, they notice a dozen or more hare forms or beds within a few yards of each other. They may conclude that

Animals at Rest

hares swarm in those fields. Probably the reason
for the many forms is that a hare likes to face the
wind when sleeping, and so scratches out many beds
to suit the wind's changing directions. Among
animals that sleep very soundly is the hedgehog—
he has little to fear when asleep ; in case of danger,
he has only to erect his spines, to discourage effectively any disturber of his dreams. While hedgehogs,
dormice, and badgers sleep deeply through the greater
part of the winter, the squirrel is the lightest of
sleepers ; on dry, bright winter days he enjoys a frolic
in the snow.

It is commonly held that fieldfares roost on the
ground ; yet we never remember to have disturbed
them when roosting in that way, but have
Vigilant Fulfers often done so in the woods, in which they
had favourite parts. They come to the
chosen haunt on the brink of darkness, after the
habit of carrion crows, and they roost in companies
apparently of twenty and thirty on the older growths
of underwood. At all times the fieldfares are wide
awake, and they never fail to take wing and utter
their throaty chuckle on the slightest provocation.

There is a theory that the eyes of wild creatures
magnify things seen, so that they appear many times

larger than to human eyes.   This has been held to
explain why creatures smaller and weaker than man,
like hares and rabbits, flee desperately at
The Eyes his approach—a reasonable habit if all men
of Wild
Creatures to them are as giants.   One's sympathies
would go out to the rabbit if he sees foxes
as horses, and weasels as foxes.   If birds' eyes have
magnifying power, many miracles of flight and of
feeding would seem natural.   The swift passage of
birds through obstacles that appear to our eyes to
be almost impenetrable is something of a miraculous
nature.   Without a moment's survey of difficulties
or direction, a bird flashes through a jungle where
there is no possible way for it to be found by human
eyes.   The blackbird flies shrieking in and out of a
dense hedge of thorns ; but not a feather is ruffled
in the course of his intricate flight.   Or watch the
jay or the sparrow-hawk passing at speed through an
almost solid network of twigs and stems.   The human
eye cannot properly follow this performance by the
sparrow-hawk ; a swish and a streak of bluish grey,
and it is gone.   Many a bold jay, finding itself caught
between beaters and guns, has saved its life by this
wonderful power of flight at speed, going away without giving the slightest chance for a shot ; it will
dash out of a wall of undergrowth on one side of a
ride sheer into another wall.   No doubt the jay
knows to an inch which is the shortest cut out of
man's sight.   Hardly less wonderful than birds'
flight through crowded obstacles is the way in which

rabbits scurry and twist through masses of fern and brambles. But where the theory of eye magnification would seem most probably true is where tits and goldcrests are searching for food on the underside of fir boughs, and finding food which no man's eye could see unaided.

❦ ❦ ❦

While February 1 brings security to pheasants and partridges, hares—where any survive in spite of the Ground Game Act—are now also nearly safe

The Season's End from persecution, thanks, however, to the courtesy of sportsmen, and not to the law.

Like rabbits, hares may be killed all the year round, but, unlike rabbits, they may not be sold or exposed for sale between the first day of March and the last day of July.

The end of the season has a strong effect on the gamekeeper. February 2 marks his annual truce with his birds, save woodcock, snipe and wild-fowl. Thereafter he loses the vindictive look of the shooting season—he becomes a man of peace. For long months he has been scheming death and destruction —he has devoted himself wholly to the science of killing game. Happy, if anxious, his face has been as he has bustled his birds to guns belching forth some three hundred pellets of lead at each discharge. At the end of the day he has rejoiced over the long rows of the dead, in feather and fur, while his hand

jingles gold and silver—his reward for success in the
contest of wit and reason against cunning and instinct.   The second day of February comes—and his
whole nature seems to undergo a change.   No longer
he boasts to his rival neighbour how a week ago come
to-morrow the bag was so many hundred pheasants,
and would have been doubled if the guns had shot
" anyhow at all."   But he will make a boast of the
numbers of his hen pheasants.   The sight of hen
pheasants is the greatest joy of his days—over his
hens he watches with maternal love.   " And how
many hens was there ? "—this is the answer he will
return should you mention casually that you had seen
pheasants feeding in a field.

As to cock pheasants, his sensations are different.
The sight of a cock pheasant is a taunt.   The veteran
cocks that have passed unscathed through the shooting season now grow proud in bearing, and the
keeper thinks they seem to eye him with scornful
looks.   They are approaching the reward of their
cunning, of their keen eyes, their sharp ears, their
speedy legs—the possibility of several wives is before
them.   No matter where the keeper goes now, he is
taunted by the sight and sound of these victorious
veterans that have eluded all his efforts to bring
them low.   In summer it is the lament of the twenty
thousand gamekeepers in this country that there are
" too many cocks by half."

An idea is widespread among keepers, if not among
employers, that they are privileged, by virtue of their

office, to kill off superfluous cock pheasants for ten days after the end of the season. The mistake may have arisen from the fact that licensed dealers in game may expose game for sale for ten days after the end of the shooting season. We knew an old keeper whose antipathy to superfluous cocks was deeply rooted: the sight of too many cocks maddened him. By an ingenious argument he was able to overcome his legal and conscientious scruples as to disposing of the unnecessary game. The legal scruples troubled him more than those of conscience ; but this argument always prevailed : " It is not lawful to take cocks killed out of season to my master's larder. But if I should happen to have any dead ones to dispose of it would be a sinful waste to throw them away. Therefore, it will be best if I eat them myself."

☙　☙　☙

Among others whose days of sport end with the season are those little considered sportsmen, the beaters. While making sport for others, they Beaters' find opportunities for themselves, and it Sport would be a churlish host or keeper who grudged the poor beaters the rabbits which occasionally they knock over with their sticks. But their love of sport becomes too marked when, in a gang, they creep along stealthily on the look-out for crouching rabbits for their own bagging, instead of plying their sticks with a will on the cover to drive forward game. They show some skill of a rough sort, and considerable wood-craft. A man gives no sign that he has seen a rabbit, his stride is unhalting as he comes up, and it is without any flourish that suddenly a swift, deft blow of the stick is delivered, aimed a little forward of the head. Too late, the rabbit knows its fatal mistake in thinking that the slow eyes of man had passed it over, as it crouched in its seat.

The law forbids any man to shoot either partridge or pheasant when the last second has passed away of the last minute of the first hour after sunset on the first day of February. No doubt the law-makers were mindful that the light one hour after sunset at the beginning of February would make it extremely difficult for a sportsman to hit a flying pheasant or partridge. The law-makers wisely drew no distinction between misses and hits—pheasant-shooting means, they held, shooting at a pheasant with evident intent to kill. What is hard to understand about the law is why the season does not end with the last day of January. Remembering that February 1 is often the day when the keeper goes from the old shoot to the new, we think it would be decidedly better for game that the day should be put out of season. It would be the worse for the poacher. As things are, February 1 is often a day of anarchy. And it would be a good plan if dog licences and the game season were made to end on the same day—

the one expiration would serve as a reminder of the other.

＄　＄　＄

If a pheasant is seen without a tail in the early part of the shooting season the cause may be put down as fox. Probably the tail has been lost through **Tailless Cocks** an ill-judged effort to capture the pheasant made by some inexperienced cub—the old fox well knows how important it is to grip the body of a bird, not merely feathers. But the end of the season also is a likely time for seeing birds, especially cocks, without tails. The cause then is not foxes' failures. Long before Christmas, even the foxes of the year are old in cunning, while the birds whom they robbed of tails in the days of their callow cubhood will have grown fresh feathers long since. The cock pheasant who must face courting days without a tail probably owes his loss of tail and dignity to a gunner who aimed too far behind, firing at close quarters.

But if you should see several cocks without tails at the end of the season the fewer questions you ask the keeper in public the better : the birds are the superfluous ones of those captured for the laying pens, and have been for a time imprisoned to provide a spirited ending to the last days of shooting. The keeper is not proud of them, and no doubt they are sorry for themselves.

＄　＄　＄

From the young days of the year, when his hens began to lay once more, the keeper adds eggs to his store for

Prepara-tions

the sake of the birds of May. His cares and worries, his long hours and weary trudgings, and the chances and changes of the weather make the keeper grumble more and more with the years; but he is always a devoted slave to sport, and takes pleasure in each act of preparation for a new season. Every time he adds to the store of feeding eggs he is thinking of the prospects of his pheasants. He sees chicks turning to awkward poults, and poults turning to full-feathered birds, topping the lofty trees or sailing high over the valley, while the guns are coughing below. Over his store of eggs for feeding he gloats like a miser over gold. Stowed away in a cool place these eggs—after each one has been dipped for about thirty seconds in boiling water—will keep their good feeding qualities for months.

❦   ❦   ❦

From the New Year until well on in March rabbits are hard pressed to find food—not necessarily be-

Hungry Rabbits

cause the weather may be bad, but because so many fields present a surface of bare earth, where hitherto rabbits have been able to find ungrudged pickings. When barred from other food, they will be driven to bark underwood, and so cause a price to be set on their heads;

and cause people to think and say that a couple of rabbits are at least a score. When they are shut in a wood by wire netting, they will be almost certain to attack the undergrowth, whereas if free to come and go they would have done no damage to speak about, outside or in.

⚜   ⚜   ⚜

The secret at once of preserving a few rabbits and saving the underwood from their attacks is judicious feeding. Swedes or mangels, and some tightly tied bundles of clover-hay, if thrown down in the rabbits' resorts will prevent much damage, and prove indirectly an excellent investment. The food will go far towards allowing foxes, shooting tenants, farmers, landlords, and the rabbits to dwell together without extraordinary annoyance to each other. Rabbits always have to bear the brunt of much more blame than they deserve, and are continuously persecuted from one year's end to another. Yet they are essential to the well-being alike of foxes and game, and ought to be better respected—especially when foxes and game in combination are considered desirable. The man so anxious to preserve foxes for hounds that he would not object if the foxes ate his last pheasants acts foolishly if he refuses to keep a few rabbits. The foxes will turn more than their usual attention to the pheasants, or they will shift their quarters to where rabbits are to

To Save
Under-
wood

be found, and a living is to be made with the least exertion.

☙   ☙   ☙

How far animals are conscious of fear, and where the instinct of self-preservation merges into fear, are questions not easily to be solved. A hare appears to be among the most timid of creatures, making off with speed at the slightest alarm—yet confidence in her own power to escape danger may drive all real fear from her heart. Instincts of fury, bravery and fear are nearly related.

Studies in Fear

There is a common idea that wild animals have an inborn fear of man. But it seems probable that where fear of man is marked it has been impressed upon the animals by example of parents, or experience. Fear, or at least a strong suspicion of what is unknown and strange, is evident among creatures of uninhabited places, though wild-fowl on waters visited by man for the first time may take no notice of a boat that sails through their flocks.

Flight is usually the first instinct of self-preservation. The zigzag start of a flight is cultivated by many besides snipe and woodcock—by hares, which bound from side to side of their line, and double back with a wonderful turn, when hard pressed ; by deer pursued by wolves ; by stoats when danger threatens ; or by the rabbit nearly taken unawares by the spring of a cat or dog. But often a wild animal, surprised, will pause for a moment to snort or grunt, and strike the ground angrily with a fore-foot before making off—a stag for example. A stamp is a common signal or sign of annoyance, curiosity or danger. Both the weasel and the squirrel stamp impatiently with their front feet on occasions—as when they seem divided between curiosity and alarm at the presence of a motionless man. The stamp suggests an attempt to discover whether the man is friendly or hostile, alive and capable of action, or paralysed. The alarm signal given by rabbits, by striking the ground with their hind feet, produces a thumping noise, no doubt to be heard for a great distance underground. So far as danger from man goes, it is usually anticipated before it becomes pressing. Walk along a hedge within a yard of a partridge on her nest, or a leveret in its form, and no notice may be taken so long as you keep on walking. But stop, or even hesitate in your stride— the partridge or the leveret goes on the instant. Wary rooks will feed within a few yards of a man hoeing in a field—but let him stop his work, and take a look at them, and they wait for no stronger hint of danger.

Rooks are the most conservative birds, and sometimes nothing will induce them to form a colony where their presence and their cawing would be the perfecting touches to the trees of some ancestral park. The most hopeful plan to tempt them is to put up old empty nests or brooms, or to put rooks' **The Rookery** eggs into a nest that happens to be in the desired place for the colony. Their strong preference for certain sites is curious ; they will crowd nest-trees on one side of a road, and yet pay no attention to other trees of the same sort, seemingly more perfect for their needs, and only a few yards distant. We have watched a case where for twenty years the rooks remained faithful to the original nest-trees of the colony. About ten years ago half these trees were cut down, and even then the evicted rooks would not build in trees across the road, though their tops touched the tops of the favoured trees, which became more crowded with nests than ever. But two or three seasons ago their favourite nesting-tree, a beech with far-spread top, began to show signs of disease ; and then, after a deal of wrangling, two or three pairs were permitted to nest in the trees near by, hitherto despised. In the next season there were nineteen nests in these trees, and in the next twenty-six. The old beech meantime grew more and more feeble, as the rooks perhaps discovered by some brittleness in the twigs at the top ; and after one more year, though it bore foliage, but not so luxuriantly as usual, the tree gave shelter to only two nests. And now the long-despised trees are the home of almost the entire colony.

In February, the rooks pay visits to their home-trees, wheeling and squawking round about, and demolish-

When Rooks Build ing old nests. On fine February evenings they linger after sunset before setting off to their winter roosting-place. A few,

who have begun work on new nests, turn back to the trees undecided, then turn again after their companions. Not until the beginning of March do the rooks seriously set about their building, in mid-March deserting the great roosting-places of winter and mounting guard over their rough nests of sticks.

❧   ❧   ❧

Rooks would seem to believe that while there is life there is hope. A dead rook displayed before other rooks for the first time attracts no particular

Ways of the Crows attention beyond a casual inspection. But if a rook is wounded, and especially if it hops about with a broken wing, other rooks will

swoop about it, and hover above with wonderful perseverance, squawking all the time excitedly, even in spite of a man with a gun. We have seen a hundred rooks perch on a fence to take stock of a relative caught in a trap set to pheasant eggs.

The cunning of rooks, crows, and magpies is very marked at nesting-time; and the keeper who would shoot them by hiding and waiting within shot of their nests may wait for hours in vain if the birds have seen

D

him approach—as they seldom fail to do. The birds
are cunning enough to watch from the top of a tall,
distant tree, until they see the enemy go away, when
they will return at once to the nest in full confidence.
But they may be tricked quite easily. Let two men
with a gun go together to stand below a rook's
nest. Away go the nesting birds. Then let one
of the men take his departure, with or without the
gun, while the other waits. The birds will return
promptly, as though they imagined both men had
gone.

The keeper has small sympathy with the crow tribe,
and takes every opportunity to reduce their numbers.
Sometimes he will carry a ferret to an open spot, over
which crows or others are likely to fly, peg the ferret
down, and himself lie in wait with a gun. No rook,
crow, magpie or jay can resist the temptation to mob
the ferret. So the keeper takes advantage of the
widespread bird-hatred of the weasel tribe. He traces
a lost and wandering ferret by the wild clamouring
of the jays that have caught sight of the bloodthirsty
creature, or by hints from other birds, great and small.

Carrion crows hold mysterious sway over rooks ; a
single pair of crows will drive a great crowd of rooks
from a rookery. Yet a crow, when compared to a rook,
does not seem to be much more powerful or armed
with a much more formidable beak. A casual observer

would find little difference between a rook and a crow in the hand. If a pair of crows were pitted in a duel against a pair of rooks, the balance **The Crow as Terrorist** of power would make the odds slightly in the crows' favour no doubt. But one imagines the rooks would still have a sporting chance. Probably crows have a black enough reputation among other birds to inspire a general fear. And rooks are cowards. It is a common sight to see them put to shameful flight by peewits or misselthrushes when they have ventured near the others' nesting-places. Yet a rook could kill a missel-thrush or peewit if it had the pluck to fight. The gamekeeper knows that the hissing and spitting of a sitting partridge will cause a rook to approach her very cautiously. A jackdaw, one would say, has ten times the spirit of a rook.

⚜   ⚜   ⚜

We have a little story of how some rooks paid a pretty compliment to an Empress. The preceding tenant of **Imperial Rooks** the Empress Eugénie's place at Farnborough is said to have spent hundreds of pounds in a vain attempt to induce rooks to build in the trees. Old brooms were hoisted—real rooks' nests, with and without eggs, were fixed in the most tempting sites among the tree-tops—young rooks were procured and given every attention—and some were even hatched and reared artificially. But the rooks refused to colonise. Then came the Empress ; and promptly the rooks came also. Soon a flourishing rookery was established. Perhaps the new-comers, too, were exiles.

❦ ❦ ❦

Though May is still the month of rook-shooting, this sport has passed out of fashion, and rook-pie is no

Rook-Pie longer an honourable dish—it has sunk, indeed, into a place of disrepute from which no amount of steak, seasoning, and hard-boiled eggs can rescue it. In old times a dozen rooks would be sent and received with compliments, like a brace of pheasants ; and labourers prized a few rooks as much as the charity beef at Christmas. But now one might search far before finding a cottager who would deign to eat rook-pie. The rooks are shot and buried, or are left where they fall beneath the rookery trees, for foxes to find and carry to their cubs.

The farmer and the gamekeeper have a common cause against the rooks, which, when they are not attacking the interests of the one are pilfering the produce of the other. An April blizzard consoles the keeper for the pheasants' eggs it ruins by blotting out a generation of rooks. For when such a disaster overtakes a rookery late in April, as young birds are nearly ready to leave the nests, the parent birds are hardly likely to make another attempt to rear a brood. But when rooks' eggs are frosted before or during hatching there will be late broods, not hatched until the trees

are in full leaf. Then the young rooks might escape
the watchful eye of the keeper were it not for the habit
of squawking for food, and for the garrulous chuckling
of the parent birds when feeding the hungry mouths.
These late broods increase the toll of the eggs and
young game birds, parent rooks taking five times as
much food as the others.

Old rooks are very cunning in search of prey. On
one excellent partridge-shoot there is a hedge bordered
by telegraph poles. It is the only hedge on the place,
and in seasons when grass and corn are backward it is
packed with partridge nests. The rooks of the neighbourhood have learnt the trick of sitting on the telegraph wires, the better to find the way to the nests, as
revealed by the movements of the nesting birds.
Thus, waiting and watching in patience, in time they
find out every nest in the hedge.

In February the work begins of catching up pheasants
for stocking aviaries, to supply the coming season's
eggs. In mild Februaries, keeper after
keeper tells the same sad story—he "can't
catch no hens." Many of those caught in
food-baited traps in mild weather are weak
and unsound, and some are injured by shot, and so are
not desirable for stock. The birds most capable of
producing plenty of fertile eggs and strong chicks are
those that scorn to enter a cage, except during hard or

Birds
for
Stock

snowy weather. Some keepers make a practice of catching up the desired number of stock-birds before covert shooting begins. Otherwise they are caught up early in February—so that they may settle down to the new way of life before the laying season is upon them.

"Catching up" is, in its way, a fine art. One secret is to place the cages, before use, in the principal feeding-places without setting them for action, for a few weeks. Cages of wire-netting with a roomy, horizontal opening at one end, after the style of a lobster-pot, are most effective; a scanty trail of corn leading on to an ample supply within. These cages are ever ready, and so catch bird after bird; they have the drawback that if the captives become restive they are liable to bark their heads on the wire. Less satisfactory traps are made with lengths of wood (local underwood is used preferably, to allay suspicion) and only so high that when the trap is thrown the birds cannot injure themselves if frightened. These traps seldom capture more than one bird at a time, and they may be thrown accidentally. A small annoyance of pheasant-catching is provided by the active little tits of the wood, who carry the corn outside the cages, and scatter it far and wide for the pheasants to pick up without running any risk. When pheasants come regularly to feeding-places in fair numbers, a large and effective cage is built of hurdles, one hurdle square. The birds are allowed to grow accustomed to feeding therein. One day the keeper lies hidden, and makes a family catch by stealthily dropping a shutter attached to a string. Where a wood with plenty of pheasants joins a belt or wide hedgerow the keeper may erect guiding wings of wire-netting, which converge on a covered-in tunnel, and then gently beats the wood through in that direction. The pheasants are run into captivity in a short time, and with little trouble.

❦ ❦ ❦

In the gamekeeper's eyes a hen pheasant becomes an old hen when she enters upon her second nesting season. But all cock pheasants are old birds when they have seen their first Christmas— only seven or eight months having passed over their glossy, green heads. With the New Year the youngest of the cocks is old in craft, guile and cunning, and all the keeper's skill is taxed to checkmate his endless ways of escape. A beat of the wood has no sooner started than all the birds depart to the point farthest from the beaters.

Old Hens

❦ ❦ ❦

When catching up pheasants for the laying-pens, there is always the difficulty of preventing their escape from the wire-net enclosures, and it is interesting to see the different devices by which this trouble is met. The enclosure must not be covered over with wire-netting, for the birds, whenever startled, would fly upwards and injure themselves—and it is wonderful with what perseverance a pheasant will fly up again and again, until its pate has no skin left, and sometimes until it can fly up no more. So the keeper sometimes covers the enclosure with string netting, small enough to prevent the birds escaping, and large enough to prevent them catching their heads and hanging themselves. Others follow the hawker's system, called brailing, attaching **Y**-shaped pieces of leather to one wing so that it cannot be opened for flight—or the wing may be tied with a piece of tape. The wings are treated in this way in turn, lest one should grow stiff through having no work.

A Gamekeeping Problem

Pheasants bred simply for stocking purposes are pinioned when small birds, as are wild duck; but this reduces their value when their egg-laying days are numbered. Some keepers cut the flight feathers of one wing, but the birds cannot then fly again until the shortened quills have moulted and new ones have grown. But a bird whose flight feathers have been pulled out in the spring will grow fresh ones by June, when she is turned out of the pen. At this time the bird with cut wings is at a heavy disadvantage, alike in escaping the dangers and in mothering any brood she may succeed in hatching out in the woods.

How shall a pheasant gather her chicks beneath her wings if she have only a wing and a half?

In March many keepers are worried by hare poachers. To lose a hare by poaching during the shooting season

The Hare Poacher is bad enough, but to lose one of those left for stock is a calamity to the keeper—though to the poacher a hare means a meal for his family, or a week's supply of beer. The chances are ten to one that a hare snared in March will be a doe—for the does run pursued by a pack of bucks, and so go first into the snare. Hare-poaching would be a matter of less concern to the keeper if the buck hares were always taken, for he could often spare a few, as they will race does to the point of utter exhaustion or death. At rutting times the poacher's task is easy. He selects three or four runs which, from their well-used appearance, are promising, then slips down his snares of brass wire, dulled by exposure to smoke to be the less easily seen by hare or keeper. The poacher chooses runs close together, and should he be a man who goes to work, prefers that they shall be near his line of march, so that he may keep an eye on the snares without stepping out of his lawful path.

Slouching along, with a lie ever ready on his lips in case he should meet a keeper, he can see when a hare is caught merely by moving his eyes, and without turning his head. And if a hare is caught, he will pass on his way unconcernedly, returning without a sign. Meantime his mind has been scheming out the best way to take possession. Probably he will wait for night and darkness—or, instead of going to work the next day, he may devote a large part of it to waiting for the chance of a clear coast, so that he may fetch the hare in broad daylight.   But give the cunning poacher the smallest hint that the keeper knows about his snares and he will leave them alone altogether.   He will only visit his snares when he has no reason to suspect that a keeper has heard of them—otherwise the keeper may be watching to " put a stop to these here little games."

❦　❦　❦

The March hare is certainly mad ; what but madness could cause him to go capering round and round a field for hours at a stretch ?   The battles of **March Hares** the hares are waged in companies ; you may see a score of militant, amorous hares together, and several couples will be engaged in duels. The combatants rear themselves on their hind legs, and spar furiously with their front feet, and when one of a fighting pair has had enough of it another instantly takes his place ; while the hare that refuses to fight may be chased until forced to turn and square himself to the battle.   The whole company may set upon some poor coward, and worry his life out of him. It would seem that when once hares and rabbits have finished their duels, so common a sight in the country in March, they live peaceably enough through the rest of the breeding season.   After these early days of courting, one seldom sees more than a slight skirmish between a couple of hares or rabbits, though the does breed again and again through the summer.

Fights at courting times among wild creatures are usually due either to a local or temporary preponderance of males, or to some special attraction of particular females. At this time of year, it might appear that fighting and courtship went naturally together; but we doubt if wild creatures who pair are given very much to fighting and quarrelling. It is when one has many wives, as the cock pheasant or the stag, that the most desperate fighting is done.

A majority of fox cubs are born about March 25, five or six to a litter. With such crafty parents there is small chance that they will go **The Cubs' Birthday** short of food, and fortunately they come into the world just when baby rabbits are most plentiful. Much else than rabbit goes down their throats, as the entrance to any fox's earth makes evident—there you see remains of quantities of frogs, mice, rats, hares, and, of course, of countless pheasants and partridges, and of many a fowl. The dog fox is not one to show any great attention to his mate : he pays her many visits, but he enjoys himself in his own way. Nor could he be expected to take a deep interest in the welfare of his half-dozen families, several miles apart. But some foxes make better fathers than others; one we have known to rear a litter of cubs on the death of the vixen. Of course a dog fox could do little if

the cubs were dependent on a milk diet. A curious
case of an exemplary fox was that of the unfortunate
one which met his end while carrying a shoulder of
carrion mutton to two vixens and two litters inhabit-
ing the same earth.

❧   ❧   ❧

March brings the gallant cock pheasant to his courting days. He knows that he is safe from men and
guns, and stands recklessly within easy gun-
Courtiers shot, a figure of defiance. Should he step
in Pens away he lifts his feet with a pompous and
disdainful air. He keeps a sharp eye on the hen
pheasants of the wood : the time is near when he will
be the sultan of half a score of hens ; that is, if he
remains at large in the woods. If confined in the
keeper's pens, the number of wives is sternly regu-
lated, and five, or at the most seven, are allowed to
him. It is curious that in captivity the number of
the cock pheasant's hens must be kept down, whereas
the mallard, who pairs when wild, will cheerfully
accept a polygamous state, and will faithfully husband
two or three ducks if kept in a pen.

When partridges are penned up for a few months
in the breeding season, on the French system of rearing, they remain faithful to their rule of pairing.
Keepers have found that it is useless to try to regu-
late the partridge courtships : the birds must be
left to their own instincts in choosing mates. It

will not do to put any cock and hen together and
expect them to pair.   The hen is quite as particular
in accepting a mate as the cock in selecting one for
his attentions.   Sometimes a hen wins the hearts of
several suitors, and then there will be fighting, the
strongest securing the prize, the defeated contentedly
pairing off with the less sought-for hens.   When a
partridge betrothal has been ratified, the happy pair
announce the fact to their friends by keeping sedu-
lously together, apart from the other occupants of
the general pen.   The partridge is seldom quarrel-
some : in a wild state a cock bird will go far afield in
search of a mate if he cannot find one peaceably in
his usual haunts—or he may make up his mind to go
through the season unwedded.   Sometimes, but rarely,
it will happen that trouble arises through an amorous
cock partridge losing his mate late in the nesting season
and trying to run away with another's wife.   But while
some partridges show a pugnacious temperament, as
they boast no spurs, like cock pheasants, their duels
mostly take the form of chasing and running.

♀   ♀   ♀

In March the hawks pair—and the pairs visit and
examine all sorts of old nests.   The nest of a kestrel
is usually found in the heart of a wood—though it
may be recognised as a kestrel's only by the sight
of the birds flying off, for they rear their young
in old sparrow-hawks' nests, or in a magpie's,

a crow's, or in a squirrel's abandoned drey. The sparrow-hawk builds its own nest, as a rule, of rough sticks, with twigs as lining, usually placed near the tree's trunk. It will return to the same nest year after year. But at times the nest of a wood-pigeon is adopted, or of a carrion crow. The cock sparrow-hawk is a polite mate, perhaps of necessity, being so inferior to the hen bird in size and strength. He is energetic in inspecting nest-sites, in advance of his mate. This habit has proved fatal to many, for it is a favourite plan with some keepers to place a circular gin in likely nests—a cruel trick, and illegal, for the law which prohibits the use of the pole-traps forbids also that traps shall be set in nests. Faithful as are hawks and magpies to each other, it is strange how swiftly a new mate is secured should an old one suffer a fatal accident. In the earlier part of the breeding season, a hen sparrow-hawk may lose her mate time after time; yet a new mate is quickly at her side, though no other hawks are to be seen about the country, except those in pairs.

When Hawks Nest

☙   ☙   ☙

The little blue pigeons, the stock-doves, call "Coo-oop, coo-oop, coo-oop," all day, in the old elms in the meadow, or high among the massed twigs of the lime. Pigeons and doves are fantastical love-makers like several other birds — the blackcock and cock grouse hold regular love-levees, going through ridiculous antics and gestures; ducks skim absurdly about

Love-Dances the water, bobbing their heads up and down as if bowing compliments to each other; and even the sober rook will perform a kind of love-dance. At courting times, the wood-pigeons assume a wonderful lustre of plumage, and the white of the neck-ring is very striking, like the edging of a woodcock's tail. The cock wood-pigeon is a laughable sight as he goes sidling down some bare branch to greet his prospective bride; nearer and nearer he works his way, bowing incessantly with a sideways motion of the body, until at last, with neck bent low, bill meets bill in some kind of bird-kiss.

❦　　❦　　❦

The Cockney in the country is perplexed by the countryman's names for birds and beasts; especially

Names that Puzzle Cockneys by names denoting gender. The countryman seems to the townsman to be particular in drawing his distinctions, and his precise way of referring to an ox or a steer, a bull-calf or a heifer, is found very puzzling, particularly to ladies—who hold all cows to be bulls. And when the countryman speaks of a wether-sheep, a barrow-hog, of a hummel-stag, he is speaking in mysteries. Even the terms of the poultry-yard—cock, cockerel, pullet, fowl, hen, or capon—are not always understood.

Custom grants some creatures only one sex. A cat is usually a she, and a hare nearly always. To be precise, as to hares, one should refer to the male as a jack and a female as a jill, the terms buck and doe being more properly applied to rabbits and to fallow deer ; red deer are distinguished by the terms stag and hind. Ferrets in some parts are known as hobbs and gills. Rats, like badgers and hedgehogs, may be boars and sows. The males of otters, stoats, weasels and foxes are dogs, but only the female fox is a vixen. Rams are sometimes " tups." The terms bulls and cows are applied to many kinds of animals, such as elands, moose, whales, elephants, and the seals ; but the young seals are pups, and gather in rookeries. The terms for birds offer some difficulties ; all common wild duck are mallards, to distinguish them from widgeon, teal and so on ; but while the male may be called either the mallard or the drake, the female is always a duck. Grouse are cock and hen ; blackcock, blackcock and greyhen ; and all woodcock are 'cock.

No less confusing to the Cockney in the country are the terms for quantities of game. He speaks of a " brace of rabbits," and the gamekeeper's eye-brows rise at the term. Two rabbits are a " couple " —when they are not a pair. Two pheasants, two partridges, or two grouse are a " brace," three form-ing a " brace and a half " or a " leash " ; but we speak of a " couple " of woodcock, snipe, duck, or pigeons.

When the gamekeeper speaks of " pairs " of birds he is referring to birds that have paired ; but a cock and a hen pheasant remain a cock and a hen. Some confusion arises from the terms applied to gatherings of birds or beasts. Young families of birds are usually " broods," and families of animals " litters." One speaks of a brood (or pack) of grouse, a covey (or pack) of partridges, a bevy of quail, a nid of pheasants (meaning a young family), a wing of plover, a wisp of snipe, a team of duck, a company of widgeon, a flock of sparrows, rooks, or pigeons, a skein or gaggle of geese, a herd of swans or deer, and a sounder of wild pigs. The gamekeeper knows better than any one else just what is meant by a litter of cubs. There is a distinction between a big " rise " of pheasants and a good " flush." If a thousand pheasants fly up at the same time it is a big rise, but not a good one, because few can be shot. A good flush does not mean necessarily that there are many birds, but that they rose, or were flushed, so that most of them offered shots—a few at a time.

❧   ❧   ❧

A wet, cold spring means death to the majority of early leverets. They are given a good chance of life, coming into the world as perfect little hares, with complete fur coat and open eyes ; and, like partridge chicks, they can run on the day they are born. But they are not always strong enough to

E

withstand the English spring. A leveret, no larger than a man's fist, runs with extraordinary speed, and

Hares and their Young

often escapes from a dog, while a man must be sound in wind and limb to overtake it in the open. Rabbits, born naked, develop a very fair turn of speed so soon as they come above ground, but they quickly give up in despair if pursued.

There is a widespread idea that hares breed only once in a year, and produce only one leveret. The gamekeeper knows well that puss may produce several leverets at a birth, and will have family after family from as early as January to the end of September. As with rabbits, the leverets born early one year themselves may breed in the late summer of the same year. No doubt the hare is credited with only one or two young ones because only one or two are found together. Occasionally, it is true, several very young leverets may be found in one place ; but they are usually cradled in separate seats, not far from each other. We once found a family of eight little leverets crouching in a bunch under a heap of hedge-trimmings. Evidently we discovered them within a few moments of their entry into the world.

The mother hare is wise to separate her family. Many dangers threaten the leveret's life ; but if families were kept together the young ones would be even more open to attack from rooks and crows, and scent-hunting vermin in fur. The leveret with its eyes pecked out by a rook, yet still living, is a sight which pleads for the mercy of a swift death at the gamekeeper's hands. The mother hare is keenly alive to the dangers besetting her family. If you find a leveret one day nestling in a tuft of grass, or against a clod of earth, whether or not you handle it the mother will certainly remove it before the morrow. She will wind danger in your scent.

❦ ❦ ❦

The old name for March, "Starvation Month," is usually justified, if winter, with snow, carries on into March. Countless birds die of starva-

Starving Birds tion. After a hard winter there is little food to be found ; but large berries remain a long time on some of the ivy bushes, and come into favour among robins and blackbirds. There has been little green growth since September, though the larger celandine shows bigger leaves, coltsfoot is out, wild arum leaves are green in the hedges, and there is green growth on elder-bushes, woodbine, privet, and brier bushes. Insect life for food is of negligible quantity : though myriads of gnats may be hatched by the sun, they are poor eating. Of flowers there are hardly any, and the sparrow, pecking at the crocuses in his need, earns the hatred of gardeners. It is a time of hunger with many animals awakening out of sleep ; with the field-voles uncurling from their beds of grass, and with the hedgehogs shaking themselves free of their balls of leaves. A new activity is stirring, birds are living at pressure, many animals have young, hundreds of birds come in daily from overseas—but supplies for all seem at the lowest ebb.

❦   ❦   ❦

In the keeper's year there is no moment so delightful as when he finds his first wild pheasant's egg.   The

The Egg of Eggs earliest egg of the season is looked on almost like a nugget of gold.   You may observe a keeper turning out of his way to pass along the sunny side of a hedgerow favoured by pheasants, craning his neck to look at the far side of a tuft of withered grass, and with his stick turning over the dead leaves of a likely hollow.   Day after day, in early April, he perseveres in his quest ; and though he may find scores of depressions scooped out by the hens—" scrapes " he calls them—it may be a long while before his search is rewarded by the sight he yearns for.   He is appeased—though he has but found something found thousands of times before, only a pheasant's egg.   But it is the first of a new season, and precious beyond all others.   There may have been eggs already in his pens.   The penned birds are protected from wind and cold rains.   They live on a well-drained plot facing the south, and they are treated so liberally to rich foods, spices, and tonic drinks that they can hardly help laying early.   The first egg is a satisfaction, but nothing like the first wild-laid egg.   At the earliest chance, the finder meets a brother keeper, and his story of the finding loses nothing in the telling, while it gains a good deal from the envy on the brother keeper's face.

☙ ☙ ☙

By the middle of April, the gamekeeper finds that a few of his pheasants are sitting. They are the older hens. Those that begin to lay early in April **Pheasants' Eggs** do not often lay more than ten or twelve eggs before beginning to sit. But it is not unusual for a young hen to lay fifteen, seventeen, or even more eggs. That the older hens should lay fewer eggs suggests that they have no more than they can furnish with the heat necessary for hatching. Later on, in warmer weather, a pheasant can manage half as many eggs again as in early spring. The old hens have eggs well on the way towards hatching before hens still in their first year have begun to lay. Pheasants commonly lay eggs in each other's nests. We have known a pheasant even to lay eggs in a thrush's nest, built on the ground beneath a furze-bush. Like the nest, three of the four thrush's eggs were destroyed by the intruder. The keeper well knows how to take advantage of this slovenly habit of his pheasants. About ten days before the time when he expects them to begin to lay in earnest, he makes up a number of false nests, into which he puts either imitation nest-eggs, or addled eggs saved from the last season. Having some respect for the sweetness of his pocket, he takes the precaution of boiling the addled eggs for several hours in lime-water. He makes up the false nests in places where the eggs shall be comparatively safe ; his great object being to induce his birds to lay at home, and not to stray away into his neighbour's coverts. The method saves much time in searching for nests. But even when he has the best of luck, a keeper would not be a proper keeper if he did not complain that his hens are laying on his neighbour's ground. Not unusually, three or four hens lay in the same nest— we have known six to lay in one nest, and on one day. From three nests within fifty yards of each other we have counted more than one hundred eggs—and this in a place where pheasants were few. It is a great satisfaction to the keeper to find one of these co-operative nests. He knows that if he leaves the hens to themselves, their eggs will soon be piled up in the nest on top of each other, like a heap of stones. No one pheasant could hatch out such a prodigious clutch, even if left in undisputed possession. What usually happens is that some hens want to lay and others to sit, so that between them the eggs are spoiled. The keeper anticipates trouble by collecting the eggs and distributing them elsewhere for hatching. He knows that his fowls will not hatch out as high a proportion of pheasant eggs from large nests as from smaller ones, since few are given the regular turning necessary to preserve their fertility. But, in spite of this knowledge, there is a deal of friendly rivalry among keepers as to who shall find the nest with the most eggs.

A mule pheasant is a sterile hen who has assumed more or less the plumage of a cock. We cannot

Hens in Cocks' Feathers say we have ever heard one of these transformed hens give vent to a crow. But once we owned a game-bantam hen, who, without changing into cock's plumage, crowed in a way that would have done credit to any fine rooster. The keeper does not appreciate a barren hen pheasant, whether or not she wears cock's feathers. She is an unproductive loafer, and is likely to be destructive to the chicks of other hens, both to wild ones and those reared artificially. Disappointed in motherhood herself, she is jealous that others should be mothers.

♀   ♀   ♀

Pheasants' eggs vary strangely in shade : they show a much wider range of shading than partridges',

About Nesting Pheasants from almost white through the most delicate gradations of blue-green and olive-brown to the rich, warm hue of the nightingale's egg. The keeper prefers the eggs with the deeper tones, persuading himself that they will produce the strongest chicks. He has small faith in the fertility of eggs that are very light in hue, and he holds to an idea that if a light, sky-blue egg hatches at all it will produce a pied chick. When a hen lays in another's nest, it is rather by some subtle distinction of shape than by colour that the keeper discovers the trespasser's eggs : for the eggs of one bird may vary much in shade. The nest is a simple affair, merely a shallow hollow, scratched out, ringed by dry grass or leaves or any dead material of the sort within easy reach ; if dry grass is plentiful a generous supply fringes the hollow, but a pheasant is not one to trouble to fetch and carry for her nest. Cunning as she may be in the choice of a site, no instinct or reason prompts her to go a yard away to collect material, however plentiful at that short distance, for comfort and warmth. Her fabric, plentiful or scanty, is arranged in a typical fashion. Standing in the middle of her scraped-out hollow, she throws the bits of grass or the leaves over her back, so that the margin of the nest corresponds to the size of her body. Sometimes a fowl is seen going through this performance ; the goose also employs this primitive instinctive manner of gauging her nest's dimensions.

All game-birds lay their eggs on the ground. Though pheasants are peculiarly fond of perching in trees, by day as well as by night, they rarely make a nest off the ground ; though now and again one may see a nest placed a few feet high in a tree, resting on a mattress of ivy or on the ruins of other nests— the derelict homes of pigeons, perhaps occupied later by squirrels. Pheasants will also sometimes make use of those convenient hollows to be found on the top of underwood stumps ; and doubtless would do so more often if it were not for the unyielding nature of wood, which they cannot scratch into

shape as instinct prompts. In rides where the old
underwood stumps have not been grubbed, pheasants
love to nest on the stumps' tops. In spite of annual
trimming, the stumps for years continue to throw up a
mass of leafy shoots. The pheasant creeps between
them, and is perfectly hidden—at least, as to her head
and body. We recall a nest in such a spot within a
foot of a path where many people passed daily. Not
one discovered the pheasant's secret, except a keeper
who saw her protruding tail. The pheasant had
forgotten about her tail. Naturally the keeper was
annoyed at her stupidity in thinking that because her
body was hidden her tail could not be seen. Fearing
lest others should discover the nest on this account, he
went for a pair of his wife's scissors, and made sure
that the tail would tell no more stories.

❧　❧　❧

The wisest poultry-farmer does not understand
broody hens better than the gamekeeper. The
ways of the broody hen are at once deep,
**The
Broody
Hen**
and stupid, and annoying. No power on
earth will force a broody hen to sit when she
is in a revolting spirit. To take a hen from
the nest of her choice and expect her to sit properly on
a fresh nest, where even pheasants' eggs costing a
shilling apiece await her, usually means disappoint-
ment. Yet it is as risky to put the pheasants' eggs in
the broody hen's chosen nest. Other hens will disturb
her, rats are likely to steal the eggs, dogs may worry

her, and she cannot be relied upon to return to her own nest after going off to feed. And if she may leave the nest at her own free will she is liable to sit too long without a break. Her eggs in that case do not have enough fresh air, and the heat of the hen diminishes through want of food, so that weak chicks develop, and may fail even to break their shells. So the keeper is obliged to provide a suitable nest, and to try to induce the broody hen to take to it kindly. He finds that an empty cheese-box with a lid will make a capital nesting-box for occasional use. If rats are feared, he encases the box in an armour of wire-netting. Then within he fashions a shallow nest, using firm mould, and adding a little bruised straw ; if the hollow is too deep the eggs may be piled on each other, and the hen cannot plant her feet comfortably or sit evenly over the eggs. The hollow is lined with a ring or collar of twisted straw, to retain the warmth of the hen, and prevent her eggs falling out when she moves her feet to turn round. Then the keeper goes off for the broody hen, which he carries in a sack of open texture. Whether or not a hen is really broody may be determined most easily at night. A hen chosen by day, though she imitates the broody plaint, may be intent only on laying eggs —not on sitting. But the hens who are in earnest will be found in the nests after dark ; and they are known by their dull combs. Into the sitting-box the keeper shuts the hen of his choice, leaving her with a nest-egg or two by way of encouragement.

He is in no hurry to give her live eggs. He waits until she is well settled after the move, and has had time to round up the nest to her liking. At first she may be inclined to stand, or at least not to go down properly; but after a little while she will be found spread out in the proper fashion of the hen who intends to hatch eggs at all costs, and she will complain loudly, and peck fiercely if touched. And then she is entrusted with the precious eggs.

Once a day the keeper gently lifts each broody hen off the nest to feed, tethering her by a string tied to her leg or shutting her into a coop. On the first day she is taken from the eggs only for ten minutes; but her time off is gradually increased, as the eggs require more oxygen, to half an hour during the second week of sitting, and then to three-quarters of an hour or longer towards the end of the third week, if the weather proves genial. Plenty of air is good for the chicks in the eggs, especially during the last days of the hatching. A hen was accidentally kept from her eggs for a whole afternoon on the day before they were due to hatch; yet all the thirteen eggs hatched out, and stronger chicks were never seen.

The red-legged partridge begins to nest quite a week earlier than the English birds. The keeper expects to find his first partridge's egg about April 25: and probably it will be a Frenchman's.

Great will be his satisfaction if the first egg should happen to be an English bird's. The same friendly rivalry exists between neighbouring keepers as to who shall find the first partridge egg as with the first pheasant's egg. Not until May will the partridges' laying season be in full swing. English partridges nest always on the ground, but Frenchmen sometimes nest so far aloft as on the top of a straw-rick. So they escape the fox, which tears the English birds off their nests on all sides. There is an idea in the heads of country folk that the French partridge habitually deserts her first clutch of eggs without cause. No doubt this delusion has arisen from the forsaken appearance of the birds' nests and eggs ; when stained by soil, the eggs look decidedly stale. While the mother bird never deserts her nest without good cause, she is in no hurry about nesting ; and there are often long intervals between the laying of the first egg, the completion of the clutch, and the beginning of sitting operations. We have heard of a case where this interval was one of six weeks. Yet a full brood was hatched.

The French-men's Nests.

French partridges have a good deal in common with guinea-fowls. The call which members of a covey of Frenchmen make to each other bears the strongest resemblance to the guinea-fowl's " Go-back, go-back." They are alike in making a deep " scrape " in the soil for their nest, which is complete when the hollow has been scratched to their liking. Then the dingy-white ground-colour and the rusty speckles of their eggs are similar; and the eggs of guinea-fowl and of Frenchmen are commonly found well plastered and stained with soil, through being turned over in the unlined nest. The eggs have notably thick shells.

❦   ❦   ❦

The ancient art of making hurdles is fast dying out. In a small Hampshire village, where a score of hurdlers could have been found a quarter of a century ago, to-day but one or two old men remain who can make a hurdle of the genuine sort. The reason is not that hurdle-making is profitless, for there is a demand for good workers, and the rate of pay is higher than of old— from four to five shillings for a dozen hurdles, which represent a day's hard work. But few boys follow the old calling of the hurdler, probably because a long apprenticeship must be served. There is difficulty in finding a qualified man to take a boy in charge; and for a long while the boy would be useful only to strip the rods of knots, and would earn but a nominal wage. At other work his earnings would be enough at least to pay his share of the family expenses at home. So that few hurdlers see their way to teach even their own sons this honourable trade.

The first stage in making a hurdle is the splitting of the rods ; and this is an art calling for years of practice before such perfect efficiency is **Hurdlers' Science** attained that the worker can divide each rod exactly down the centre with his eyes shut. The bill-hook is inserted at the rod's smaller end, the other end is held between the knees, and the straight, clean split is made by directing the pressure of the bill-hook one way or the other—the edge of the hook being turned towards that side of the rod which threatens to splinter. When the rods are split, the " salins "—the upright stakes which form the framework of the hurdle—are fixed into the " mole "—a solid piece of wood, slightly curved, and drilled with holes. "Spurs" are the small, round, unsplit rods woven over the top and bottom to prevent slipping. The weather has much to do with the ease and speed of the work. Cold, sunless days with east winds tend to make the rods brittle, and then when a binding spur is being wound into place it will break, and part of the hurdle must be remade. Drought hardens the wood, and the rods lose elasticity. A hard frost may freeze the wood's moisture, and the rods may then snap. The most favourable weather is sunny, but not scorching, with occasional light showers. In wet weather the strongest worker is terribly handicapped, and rheumatism, sooner or later, is almost certain to take hold of him.

❦   ❦   ❦

Not all who work in the woods are entitled to the name of woodman : a word standing for an ancient and an honourable calling. The woodman proper is an estate official, a sort of general foreman over the underwood and the timber. He ranks a grade below the gamekeeper. A man of parts, he knows his woods through and through. He can tell you the exact age of the various growths of underwood, for it is his duty to advise what shall be cut each year, to map it out in lots for sale, to undertake the marking and felling of timber, and to see to the upkeep of covert fences, and the trimming of rides. He receives a retaining weekly wage, except when he is turning underwood to account or laying a hedge, when he is paid by the piece. In time of need, the gamekeeper calls on the woodman's assistance, and he seldom goes long in want of a rabbit. The keeper is always generous with his friends and allies.

The Woodman

❧   ❧   ❧

Below the woodman in rank, and not rightly to be called a woodman, is the copse-worker, or copser ; a piece-worker, free to work for any one who will give him a job. He is a skilled craftsman, one of a dying race, for his boys are kept too long at school ever to take kindly to his calling. This is his constant complaint : and he will air his views freely on " eddication " and

A Dying Race

the making of "scholards." He himself had
only enough learning drubbed into him to allow
him to make every night an entry of his day's
work—so many bavins, so many bundles of pea-
sticks, so many fencing-poles. His daily earnings
fluctuate with the quality of the wood, which
he is sure to declare is nothing like what it was
in the days of his youth.

❦   ❦   ❦

It is the keeper's lot to make the best of many a
bad job. If he could have his way, all underwood
would be chopped and stacked in neat piles
by the middle of April, so that his nesting
birds might enjoy undisturbed peace in his
woods. In olden days, all underwood was
cut, worked up, and cleared off the ground by certain
fixed dates so that the new shoots of the shorn stumps
had full measure of light and air. But the dates are
no longer remembered, and the work is carried on
into early summer. The birds benefit in some ways.
Pheasants find the long rows of felled underwood
very attractive as nesting-places, and many pairs
of partridges decide to give them a trial. Pheasants
and partridges prefer to nest in dead material—it is
warmer and drier than greenstuff, does not hold
dew or rain, and cannot grow, and so possibly upset
the nest. Dry leaves are driven by the wind beneath
the rows of wood, so nesting material is plentiful.

*Choice
Nesting-
Places*

And there is no dense canopy of leaves to shut out the sun that is so loved by the sitting birds.

❧   ❧   ❧

Much underwood remains in the long drifts where it was laid after cutting until well on in May, and even into June. The keeper may search carefully, but unless the rows are very narrow and thin he can hope to find only a few of the many nests they shelter. Especially difficult is it to find the partridge nests. The finding is almost as much a matter of luck as of skill, for the eggs are covered completely by the birds with a drab quilt of leaves, perfectly matching the surroundings. The eggs of pheasants, too, though the birds seldom cover them, are often hidden through the play of the leaves in the wind. Even should a bird be sitting on her nest, she is not easily found—unless the keeper catches the glint of her dark eye. Her feathers are merely one shade more in the prevailing blends of brown. The woodworker, keeping the most careful watch for nests, often does not see the sitting bird until he strips the underwood from her very back.

Hidden Nests

❧   ❧   ❧

Between the gamekeeper and copsers in his woods there is an unwritten agreement, making for the good of all. The workers take heed and care of the game-nests, and the keeper sees

F

that they are rewarded according to the care.
He does not pay people to find nests, but to protect
those discovered in the course of daily work
A Mutual —a small sum, by way of encouragement,
Under-
standing usually a shilling for each nest. But the
copser, while chopping up the rows of underwood, finds a good many small nests, with three or four
eggs each, and the keeper may agree to pay him a penny
for each of these odd eggs, as he calls them, and a
shilling for each more respectable nest saved. The
copser must leave cover for a few yards around the
nests, and do nothing to disturb the tenancy. When
the nest is so situated that it causes no inconvenience
or delay to the copser's work, the shilling is paid
only when the eggs hatch ; in special cases the keeper
takes the risk of safe hatching. It is a proud moment
for the copser when he makes a satisfactory report
of a nest. " That there old bird over agen they ash-
stems," he will say delightedly, " she be hatched
and gone, master."

❦   ❦   ❦

Often a keeper must give judgment as to who is
entitled to the reward for a nest found and protected
by two or three men. It would be easy
Many if the spirit of justice were satisfied by
Guar-
dians handing the shilling to the man who first
found the nest ; or if a shilling were given to
each man ; but this would make up an alarming
account for nest-money. So the keeper may give

the first finder a shilling, and the others a couple
of rabbits each. It would not be policy to foster
a man's interest only in the nest which he finds himself, and is the first to find, for a nest may need the
guardianship of many workers. First it may be
found by a copser, working up underwood ; he keeps
an eye upon it for a week, finishes his job, and departs.
Then a hurdler comes, or perhaps a hoop-maker, who
starts work, sees the nest and guards it for awhile.
And then the nest catches the eye of a carter when
he comes to fetch a load of wood ; he notes the
position, lest it should come to harm under the
hoofs of his horse or the wheels of his waggon—and
after his day's work he may walk a mile or two to
lay his information at the keeper's cottage.

When three men work in the same part of a wood,
one may have the luck to find several nests, and
the others may have no luck. So the men, if good
mates, arrange to pool the nest-money ; but sometimes the lucky man is avaricious. The keeper
must study the vagaries of luck and character.
Some men will be spoiled by too liberal rewards ;
but an extra shilling or two may be well spent if it
prevents a sour man from thinking he has been
harshly treated. The keeper knows the labourer
as a man who broods much, and is slow to forgive
an insult, or to forget an injustice. And he knows
it makes all the difference to his own work if the
men who labour in the woods for six months in the
year are his friends and allies. This, in turn, is no

bad thing for them—many odd jobs the keeper puts in their way when work is slack, and he puts many rabbits into their hands to the comfort of their hearts.

   ❦ ❦ ❦

The twenty-fifth day of April is one of the keeper's high days.   A large number of the twenty or thirty thousand gamekeepers in this country then

Mark's Day

commit their first batches of pheasant eggs to the care of broody hens. Some keepers cling to this date because their fathers did so before them, in the same way that ancestral etiquette decrees that on a certain fair-day cabbage seed must be sown. No decided advantage is to be gained by very early hatching ; but by April 25 the keeper usually has a goodly collection of eggs, taken from wild birds' nests, and their quality does not improve if kept, in an artificial way, longer than a fortnight. Eyes ignorant of woodcraft would pass a pheasant's nest which no keeper could fail to see ; and would pass unseeingly over the brown form of the sitting bird, heedless of the bright, dark eyes that keenly watch the intruder's movements. Pheasants like a little light cover, but do not care to nest in thick and tangled undergrowth. They love sunshine, and prefer a site where falls a shaft of the morning sun ; if you note the position of a sitting pheasant, you will probably find that her face is sunwards. The mother bird is very jealous of the sanctity of her nest ; if disturbed she does not often return. The keeper, passing by a sitting pheasant, passes by as though he had seen nothing.

☙   ☙   ☙

The story of pheasant-rearing begins with the collection of eggs from wild nests and from penned birds.

The Old, Old Story Then comes the collection of broody hens to play the part of foster-mother. Then the lime-washing of the nest-boxes. Hundreds of wooden boxes, each compartment measuring fifteen inches square, are placed in lines in a shed or an open field; the nests are roughly fashioned in the boxes, of turf and soil, moss, meadow-hay, and straw. And on the nests are set broody hens, beneath which, when they have proved their worthiness, are placed from fifteen to twenty eggs. Heaps of soaked corn and pans of water are made ready, and once a day the hens are lifted off their nests to be fed and watered, and to allow fresh air to play on the eggs. A rope runs on the ground before the boxes, and to this the hens are tethered. The keeper lifts off and tethers his hens at the rate of three or four to the minute.

☙   ☙   ☙

Seventeen is the regulation number of pheasant eggs to be put beneath each hen, and seventeen chicks are put with each hen in the coops in the rearing-field. The most motherly hens are selected for service on the rearing-field. Less careful mothers are turned out when they have hatched the eggs, or, if they are willing, are supplied with another clutch. A hen that will hatch several clutches is too useful to be honoured with the task of bringing up a brood, and must be content to play the part of living incubator. The keeper knows his hens through and through—and he can tell when a hen has chicks without seeing them, by the bristling of her feathers at his approach, and her instinctive clucking.

The Luck of Pheasant-rearing

An incubator helps the keeper to cope with the whims and frailties of broody hens. It is always ready to receive those unexpected eggs which may be brought to his cottage at any moment, as when sitting birds are disturbed by sheep or cut out in the mowing grass. And it is ready to take charge of the eggs abandoned by a fowl, or the chipped eggs of a foster-mother which shows an inclination to crush the chicks as hatched. Yet it will be long before it ousts the broody barn-door hen from the rearing-field.

In the days before incubators, keepers who found themselves with more eggs than hens were forced to strange shifts. One keeper saved the situation with the help of ducks. Wild duck nested in numbers on an island in a lake, and one spring day he took six hundred pheasants' eggs to the island, exchanging them for the eggs of the sitting ducks. The ducks proved excellent sitters, but as his hens became available he would punt to the island to relieve the ducks of their charge. Pheasants were more prized in those days than wild duck. Such a sacrifice of duck for pheasants would be saved to-day by the ever-ready incubator.

While pheasant-rearing is chiefly a matter of skill, luck plays a part in success, and of course a light warm soil, a good situation, a good supply of natural food, and good weather make all the difference. If eighty eggs hatch out in a hundred this is considered good ; if less than seventy hatch, this is bad. A keeper may congratulate himself if he turns a thousand pheasants into covert from fifteen hundred eggs set ; anything below one bird turned into covert from two eggs is considered a poor result. Keepers believe that chicks cannot be hatched too late in May or too early in June.

After about twenty-four days the eggs hatch, and the little chicks are taken with the hens to coops placed in readiness in the rearing-field ; a place so jealously guarded by the keeper as to be in his eyes sacred land. Four or five times daily the chicks must be fed—at first on eggs, to which is added later a mixture of biscuit-meal, rice, greaves, and small bird-seed, until boiled corn becomes the staple food. Every night the chicks must be shut carefully into their coops—a long and tiresome task. The danger of enteritis looms up—ten thousand chicks may be swept off in a week. When five or six weeks old, chicks, hens, and coops are carted away in waggons to the woods, where the chicks must face the dangers of vermin by night as well as by day until they learn to go to roost.

For the keeper the days and nights spent in his rearing-fields pass in incessant anxiety. He never counts his pheasants before they are hatched.

From Egg to Larder He may count them as morsels of fluff; when they begin to use their babyish wings; again when they fill the broad ride with a mass of seething brown—but not until the bracken is dead, and the trees are naked, and the game-cart has borne away its burden, does he count them as his own. Nor does his anxiety cease until the long tails hang safely in his larder.

꽃   꽃   꽃

" They be a good lot of eggs," the keeper will inform you as he reveals his store, ready to be given to the quickening warmth of broody fowls. " I don't know as ever I set eyes on better," he will add, " and I don't expect you have neither." If you denied this he would not believe you. His pheasants' eggs are like the apple blossoms : each year more beautiful than ever. And the more plentiful the more beautiful. Noting the keeper, as he goes out in search of broody hens, you might mistake him for a dealer in rags and bones. He tramps all round the countryside with an old sack slung over his back —one of the light, thin kind in which dog-biscuits come ; or sometimes he drives in a gig, and poultry-farmers welcome him gladly. He pays half a crown or three shillings for each hen in broody mood,

Fine Eggs and Good Mothers

and so helps to make poultry pay. His difficulty is to find broody hens at the time when he most needs them. The ideal is a healthy bird, not one with pallid comb or inclined to mope ; she must be of medium size and of light weight, with short legs, small feet, and a wealth of downy feathers. Above all, she must be quiet in demeanour. The fidgety, fussy hen may have excellent intentions, but is likely to cause disaster to her eggs and chicks. A big hen with the sprawliest feet, but of gentle disposition, and slow to anger, will often prove a better foster-mother than one a model in form, feather, and feet, but in temperament a spitfire.

♀   ♀   ♀

Illicit traffic in fox-cubs and partridge eggs is hard to stamp out. So long as men will buy fox-cubs and eggs there will be men to supply them. **The Cub-stealing Shepherd** If there were no buyers there would be no middlemen, and there would be fewer cubs which bear the label, " From Germany." Cubs, wherever they come from, fetch a good price, giving ample profit for an hour's hard digging—say ten shillings each. Cub-snatching is less risky than egg-stealing. So far as we know, even to kill cubs is not an offence against the law, and so there can hardly be a penalty for taking them alive. The worst that could happen to the culprit would be a prosecution for simple trespass and damage. A cunning, rascally cub-stealer of our acquaintance was employed by none other than the local M.F.H. He was a shepherd, and nothing pleased him better than to hear that foxes were plentiful when hounds came his way. He knew that in the spring he would reap many pounds by cub-snatching, and with small risk of rousing suspicion. But one spring morning he was caught in the very act of cub-snatching, and then he ceased to be that Master's shepherd.

❧   ❧   ❧

The old-fashioned professional rat-catcher is seen as rarely as the mole-catcher, with his rude traps of wood, wire and string, actuated by a spring
Lures and Charms of green wood from the hedgerow. And with the rat-catcher have passed the secrets of his calling—how, when and where to use oils and essences to attract rats to their doom. He knew how to handle rats alive with his naked hands, and the trick of squeezing the life from their bodies. The experienced take rats by the back of the throat, but unless the grip is made in just the right way a dangerous bite may be received. The safest plan for the inexperienced is to take live rats by the tip end of their tails; then they are helpless, since their own weight keeps their heads down. Mice, treated in this way, would curl up and nip their captor's fingers in a twinkling. He was a deep character, the old rat-catcher. If there were

many rats he would destroy many—but if few he would take good care to leave behind him some fine specimens for stock. No doubt the oils and preparations invented by himself, or handed down to him by his ancestors, would not only attract rats for his catching, but would attract others after he had gone, so that his trade was kept alive. Thus, perhaps, arose the old saying that if you kill one rat twelve friends will come to its funeral. Oils are still used as lures by the fish-poacher, and also by the game-keeper. To draw rats into his traps the keeper sprinkles them with the sweet-scented oil of rhodium-wood and oil of aniseed. To attract cats he uses tincture of valerian; the essences in the root of that plant having so great a charm for cats that it will draw them from far and near. To attract stoats and weasels he uses oil of musk. To entice a fox, a dead cat is one of the best lures : many a fox, to our knowledge, has owed its death to an over-keenness in unearthing a cat that had been shot and lightly buried. We have heard that dog-stealers induce dogs to follow them by carrying a piece of wart from a horse's leg—we know a simpler plan. The keeper's woodcraft teaches him many ways to charm wild creatures to their destruction. A common trick to bring rabbits from their holes is to imitate the squeal of a rabbit in fear, by applying the lips to the back of the hand, and producing a tremulous sucking sound. Possibly the rabbits think that a brother is in distress, and come to see from curiosity.

The eggs of plovers in some parts are now receiving protection all the year round, the Board of Agriculture having given notice that peewits feed **The Law and the Peewit** wholly to the benefit of field crops and do no injury whatever to the interests of farmers. The greedy and the thoughtless have taken plovers' eggs in unreasonable numbers, and total protection is to be welcomed. It may be argued that peewits' eggs are a rare delicacy, and wholesome food ; that where they may be taken a limited number of old men may earn a few shillings ; that a law superior to find-and-take would be difficult to enforce ; also that taking the eggs until about the middle of April does not materially affect the numbers of peewits. What with the effects of frosts and the destruction of eggs during the tillage of fields, such as harrowing the fallows and rolling the grass and cornfields, where peewits mostly nest, the greater portion of the first layings cannot in any case survive. But those allowed to take eggs for the sake of profit will not stop at early ones, and peewits are such useful birds that thorough protection for all the eggs would be the best policy.

❦   ❦   ❦

The partridge and the peewit seem to lead almost blameless lives. We could claim that the productive value of land is improved by the presence of partridges and peewits. There is no end to the good work of partridges.

Even when they devour grain, they are innocent
of doing harm, for they eat only such grain as is
shed on the stubbles—waste grain which none

The Partridge and the Peewit could grudge them. They never seek out
grain newly sown, like the rooks. When
a field has been harrowed, directly the
men and horses have gone, the partridges gather
in numbers to feed, and though they may come after
the field has been sown, they come as readily before,
as it is not the grain, but the slugs, grubs, worms,
and insects they are seeking ; bits of weeds and their
seeds, aphides, earwigs, and ants' eggs are eagerly
devoured.

The partridge is disheartened when a broad acreage
is laid down to grass ; insect food grows scarce,
and he soon takes his departure. On arable

A Friend to Agriculture land thrown out of cultivation the birds
will thrive, because of the hosts of weeds
that spring up, and give them food and
shelter ; insect food is found on the surface, and partridges multiply. But nothing suits
them better than highly cultivated arable land.
The more the soil is worked, as by harrows, the more
food they are able to find—and the more good they do
by destroying insects and grubs that injure delicate
roots. Where land is needed for partridges there
is every need also of the peasant ; and partridges
bring the peasant many a shilling for nests, and,
when work is scarce, many a day's employment at

good wages (such as wages are), with a hearty lunch into the bargain.

❦   ❦   ❦

No doubt one reason why farmers fail to co-operate properly with gamekeepers in keeping rats down is because they do not see the damage which **The Rats in the Stacks** rats inflict upon them. A farmer is deeply troubled if he sees a blade of corn or grass nibbled by a rabbit; he will make frantic efforts to secure that rabbit—which has a market value. But a rat does little visible damage, and when dead is worth nothing. Another cause of apathy is that the farmer knows how useless it is to deal with the rats on his own premises when the supply is promptly renewed from his neighbours'. In a single corn-stack he entertains cheerfully, perhaps, 500 rats. Assuming that each rat eats three pints of corn a week, the 500 rats in three months eat fifty pounds' worth of corn, to say nothing of the grain and straw they damage. In a day, ten rats will consume enough food to keep a man. If anything further were needed to impress a rat-cherishing farmer, we might point to the statement that a female rat may be responsible, theoretically, for between twenty and thirty thousand descendants in the course of twelve months. But it is left to the gamekeeper to be the rat-catcher of the countryside. The farmer goes cheerfully to bed, unaware that rats are enjoying themselves in his stacks to the tune of two or three

pounds a day.   Many keepers destroy two or three
thousand rats in a year.

☙   ☙   ☙

As a hunter of rats the gamekeeper has no equal,
though he could do little without the help of his
trusty ferrets and ratting terriers.   He and
Thoughts his assistants are on terms of thorough
on Rat-
hunting understanding.   We know an old keeper
whose ferrets seem to have a strong affection for him ;   they are quiet to handle, and are
treated as pets, but they are the best ratting ferrets
in the world.   The keeper does not care to use good
rabbiting ferrets for ratting :   they may be lost and
bitten to death—a rat bite is always dangerous.
Ratting ferrets need peculiar qualities, and are not
necessarily the most ferocious of their kind.

The keeper's ferrets seldom nip him, for he knows
how to handle them.   A ferret nips, and is not to
be blamed for it, when a hand suddenly makes a
grab at him without warning.   The keeper's way
to attract a ferret's attention is by speaking before
touching.   " Come on, Betty," or " Come on, Jack,"
he says in soothing tones, as he boldly puts forward
his hand.   His passwords of friendship are useful
for coaxing a ferret from a hole or from impenetrable
bushes.   The ferrets tell him if a rat is near by the
action of their tails as they enter a burrow, working
them after the manner of a cat about to spring on a
mouse.

Why should cats and ferrets at times lash their tails when approaching prey ? The tail-lashing suggests suppressed excitement, also a way of gaining impetus or steadiness for a spring. But we think it should be read chiefly as a sign of hostility and ferocity. A ferret enters a burrow, discovers that there is a rat a little distance from him, is angered, grows excited at the prospect of a fight, and lashes his tail. But we have never observed a ferret to lash his tail when approaching a rabbit—comparatively a harmless prey. A cat gives the same storm-signal when annoyed, as when her fur is rubbed the wrong way, or when she is about to spring on a mouse or a rat, each capable of retaliation. But she seems to lash her tail chiefly when her prey has come suddenly to her notice without warning ; when she has been lying for a long time in wait for a mouse, her tail hardly twitches, in spite of her excitement ; she is cool and collected, and her spring brings certain death.

When Cats are Angered

☙   ☙   ☙

When rat-hunting, and working hard, ferrets and dogs grow excessively thirsty. One old keeper friend always takes the trouble to carry with him a small flask of water for his ferrets, offering it to them at intervals in the palm of his hand. For his dogs also he carries water and a tin dish—while he seldom goes out ratting without a gallon jar containing what he describes as " a little summat " for himself.

Hunters' Thirst

Now and again it happens that a ferret is killed accidentally while at work. And sometimes dead ferrets return to life, health, and strength in a way to put even cats to shame. We recall how a rat-hating keeper's wife, notorious for the quality of her right arm, was one day helping her husband to hunt rats in a wood-shed. On the ferret suddenly popping out his head from a wood-pile, the good woman lost her wits, and aimed a shrewd blow with her poker at the ferret's nose. In tears, she left the poor little beast still and stark. A gardener was asked to bury it, and plant a carnation over the grave. He found it in the dustbin, eating the head of a duck.

Life-in-Death

In another case, a rat-hunter knocked a ferret with a hurdle-stake from the eaves of a corn-stack far out into a field, where it was picked up apparently dead, and put into a bag. Some hours later the body was tipped from the bag into a little grave, when it startled the gravedigger by gasping for breath. In a little while the corpse celebrated its resurrection by slaughtering all the pheasants in a pen, and just as they were beginning to lay. Once we saw a ferret struck by a pellet from a gun, which went through its head, a hair's-breadth below the eyes. Both eyes were blinded ; yet the ferret recovered, and lived and worked as long and well as most of its kind. Ferrets are tougher than they look. The weak spot, no doubt, is in the lungs.

❧ ❧ ❧

G

The present type of show fox-terrier is too big and too long in the leg for ratting in hedges. Little dogs are called for, full of sense and pluck, with wide heads, strong jaws, bully chests and short bodies on short legs, which carry them as quick as lightning almost anywhere among the thorn hedges. The keeper does not care for his ratting terriers to hunt anything but rats—and the difference in the work of a rat specialist and a general-purpose dog must be seen to be believed. He does not enter his puppies to old rats, for the puppies may be badly bitten, and perhaps their ardour and dash will be ruined, and they will never look at a rat again.

Ideal Ratters

The general-purpose terrier develops grave faults. If a rabbit or a hare is started, he prefers giving chase to going on with the rat business : he attacks ferrets as well as rats, and he prevents rats from bolting by jumping about over the burrows and poking his nose into them too freely. A terrier must be taught to restrain himself until a rat has bolted. The keeper holds him down, cuffs and rates him soundly each time he tries to go too soon, but gives lavish praise if he waits until the right moment. After a time, the little terriers so well understand the necessity for allowing rats to bolt that they will crouch as motionless as statues, with their noses almost touching the edge of the hole. So crafty was one we have owned, that she would crouch in this way, with her body round the corner, out of sight.

All plans for the destruction of rats are welcomed by the keeper, because rats are the most numerous of all egg-thieves. He heartily joins the foxes, stoats, and weasels in their war on rats, though he is for ever at war with his co-operators. He believes that there are now more rats than ever, and has figures at his finger-tips to prove the growth of the rat-plague. If, he argues, there were only one rat to every acre in England and Wales, and if each rat did damage only to the extent of one farthing a day, the loss in a year would be £15,000,000. And he quotes a report which says that a single poultry-fancier in Dorsetshire lost £80 in a year through rats ; that the owner of a flour-mill lost £150 in a year, through the gnawing of sacks alone; that men have attributed their bankruptcy chiefly to rats ; and that the damage done by rats in this country is greater than the damage done by the cobra and tiger in India.

The gamekeeper holds that there ought to be complete, organised co-operation against rats over wide areas, and heavily blames the farmers for not giving proper assistance to keepers in their rat-war. By delaying over-long the threshing of their corn-stacks farmers certainly give rats a grand chance to increase and multiply ; and when ricks are left unthreshed until April the rats leave them without let or hindrance, to spread over the countryside as the weather grows warmer, and food is to be found everywhere. The keeper argues that ricks should be

threshed betimes, to allow the rats to be properly
dealt with. A day or two beforehand he would
have the rats which lie in outlying burrows, in neighbouring hedges, driven into the rick; this can be
effected by tainting the burrows with paraffin—a
simple plan is to blow in smoke from paraffin-
steeped rags with a bee-smoker. Then the keeper
would have the rick surrounded by half-inch wire-
netting. At the time of the threshing he would like
to be summoned to the scene, and he would see to it
that there were six or seven smart ratting-dogs
present, and that they were constantly supplied with
drinking-water. In one case where this plan was
tried, six hundred rats were accounted for from one
rick. Even after threshing and rat-killing on these
lines, rats will be found, if sought, in hidden holes
where the rick stood—packed to suffocation to the
number perhaps of seventy or eighty.

☙   ☙   ☙

The keeper does not always take his ferrets with
him when he goes ratting. Usually they are too
large to enter rat-holes freely, and even the
Ratting small rat-ferret has difficulty in turning
without
Ferrets round. And when a ferret has once entered
a hole a rat cannot pass him, and so may
be prevented from bolting and showing sport. The
sport takes place underground, unless the ferret
retreats while there is time. The fight ends either
in severe punishment for the ferret or in the death of

the rat ; when the ferret proceeds to gorge himself on his victim—and to lie up.

Again, it is more difficult to find a lingering ferret in a rat's hole than in a rabbit's burrow ; a line-ferret sent in to explore cannot move about in the small rat passages as in the roomy tunnels of rabbits, and so cannot locate the free ferret. To dig for a ferret in a rat's run is always risky ; the diameter is so small that the spade may cut through without any warning, and also cut through the ferret. When the spade breaks through the crown of a rabbit's hole, on the floor of which is the ferret, the man with the spade naturally eases his pressure. But the ferret fills the rat-hole to the roof.

There is still another danger in ratting with ferrets ; the dogs, unless very well trained, may bring about a tragedy. Even when a dog is ferret-proof the ferret may plunge teeth into the dog, who naturally retaliates. On all these accounts the keeper may prefer to go ratting with an iron bar in place of a ferret.

By using an iron bar instead of ferrets for bolting rats, all kinds of difficulties and delays are prevented ; and the keeper is free to go home at any time without having to wait for loitering allies. To strike an iron bar into a rat's hole is to strike terror into the rat's heart. One might probe a rabbit's burrow with a bar for a month, and no rabbit would bolt— indeed, the more one probed the tighter would the rabbit sit. In rabbiting, a bar is used only to find holes and save digging.   But thrust a bar anywhere near a rat's subterranean lair, and probably the rat will bolt, as if possessed, at the first time of asking. Such an effect does probing have on rats that they will fly before the crowbar well knowing that enemies await their appearance.   Even with a dog at the hole who has grabbed at the rat more than once, the rat will fly before a shrewd thrust.   The art of thrusting is to drive the bar into the hole behind the rat, not blocking the way by which it will bolt.

Rats seem to have a deep-rooted terror of anything that probes and prods.   Perhaps some of them when their holes are disturbed associate the trouble with pitchforks.   For hundreds of years rats have lived in corn-ricks, and at threshing time when the sheaves have been lifted by pitchforks have bolted furiously.   The first thrust of the pitchfork into a protecting sheaf puts out the rats, though well aware of the presence of men and dogs.   When the iron bar comes crashing into the burrow, perhaps the rats half expect the soil to be uplifted as if it were a sheaf of corn.

SUMMER

THE gamekeeper has a way of putting things to surprising and ingenious uses. Usually he carries a dog-lead concealed somewhere about his person—a yard or two of string attached to a simple spring clip; and this lead serves a hundred purposes apart from restraining dogs. One case we remember well, where a dog-lead saved a situation. The vocal services of a keeper had been impressed for a festival of choirs; but when he arrived, just before the procession was timed to start, it was found that the one cassock which would encircle his figure was so long that he could walk in it only with danger of falling. Of course there was no string anywhere to be found, except in the shape of the dog-lead. The dog-lead saved the day, and the robed procession started off, lustily singing. It chanced that the keeper was one of the two leading choirmen, and when he noticed that his companion was rather headstrong in taking a corner, " Heel, will yer," he was heard to mutter, absent-mindedly, as he flicked his friend with the snap of his dog-lead from a besurpliced arm-hole; " heel, sir, heel."

A Keeper Chorister

There was something pleasing about the old familiar name for the gamekeeper—" Velveteens " : but it has been dropped almost completely, because no longer appropriate.   In the old times all gamekeepers were clad in ample coats of velveteen.   To-day, for one in velveteen you may see a hundred in tweeds.   And it is only the Cockney who calls the keeper " Velveteens " to his face— thereby putting him on his dignity at the least, if not insulting him.   The old-time coat was pleasant to the eye, so long as it was kept unspotted by rain. But its bloom departed after a few minutes' exposure to a generous shower, and no amount of drying or brushing would bring it back.   Moreover, the shirt of the man beneath the coat would probably suffer also from the wetting.   The best of velveteen was its thorn-resisting qualities.   Tweeds resist rain besides the thorns—the thick, heavy, closely-woven tweeds of the neutral brown tint that are now the fashion for keepers' clothes.   It is a long time before they can be thoroughly wetted—and the keeper's wife will tell you it is as long before they can be thoroughly dried.   They have two drawbacks—if made to fit closely and well they are uncomfortable for shooting until almost worn out ; and they are too hot and heavy for summer wear. Employers would be investing profitably if they allowed their keepers, instead of the one suit a year, a summer and a winter suit.   Comfort in dress makes a wonderful difference in the keeper's work ; hence the keeper's affection

Vel-veteens

for his oldest things and his scorn of appearances. His old breeches and gaiters become part of himself. A keeper who always donned trousers on Sunday invariably wore the old gaiters beneath them so that his legs might feel properly encased.

❦   ❦   ❦

Small birds, like men, misunderstand the owl— and it is always a curious sight to watch the mobbing of a night-bird by other smaller birds. Presumably the angered birds mistake the owl for a hawk. At any rate, they know him for a stranger, and no proven friend. When the swallows are alarmed by the appearance of an owl in day-time, they perform wonderful feats of flight, as they dart at the great bird from every angle, and swerve about him in every degree of curve. We have counted fourteen swallows' nests built in a shed against a pigeon loft wherein a pair of barn-owls were rearing their three young ones; we wondered how far the swallows were aware of the owls' presence, and what they thought about it. If they mobbed a parent owl by day there could be little real cause for their wrath—as little as when a missel-thrush or a jay joins in the outcry raised in the wood against the brown owl.

Owls and Hawks

Enlightened keepers leave all hawks unmolested, except perhaps on the rare occasions when they catch one in the act of gamecide. Beyond question, hawks as a rule do far more good to game interests than harm; and the kestrel, if he ever does any harm, pays for it a hundred-fold by his tireless industry in keeping down mice and voles. Once we carefully watched for several weeks the nests of three pairs of sparrow-hawks; and among the remains of their feasts the legs of only one young pheasant were discovered.

❦   ❦   ❦

It is time, and high time, that sparrow-hawks were placed under the protecting wing of the law. Generations of gamekeepers have persecuted them
The Bold Sparrow-Hawk relentlessly: it says much for their courage, strength, and craftiness that any should remain to offer a target for the keeper's gun.

But they grow scarce; they are seen far less commonly than kestrels, whose usefulness and innocence of gamecide is beginning to be a little understood. If sportsmen would consider the evidence for and against sparrow-hawks as despoilers of game—if they would rely no longer on prejudice and crass ignorance—we feel sure they would take steps to stay the wanton slaughter by their gamekeepers of these handsome, useful birds. Keepers ought to be forbidden to destroy any sparrow-hawks, except those which clearly prove themselves guilty of killing game as a habit. How thoughtless, ruthless, and mistaken is the keeper's zeal in killing them, we could show by a hundred instances. To take one:

It chanced that part of a patch of buckwheat had
been left unharvested, so that the pheasants might
help themselves to the grain.   Thousands of small
birds flocked to feed on the choice feast.   A gamekeeper noticed that sparrow-hawks found this patch
of buckwheat a fine hunting-ground, and would
perch in a clump of tall trees near by.   He therefore
hid himself in the trees, with a gun, and bagged four
hen sparrow-hawks, which had been well employed
in thinning the ranks of the small birds.

Countrymen will speak of the cock sparrow-hawk
as the little blue hawk, as though it were a separate
variety : not knowing that the cock bird is about
half the size of his mate.   Blue hawks, pigeon hawks,
and five-barred hawks are among the sparrow-hawk's
local names, arising from the blue-grey colour of the
upper parts of their plumage, from their occasional
habit of attacking wood-pigeons, and from the five
striking bars of brownish black on their tails.   Less
common than kestrels, sparrow-hawks are far less
conspicuous : while the kestrel hovers high in the
air on the lookout for prey (whether a mouse or a
grasshopper), the sparrow-hawk's way is to glide low
over the fields and along the hedges, swooping suddenly through gaps to pounce on unsuspecting small
birds.   The size and shape of the wings, and therefore
the flights of the two birds, are very different.   The
sparrow-hawk's wings are inclined to be rounded and
short ; the kestrel's are long and pointed.   While the
young of the two birds have a great deal in common,

the fledged young may be distinguished readily
by the white spot on the lower part of the back of
the sparrow-hawk's head. Each bird has a fatal
way of coming to investigate the sound of a gunshot.
If a shot is fired in the direction of a hawk flying
far out of range, say a hundred yards distant, it will
instantly dart down and towards the gunner, nearly
always within easy range. We have seen this happen
many times.

Like the kestrel, the sparrow-hawk is content with
a slovenly nest, which it builds of dead twigs on
the ruins of other nests—usually those of
magpies, crows, or pigeons. Or it uses a
squirrel's drey as a foundation, or comes
year after year to its own old home. Usually
the chosen site is not very high in a tree—larches
and oaks are favourites—and the nest will be found
near the trunk : in short oaks it may be in the cup
formed where several branches spread away. We
have found a nest within ten feet of the ground.
The nest, when you climb to it, is much larger than
it appears from below, and only a man with long
arms could encircle it. There may be five eggs,
pale white, blotched with dark chestnut-brown, the
markings of eggs in one clutch sometimes showing a
beautiful variation, while the markings of the clutches
of different birds differ considerably. The shells,
like those of the kestrel's eggs, are very thick—even

*Nest
and
Young*

the hawk's sharp claws would hardly puncture them without intentional effort.

Should you hear a soft whistling in a wood—not unlike the whistling of the farmer's wife when she calls her chickens to meals, but much subdued— you may know there is a sparrow-hawk's nest not far away. A glimpse of the whistler gives rise to a general alarm-cry among blackbirds. If the whistling leads to the discovery of young hawks, on your approach they will assume attitudes suggestive of disgust and resentment. In their poses and markings there is something owl-like about young hawks : and, as with young owls, there is a good deal of difference in the size of the fledglings, and in the state of their feathering. The strongest young one has the pick of the food, and quickly outgrows his brothers and sisters. Should the mother bird be killed, the cock will rear the family unaided on the small birds on which they thrive. The preservation of woods has meant a steady increase in the hosts of small birds, and hawks in consequence are under no necessity to prey on game-birds. Some sparrow-hawks will acquire the game-feeding habit : others will pounce by chance on a small game-bird ; but sparrow-hawks are in no way dependent on game, living for the most part on finches and the like, thereby helping to preserve the balance of scales of which the gamekeeper and his master take little heed.

One evening we were passing through a large, old-fashioned wood, when we came upon a keeper feeding his pheasants—many hundreds of them :
and the talk went round to the question of sparrow-hawks and game. We suggested that it was a wise keeper who spared the sparrow-hawk—that this hawk did not kill game for a tithe of its food—and that the time only came to kill it after it had been proved to attack game as a habit. But the keeper would not hear of this ; and he thanked his stars, he said, that not a sparrow-hawk remained alive in his woods. Just as he said these words we chanced to see before us on the ride, in the middle of the long rank of pheasant coops, a dead blackbird. The feathers lay scattered about the bird in a circle ; there was every sign of a sparrow-hawk's work. We called the keeper's attention to that blackbird's body. He agreed that a hawk had killed it, and then we drew from him the confession that he had not lost a single pheasant from a sparrow- or any other hawk. The keeper told us a story of how a brood of sparrow-hawks had been reared in a tree at the back of the very hut in which the pheasants' food was mixed. Though the hut was also a sort of watch-tower, yet the man who spent his days thereabouts had failed to notice the hawks until the young birds left the nest. This is not to say that the powerful old hen sparrow-hawk did not raid the pheasants ; but it is certain that she outwitted the under-keeper who

The Keeper Outwitted

worked daily at the hut, and it proves that an under-keeper may not know all that is to be known about sparrow-hawks and their ways.

❦   ❦   ❦

Among the birds not loved by keepers are jackdaws. One old keeper friend of ours has brought hundreds of jackdaws to a bad end. One evening,

A Jackdaw Nursery years ago, when walking through a park, his keen eyes noticed a hole high up in the stem of an ash-tree; and as he looked, out flew a jackdaw—never to return. Passing that way again, another jackdaw flew out, and paid the penalty of living in that keeper's preserves. He found the hole to be a favourite place for these birds, for it made an excellent nursery for the young. Season after season, the keeper kept his eye on the hole. As he went by, he would make a peculiar squeaking noise, which would call out any birds that might be at home. The stem of the tree about the hole became riddled with shot with such curious effect that when the tree fell the keeper cut out the section containing the hole; and it may be seen in his parlour, among other treasures, to this day.

❦   ❦   ❦

The gamekeeper is a trained detective. He is for ever setting a trap to catch a poacher. Across a ride where poachers may come at night, he will stretch a piece of invisible twine or wire, and he is at pains to place it just so far from a sharp stump that any one tripping will probably break a nose.

Anxious for a good night's rest, he keeps a **Detective Work** light burning in one of his cottage windows, so that the poachers may think he is out and about ; or when he goes out he pulls down a blind in his bedroom, as if he were sleeping within. Meeting workmen in the lanes near his preserves, he sends his dog for a sniff at their dinner-baskets— the dog soon tells him if there is game inside where should be bread and cheese.

☙ ☙ ☙

A dreadful idea to the keeper is the thought of cattle in his coverts. The worst that a mad bull could do in a china shop would make a faint picture **Cattle in the Woods** of destruction beside the havoc wrought by cattle in well-stocked preserves. Happy the keeper whose coverts are guarded by good fences in the days when flies torture cattle, and colts are most mischievous. If in hot weather a breach has once been made in a fence by cattle or horses, they will persist in trying to find their way into the woods. One can only pity the pheasant who sits on her eggs, on some sunny bank of a covert fence, while a herd of unbroken cart-colts go lumbering round the field, each shouldering each in an ill-judged swerve from the fence. Even in their calm moments colts are inquisitive, and leave nothing alone that is living and within their reach. We remember a case where a pheasant nested on the outside bank of a wood, and the colts in the field, pushing into the living fence, actually nosed her from her nest, and there was good evidence that they then chawed every one of her eggs. Most difficult of all creatures to keep out of woods are roaming swine. The strongest of live fences offers only a temporary check to their boring ability. And pigs have good noses, and few rabbit-stops and nests of eggs on the ground escape them. If a keeper's woods are infested by pigs he can scarcely be blamed for shooting his own bacon.

The keeper has an eye for the trim and pleasing appearance of his woods. He takes a genuine pleasure in their beauty. Jealous of the untrodden appearance of his secret paths, his annoyance is ill-concealed when the hunt cuts up his green rides. He would cheerfully forego the reward for the finding of a fox if he could preserve his rabbit-shorn sward—green and as smooth as velvet. And in his soul is a secret hatred of the traffic of the woodmen's waggons. Their great wheels crush and destroy the promising young underwood; woodmen, removing tree-trunks, ruthlessly plough up lawn-like turf; they have no care and no eye for the young growths of hazel, ash, maple, thorn or brier, to say nothing of bramble and bracken; and their waggons, carts and horses' hoofs spread a desolation which brings curses to the keeper's lips.

We know a wood near the Hampshire Highlands
that was once famous for its ash, and would be as
A Tragedy of the Woodlands famous now if the wood's owner had his
keeper's fine feeling. The keeper's heart
was cut if frost blackened the leaves ;
this was a grim tragedy. And there were
larches of gun-barrel straightness. An order
was given that the wood should be laid low. The
woodmen came with saw and axe, beetle and wedges,
they cut all the trees, and sent them to the guillotine
of the travelling steam-saw, which spoiled as fair a
meadow as any in Hampshire. Next the woodland
was thrown open to cattle, horses, and sheep. Then
the keeper was dismissed : and glad he was to go.

☙   ☙   ☙

When shooting parties begin again strange stories
are repeated about pheasants and partridges. We
Fox and Partridge remember hearing a learned disquisition on
the subject of the fox and the hen partridge ;
the argument was that the fox is only
occasionally successful when he makes a grab
at a hen partridge sitting on her eggs, and that the
hen, after fluttering from the jaws of death, will
return unconcernedly to her duties. Further, even
if the fox were so lucky as to capture the hen, the
cock partridge would most obligingly take up the
sitting and hatch the eggs. But no case was cited
where a fox had been known to attempt to catch a

sitting cock partridge—from which the inference might be drawn that the fox has a special aversion to the sitting cock.

Much nonsense of this sort is swallowed with good faith by those not closely in touch with foxes and game. We have an old book called " The Life of a Fox : Written by Himself." In this we read that a sitting bird acquires a thinness and flavour which are abhorrent to the taste of a fox ; nonsense guised as sense could hardly go further. It would be grossly disparaging to the fox's skill to say that he fails once in a hundred times when making a grab at a sitting bird ; and we are sure that a cock partridge does not take up the duties of his wife as often even as a fox fails to bring off a catch. We have never known a cock partridge to take the place of his murdered mate on the nest, but every gamekeeper knows he will rear the brood when the hen is killed after hatching.

❧   ❧   ❧

We have a pretty story to tell ourselves about the perseverance of partridges. In a district where few were found, a pair had left the fields **A Study in Perse-verance** and nested within a stone's-throw of the keeper's cottage. It stood in a green glade, sheltered on all sides by rambling old woods. For four successive seasons this partridge pair nested within a few yards of the same spot : and year after year something upset their plans, and spoiled all prospects of their hope of a covey—a hedgehog, rooks, inquisitive children, but, luckily, not a fox. The fifth season found the persevering birds trying again; their nest contained seventeen eggs. The site was an obvious one, but now the birds' luck turned. Just when it seemed that nothing could keep the nest from the eyes of any curious passers-by, a fine plant of hemlock sprang up to provide a screen and shelter. Every egg was then hatched, and every chick was reared to the flying stage. True, by September the young birds had been reduced until only nine were left. But as the keeper said, that was better than that a fox should have killed the old hen on her nest; and a family of nine was very creditable to a pair of five-year-old birds.

❦   ❦   ❦

Your gamekeeper is a skilled cook, and his open-air kitchen is a place of curious interest. For the first five or six weeks of their lives young pheasants

The Hut in the Woods are regaled several times daily with meals of hard-boiled eggs, custard, biscuit-meal, oatmeal, canary-seed, greaves and rice—seasoned with spices. Look into the keeper's hut in the woods, and you will see quite a collection of sacks filled with choice foods—cracked maize, dari-seed, groats, rice, preparations of dried meat, and finely dressed meals of wheat and barley. When the birds have learned to go to roost only one meal

a day is provided. In his kitchen the keeper prepares a thin meat soup, sometimes of sheeps' heads ;
this is boiled, then cooled, chopped lettuce and onion,
and barley and other meals are added, and then the
rations of the pudding-like mass are rolled into small
pellets. Over the keeper's kitchen the keeper's wife
has no jurisdiction. In some sheltered corner from
which he can keep an eye on his birds he builds himself a fireplace of two parallel rows of bricks open at
each end, so that he may burn long sticks and save
himself the labour of chopping wood if pressed for
time. Sometimes he will get the village blacksmith
to fashion a sort of iron gallows from which to hang
his great cooking-pots, each containing eight or nine
gallons, and of no small weight. By November
many keepers have cooked the last meal for their
pheasants—others may be preparing a final supper,
whistling till their jaws ache to call the birds to
the meal—on the morrow to do their utmost to
send the long-tails to destruction.

❦   ❦   ❦

" Mothering " is the factor which makes all the
difference between a moderately good and a very
good season for young pheasants. A hen
**Pheasant
Chicks** pheasant, when her chicks are quite small,
can easily give warmth and shelter to a
dozen or more ; after the first week or so some have
to go without, and unless the weather is fine and

warm, they perish before they are covered by body feathers. Weather conditions that have had a bad effect on partridges may have little effect on pheasants. Many suppose that if partridges have suffered from drought, pheasants, especially wild ones, must have suffered also. But wild pheasants have an advantage in several ways. The period during which they lay and hatch their eggs and rear their young is much longer than with partridges. If the last ten days of June be days of cold, heavy, ceaseless rain, they may practically annihilate the partridge chicks. But at that time a great number of young pheasants are old enough to withstand a considerable rainfall. Nor are the pheasants of tender age—only a section of the pheasant crop—so much at the mercy of bad weather as are tender partridges, for their haunts are chiefly in and about the woods and hedgerows, which afford shelter from cold and wet. In times of drought, the pheasants have the best chance of finding, among the shaded herbage, and beneath the masses of decaying leaves, enough moist insect food to carry them over to better days. It is on account of the better insect-supply in moist places that in very thin partridge seasons, where birds have suffered heavily from drought in open places, a few fine coveys may often be found on the fringes of woods. And in very wet seasons, the shelter and warmth of underwood also explain the survival of strong coveys. The end of September marks the time of the breaking-up of the pheasant broods. The

young birds no longer remain with their mothers ;
the young cocks begin to feel self-conscious and
gallant in their fine feathers, growing richer daily,
and duels are fought as by way of practice for the
fierce struggles of their first spring.   You may hear
at the roosting-time of the birds the crude efforts of
the young cocks to say " cock-up " instead of " peep-
peep."   Their utterances are an inharmonious blend-
ing of treble and bass ; indeed old pheasant cocks and
the birds of the year are as different in voice as
grown men and choir-boys, old rooks and young.

If one thing annoys a keeper more than another, it
is to have foxes turned down on his beat without
warning.   It is bad enough that foxes
The should be turned down at all—especially
Roosting before the young pheasants have learned
Habit
the trick of going into the trees to roost.
Most of the pheasants living in and about the
woods should go to roost by the middle of August,
and only late birds may be excused if they have not
acquired the roosting habit by the First.   In the
past the keeper was relieved of a load of anxiety
if all his hand-reared birds went to tree by the First
—for with the long days spent in the partridge fields
he was unable to watch over his pheasants at night.
But in these days, when there is so little partridge
shooting in early September, the keeper has more
time to give to his pheasants, and his anxieties are

less, though he is always glad when his birds take to roosting out of the reach of vermin, especially of foxes—tame or wild.

Given a fair chance young pheasants soon learn to go to a perch to sleep. Where one sets a good example, others quickly follow. We remember a partridge that was reared with pheasants, and learned to go with them regularly to roost. Five-weeks-old pheasants will flutter up to roost on the first night after removal to covert. It is less difficult to induce them to seek a perch than to break them of the habit of sleeping on the ground. Pheasants have an eye rather for comfortable sleeping quarters than safe ones. Many a keeper has suffered heavy loss from putting his birds in a covert with a thick grassy undergrowth, or within reach of a field of rough grass, or a young plantation with a thick growth of rank herbage and attractive weeds. There the fox is most likely to come.

Ideal quarters for the birds, when the time comes to shift them from the rearing-field to the coverts, is ground bare of brambles, fern, and grass, where oak saplings throw out horizontal branches—not too thick—a few feet from the ground. With his young birds in such a place, the keeper may lie on his bed in peace and thankfulness—to dream of the harvest of his toil, a harvest which needs but a fine November day and straight powder to be garnered in abundance. Where the ground is unfavourable the keeper will try to teach his birds the roosting habit; one plan is to put the hen and her coop on a raised platform. This lessens any risk the hen may have to run from vermin, and encourages her brood to fly to the roost.

❦   ❦   ❦

A badger may come to a neighbourhood and stay for a long while unnoticed. He prowls at night, unseen and unsuspected, and people may **The Badger's Stealth** suppose there is no badger within miles. In the same way otters are at home in many a stream where nobody dreams there is an otter in the neighbourhood. But let the badger's presence be discovered, and he will be persecuted to the end. The wise badger shifts his tent at once if a human nose is poked into it; all badgers would profit if they went to the fox for a few wrinkles. The foxes have a maxim : Never be at home to callers who may come again. A visiting-card, in the shape of a particle of scent, is more than enough acquaintance for a fox with a human being.

Even the gamekeeper often harbours a badger unknowingly. What he does not suspect he does not look for. And if he were to look for a month for signs of a badger he might never find one. Again and again he might pass within sight of a badger's holt, and think it to be the retreat of a fox. But by chance he might come upon a clear imprint of a badger's tracks, and after that it would not take him long to discover the badger's lair. While not a friend of the badger, he has no such bitter resentment against him as he feels for the fox. If it were not that the badger every now and then commits an outrage that brings disgrace on himself and all his kith and kin, the record of his life might be written down as fairly harmless. In these days the badger can make small claim as a provider of sport, which might mitigate the sentence most keepers pass upon him.

We knew of a badger who lived in peace, his presence unsuspected, for many long months. Then a series of mysterious poultry massacres began to disturb the district, and sometimes a dozen chickens and ducklings would be slain in one night. Some said fox, others dog ; strange stories of ghosts spread abroad ; it was even hinted that a wolf had been imported by mistake with foreign foxes. But one day tracks were seen that were not the tracks of fox, dog, or wolf, and a trail of feathers led to the discovery of a hidden draw-out. The badger was evicted and summarily shot.

❧   ❧   ❧

The bullfinch is not always made welcome when he comes to gardens at the time of fruit-buds. And there are seasons and places in which he would be welcomed—but comes not. We know a way to attract bullfinches, even to gardens in towns. You should take from a hedge-side a few plants of the wild geranium, and set them in your town garden —bullfinches are wonderfully fond of their seeds.

To Attract Bull-finches We have known the birds to find out the geranium plants in a town garden where bullfinches had never been seen before. To this garden they would come regularly, but always in the early morning. They are cheerful feeders—they live on insects and larvæ, as well as on many kinds of seeds and berries, in the spring feeding their young on seeds which have been carefully softened.

☙ ☙ ☙

Prominent among the birds that mob the barn-owl when he flies forth by day are jays and blackbirds.

Bird Warn-ings They are the noisiest, and to the gamekeeper the most useful of all the sentinels of the wood. A sudden hubbub from blackbirds and jays always has a meaning. If the birds are flying high it is a sign that the barn-owl is on the move—if low, the gamekeeper's thoughts fly to a poaching cat. A cat can hardly move a yard in a wood without a blackbird crying the alarm. His excited notes, suggesting the sound of the words "Flint, flint," are taken up by all the blackbirds within call, and soon the cat is besieged by a throng, and so closely that the keeper can follow pussy's direction, though she remains unseen. And the blackbirds give warning of the movements of stoats and weasels. The wren, too, is a lively and vigilant

sentinel, and from its movements one may determine
within a yard where the stoat is lurking. Jays, by
their screams, give prompt warning that a fox is on
the prowl, and no human trespasser, in pursuit of
game or otherwise, can hope to escape their attentions.
A lively reception awaits the fox moving in a wood
by day, and his progress may be marked through
the length of a big covert by the agitated way in
which the cock pheasants mount the trees, with
warning " cock-up." In the open the peewits
will gather to swoop and swerve in anger and
defiance above the fox's head.

❦   ❦   ❦

There was a small rabbit in our woods who might
have congratulated himself on two wonderful escapes
from death. We first made his acquaintance in a quiet by-lane, and just in time to
drive away a stoat that was loping swiftly
along on his trail. A little rabbit is pathetic
in fear, and instinctively one is angered against the
stoat which would take its life—though the stoat's teeth
represent the natural weapon of rabbit destruction.
The rabbit fled on his way—directly towards a motor-
car coming at speed round a corner. He darted to
one side, escaping the wheels by the fur of his tail,
then foolishly turned across the road, and again
escaped the wheels by a miracle. We wondered
whether the fate thus avoided would have been easier

**A
Rabbit's
Fates**

than the one delayed—no doubt soon after the stoat's
teeth bit home in the tender neck.

❦   ❦   ❦

We have seen a motor-car drive right over a covey
of young partridges as they dusted themselves on a
road, leaving half a dozen victims behind
it. But motors are not entirely opposed
to game interests. The dust they scatter
on roadside hedges greatly helps the hiding
of precious nests. Then the frequent passing of
cars along country roads is certainly a deterrent
to the poacher; the shooting man in his car takes
note of doubtful-looking tramps and gipsies, and
can spread a swift warning to keepers or police.
Even the smells of the car are a disguised blessing,
overpowering the scent of the sitting bird, and so,
no doubt, often preventing a dog from finding a
roadside nest. The motor has sent up the value of
many inaccessible shooting properties by eliminating
distance. It may be useful to a shooting party when
cartridges have come to an end, or at the close of a
day for transporting game speedily to the station,
or at any time for bringing a doctor when the bag has
been enriched by the addition of a gamekeeper.

Game-Birds and Motors

❦   ❦   ❦

On a midsummer night, in an old wood, the crooning
of the nightjar, with its whirring, vibrant, monotonous notes, now rising, now falling in key, seems

the ideal of lullaby. The beautiful night-flying swallow suffers for an evil reputation. It is a bird of mystery.

Mysteries of the Nightjar The nightjar is the last of our summer visitors, coming about the middle of May to stay until September. It is known almost the world over, but few understand its ways ; birds of the night suggest evil doings and inspire superstition. The plumage has the rich, quiet beauty of the woodcock and the hen pheasant, and the feathers have the softness of the owl's. In build the bird comes between a large swift and a small hawk, and is suggestive of swift or swallow when seen close at hand, with its miniature, hawk-like bill and a mouth surprisingly capacious when open. The eggs, like the swift's, are rounded at the ends.

It is commonly called night-hawk, or dor-hawk, because it preys on dor-beetles, and it is fern-owl, because it haunts the bracken fern. It is night-crow, because when on the wing it cries a crowing note, " crow-ic," and it is jar-owl, because of its owl-like love of night and its jarring or churring song. Wheel-bird is a name derived from the wheeling flight. Other names are churn-owl, eve-churr, and night-churr ; but the oldest and one of the most familiar names is goat-sucker, derived from the legend that the bird sucks milk from goats, thereby poisoning them and causing blindness. Probably some one saw the bird near a goat, did not know what it was, or anything about it, and invented the goat-sucking myth.

✿   ✿   ✿

Another bit of folk-lore about the nightjar is that it gave calves a disease called puckeridge; and on this account country folk still call this **The Razor grinder** innocent but unfortunate bird the pucker-idge. The disease, in fact, was caused by an insect which laid eggs on the backs of cattle, whence emerged grubs to cause the skin to pucker. The nightjar may often be seen wheeling about cattle, for the reason, no doubt, that the animals attract insects and disturb moths. Possibly for the same reason the nightjar, instead of flying away from human beings, will flit near about, keeping just in front of a walking man. Among other curious names is " razor-grinder." We met a countryman who only knew the nightjar by this name, derived from the noise made by itinerant razor-grinders at work.

✿   ✿   ✿

Perched lengthwise on a low branch or rail, the nightjar gives to its churring a ventriloquial effect by **A Ven-triloquist** turning its head while it croons. Though the crooning is monotonous, it varies in key, loudness, and duration; while the occasional cry, " crow-ic, crow-ic," reminds one of the cry of moorhens and tawny owls. As the bird flies, the snapping of the beak may be heard as a sharp click, whether it is snapped over a moth, or by way of showing resentment at one's presence— young wood-pigeons and doves snap in the same way if disturbed in the nest. The bird has marvellous control of its flight, and has a way of poising itself in the air with the wings meeting above the back, like the wings of the dove in a Scripture-book picture. The serrated claw on the middle toe is probably used for catching prey, and for clearing away fragments that cling round the gaping mouth ; while the long bristles that grow from the jaws entangle moths as in a net, as the bird flies with mouth wide open. It finds good hunting among oak-trees, and is especially fond of several of the many insects that chiefly haunt the oaks.

The nightjar is among the nestless birds, and is content to lay its two eggs on the ground. When hatched the young are covered with down like young peewits, and they grow at an amazing rate. An old nightjar, when disturbed from its young, will go through a despairing performance, flitting to a low branch near by, and flapping or wringing its wings in a disconsolate manner, as though to say, " Please go away—please *do* go away ! " The old bird seems to know how helpless is the position of the young ones if once discovered by a foe. But it is never easy to pick out the young birds from their surroundings, while the mother bird on her nest is as good as invisible.

Not all familiar with partridges know how to distinguish the cocks from the hens by the few minute differences in plumage. In flight the birds

The Cock and the Hen are so alike in size that it is impossible to tell them apart—unless, perhaps, they are in pairs, and one goes away ahead of the other on being put up, when the cock may be the hindmost bird. The usual test of sex is the chestnut horseshoe of the breast. The cocks display a fine bright horseshoe badge, while the hens have a few chestnut spots on a whitish ground. However, some insist that this test is not always infallible. One to be trusted absolutely, so far as we know, is the striking difference in the lesser and median wing coverts. In each case there is a light buff stripe down the shaft ; but the cock's feathers have a chestnut stain which is lacking in the hen's feathers, while the hen's feathers have zigzag buff cross-bars (of the same hue as the shaft stripe), which are lacking in the cock's feathers. There are other differences which the experienced eye sees at once ; and there are differences also in the neck feathers. In the adult cock they are grey, with no shaft stripe ; in the hen they are brown, with a light shaft stripe. The age of birds is to be determined to a certain extent quite simply. Those with bright yellow legs are birds of the year. Those with their first pen-feathers rounded are more than a year old, for in the young birds these feathers are pointed at the tip.

❦　❦　❦

To be able to name the different sorts of feathers to be picked up on any woodland walk is an interest

On Finding Feathers like that of the knowledge of flowers, which allows one to give each wayside blossom its name. The gamekeeper may put by the more beautiful feathers he finds for presents to his friends. The jay is killed for an egg-thief, but his blue and black wing is borne afterwards to church on the hat of a village maiden. The keeper has an appreciative eye for the burnished metallic hues of the feathers of cock pheasants of every kind. What greatly pleases him is to point out to the ignorant the existence of those two peculiar feathers in the wings of woodcock—the tiny, stiff, pointed feathers, growing close against the base of the first flight feather's shaft in each wing. These he could pick out in the dark by sense of touch. They are to be found in snipe's wings—in which they are lighter in colour, and even more minute—and in other birds, but it would be difficult to say what particular purpose they serve beyond a finish or covering for the exposed edge of the first flight feather. An unwritten law entitles the shooter of a woodcock to these particular feathers, and formerly the etiquette of sport allowed him to wear them in reasonable numbers in his hat. To-day one may sometimes see them in the hard hat of the poulterer. Painters in olden times appreciated the stiff points of the feathers for delicate work. And there was an agent on a Scotch shoot whereon woodcock are plentiful who maintained the national reputation for thrift by using the feathers as nibs for writing. But we suspect he did more woodcock shooting than quill-driving.

❦ ❦ ❦

Rats are marvellously cunning, they never fail to seize an opportunity and make the best of it. They are as bold as cunning, and take desperate **When the** risks ; but no doubt they know their own **Dog's** powers. The cunning and the boldness of **Asleep** rats are made evident when one is seen eating the crumbs of a biscuit beside a sleeping dog. Rats soon find out that where there is a dog in a kennel there will be food—not crumbs only, but an assortment of bones, and many a tit-bit, despised by a fastidious dog, from that comprehensive dish, household scraps. It is strange to watch a rat stealing a feast within a few inches of a sleeping terrier—the very rat for whose blood the terrier has wearied himself by scratching at a hole for the greater part of the day. Should the dog wake up and dash for his enemy, the rat coolly darts beneath the kennel. It is a thousand to one against the dog catching the thief.

❦ ❦ ❦

Keepers as a class have no love for rats ; but there is one keeper who regards all rats with the deadliest loathing, on account of a little experience. He had taken a new berth, and arrived at the cottage which was to be his home some days in advance of his wife, taking bread, a ten-pound cheese, and a cask of beer, on which to subsist until the more luxurious days of his wife's coming.

A Story of Rats

Having found that the outgoing keeper had carried off the front-door key, he brought his most valuable possessions into his bedroom, including the bread, cheese, and beer. Thoroughly tired with his journey and his unpacking, he slept so well through the first night that some mysterious sounds, as in a dream, failed to rouse him. On awakening, he discovered that rats had paid a call, and had eaten every particle of the bread and of the ten-pound cheese. They had even assaulted the bung of the beer-barrel, happily for them and for the keeper without success. During the first three months of his residence this keeper killed no fewer than 600 rats in and about his old-fashioned cottage.

Thinking of the rats who assaulted the beer-barrel reminds us of the story of a clever rat that drank from a wine-bottle by first inserting, then licking, his tail. Rats are so cunning that one can believe almost anything told of them. They suffer, at times, terribly from thirst. There is no doubt that a dry breeding season means a small crop of rats, which seems to support the theory that when hard pressed by thirst larger rats kill the little ones for the sake of their blood. When feeding on corn, in ricks or barns, a spell of rainless weather means much suffering, even if dews compensate in some measure for the absence of water. If you would see rats at their merriest, watch a corn-stack on a summer evening when a shower has come after scorching days. In a little while a rustling will be heard, and the rats steal out to gulp the raindrops on the thatch and the herbage near by. We have seen a rat so thirsty that in spite of being driven back to his hole each time he appeared, every half-minute he would again attempt to reach a farm-yard puddle. A farmer who shot at one rat killed no fewer than seven, which had crowded to drink from a wayside pool.

We have a cat which, when thirsty, sometimes drinks from an open tub, balancing herself on the edge. When the water is too low for lapping she **Blood and Water** will dip in a front paw and lick off the water in delicate and dainty fashion. Bloodthirsty creatures require deep drinks: stoats and weasels go often to water. But creatures which feed on green-stuffs seldom drink water directly, but in the shape of dew, or the moisture of their food. Sheep, when feeding off root-crops in autumn and winter, have little need of water, and rabbits and hares are not great drinkers. Partridges are among many birds that may drink only of rain-drops or dew, or quench their thirst with juicy seeds or insects. Dry summers always mean plenty of partridges—yet one hears, each dry summer, that partridges are dying in numbers from drought. It

is rather the absence of moisture-supplying insects
that is fatal to the birds.

***

Midsummer Day might be marked as the partridge's
birthday, since the majority of birds are hatched
about that time—a month later than the
majority of pheasants break their shells.
People are sometimes puzzled when they
realise that pheasants are preserved for
two months longer than partridges. The reason,
of course, is that pheasants mature slowly, and partridges quickly. But are partridges given fair grace ?
We think not—and would advocate a later opening
day for partridge-shooting. Not a partridge of the
year is matured on September 1, in size, or strength
of flight, or endurance. The young birds are still in
the drab-feather stage ; their legs are bright yellow,
an infallible token of youthfulness ; and it is rare,
before October, to find one with the horse-shoe
chestnut feathers on its breast, or with rufous head—
the signs of maturity. The heavy toll taken on
small shoots during the first fortnight of September
is not only unfair, but unwise, and often fatal to the
good prospects of future seasons. Another mistake
commonly made is the shooting of too many hares
in September. Many of the does are still suckling
leverets ; and does, that breed for the most part in
the fields, form a large proportion of the hares met
with in September partridge shooting.

The
Untimely
Opening

Wire netting is the cause of many a tragedy to young
pheasants.   One may see it stretching for miles on
the fringe of woods as a fence against rabbits.
'Ware
Wire   Suppose a hen pheasant, with her brood,
has been making an excursion to the fields.
She comes to the wire and finds her return passage
barred.   Seeing that most of her little ones have
wriggled through the meshes, the mother flies over,
and goes on.   But as often as not she leaves behind
her one or two chicks, and these the flower of her
flock—for they are the ones so well grown as to be
just too large to pass through the meshes.   Sooner or
later, after fluttering to find a loophole, the little
necks become caught, and after a few frantic struggles
the chicks hang themselves.   Or night comes on,
and some prowling vermin saves them from a slow
death by exhaustion through their vain efforts.

❦   ❦   ❦

Pheasants, beside partridges, are stupid mothers :
nor have young pheasants anything like the common
sense of young partridges.   The mother
Witless
Pheasants partridge is the most careful mother, and
by example soon teaches her young ones
to use their wings.   One hears the old partridges
calling all through the day to their young ; but the
little pheasants must fight their own battles with
less encouragement, and look after themselves.   One
may see a hen pheasant leading her brood towards a
dike, over which it is obvious they are not strong

enough to pass.   But without a look to see if they
follow her or not, she flits across ; then, finding that
a few are with her, having managed the passage, she
hurries on, as if she had not a thought for those left
behind.   They do their best to follow, only to fall
into the water, in which they are drowned, or, if the
dike is dry, to become exhausted in their vain efforts
to scale the steep sides.

❧ ❧ ❧

Yet it is hardly fair to compare pheasants to partridges.   The difference in their habits of life makes
it necessary that partridges should learn to
use their wings more quickly than pheasants.
Nature's Laws
They will fly when no larger than starlings,
but pheasants grow as big as full-grown partridges
before making much use of their wings.   Partridges
mature the more quickly : hatched in mid-June they
are nearly full grown by September, while pheasants,
born in May, are still in their baby stage in October.
Then the habit of the partridges to roost in coveys
on the ground fosters the instinct to spring into the
air and fly on the first sign of danger, all in a covey
acting as one bird for mutual protection.   There
is some little excuse for the young pheasants that
butt into wire with such foolish persistency—they
are so near to the wire that their legs have no chance
to launch them fairly into the air.   While the desire
of a pheasant, on meeting wire outside a wood, is
to pass through into the covert, the idea of the par-

tridge is to turn about, and fly back to the fields whence it came. The effect of a line of wire-netting on wild creatures seems to be that they imagine they are enclosed on all sides. A half-grown leveret cantered before us for quite two miles alongside netting to the left of him ; only after covering this distance did it seem to dawn upon him that by turning to the right he might go his way to freedom.

What are the ideal conditions for partridges ? First, an old-fashioned April—growing weather. Then an old-fashioned May, with blue skies and genial sunshine, to be followed by a June without a drop of rain that would hurt a fly by day, with occasional warm sprayings of rain by night, to help on the insect-supply for the chicks, and to keep the soil just as partridges like it when scratching for insects, but not wet enough to clog their feet. The ideal June—the partridge June—has warm nights and fine sunny days, without too much scorching sunshine. The fine weather must go on during the first part of July in the interests of the later-hatched chicks; and if August can behave as it should, so much the better—but the most important thing is a partridge June. Nothing can make amends to the partridges for a wet, cold June ; for nothing can bring their dead chicks to life.

We need not think of the effect of frost on partridge eggs, for the birds cover their eggs when they leave them, until they are well on their way to-wards hatching, with wonderful care, regularity, and thoroughness; and here they have the advantage of pheasants, which rarely cover their eggs when off the nest. Another advantage of the partridge is the hen's faithful mate—to help to shelter the brood from the weather and keep them warm. One bird might be able to manage this for fifteen little ones during their first week of life; but afterwards she could not possibly give the vital warmth to more than half her offspring. To the chicks of the pheasant hen a risky time is between the shedding of the soft fluffy down of infancy and the growth of feathers proof against cold and wet. Where pheasants have the advantage is that their hatching-time is spread over many weeks; so that whereas partridges may have their hopes ruined by a week or by a few days, or even a few hours of bad weather, the pheasants' hopes are never blighted while summer lasts.

It may be urged that if there are few young partridges there must be few young pheasants, and this to some extent is true. Though the breeding conditions of pheasant and partridge are very different, a bad season for one can hardly be a good season for the other. With partridges, the great trouble is that nearly all of them nest about the same time: where one brood suffers from bad weather, thousands

must suffer.   For ten days after hatching, partridges
are at the mercy of the weather.   Let one of those
marble-sized drops of rain strike a newly hatched
chick, and its day is done.   As one sharp frost destroys
all the apple-crop of a countryside, if it comes when
the trees are in full bloom, so a deluge in mid-June is
fatal to all young partridges.   Even a day's thunder-
rain, between the fifteenth and thirtieth of June,
would almost excuse a partridge keeper if he com-
mitted suicide—though we have never heard of such a
thing.

Heavy warm rain is bad enough—heavy cold
rain is simply disastrous when it falls day after day,
for weeks, from the time when most partridge eggs
begin to hatch, until all except the second clutches
are hatched—or flooded out.   It is hardly worth
considering whether the wet or the cold claims most
victims : enough that if wet fails to bring about a
tragedy, cold finishes the work.   The sunless days,
the everlasting rain, the drenching herbage, and the
sodden soil wipe out most broods to a bird.   It is
not, as many suppose, a question of a good hatch
that controls the supply for September, but it is
simply a question of the weather for the first fortnight
after hatching.   Usually, if any eggs in a nest hatch,
all the eggs hatch ; but we may say that if only half
the eggs in each nest hatched, and a fine fortnight
followed, more birds would be reared than if every
egg in each nest produced two chicks, and a drenching fortnight then set in.

In a wretched hatching season, the best luck is often with the intermediate early broods. They fare least badly. As to second nests, it never makes much difference to September's sport whether they prosper or not. A covey of a dozen, in a September following a wet June, is a good covey. The most general coveys are coveys of old birds—or coveys consisting of one young bird! There is no more reliable sign of a poor partridge crop than a good year for roots.

❦   ❦   ❦

We remember how an experienced keeper was quite at sea in his judgment of a particular covey. It

A Covey of Ancients

had been a bad season, and after the corn had been cut he knew of only one good covey; it numbered nine birds, and fine forward birds they were. On this covey he set great store against the coming of September. It happened that he was bidden to shoot a couple of brace of young birds for dinner at " the house " on the First. With his first shot at the covey he bagged the old cock. He pursued the rest of the covey, bagged another bird, also an old cock. Disappointed but still hopeful, again he pursued the covey, again he bagged another bird, and again it was an old cock that fell to his gun. He went on until he bagged the ninth and last bird, and the ninth was no better than all the others. It was a sad keeper who went home that day with his nine old birds. Ever since he has been sceptical about coveys of forward birds. But he always says now that foxes at least show gallantry in the matter of " ladies first."

❦ ❦ ❦

If June proves wet, despair reigns in the partridge keeper's breast. With hopeless eyes he looks forward to the coming season. One keeper of our acquaintance, one wet midsummer, a time when, in a promising season, he would have had no moment to spare from the care of his young birds, married, and went for a honeymoon. " Lor' love ye," said another, weary of June rain, " I might just as well 've bin in bed for a month past." A common remark made by keepers in a rainy June is the mournful plaint, " Ye don't see no feetmarks on the roads, but old un's."

Keepers' Woe

❦ ❦ ❦

The more we see of red-legged partridges the more we appreciate their powers of running. They are wonderful birds for eluding the tactics of walking-up parties ; even where the birds are plentiful it is rare to walk-up one within gunshot. The red-leg also suffers by comparison with the English birds on the table. But he is a grand bird for driving (when he is headed and forced to fly), seldom coming in coveys—so that a dozen red-legs may afford as many shots as a dozen unbroken

Red-Legs

English coveys. And they come straight, more in
the style of grouse than of the brown partridges.
The two types seldom intermingle, being of different species and different genera. In some places
an ill-feeling is still harboured against the bigger
and handsomer red-legs, and it is thought that they
drive away the English birds.

☙   ☙   ☙

It is a lucky keeper whose shoot is watered by springs
and brooks which never fail in time of drought, for a
continuous supply of water means much to
Water for the success of game-breeding. But streams
Game-
Birds have their dangers : birds will be attracted
to the banks at nesting-time, and if heavy
rains follow, their nests may be destroyed by the
floods. A greater danger lies in the streams which
are winter water-courses only and dry up in the
spring. Herbage will grow luxuriantly at the stream-
side, and birds will be enticed to nest in places where,
after a heavy rainfall, there will rush a raging torrent,
to carry away birds, nests, eggs and all. Some say
that nesting birds can foretell the weather, and choose
their nesting-places accordingly—building on the
banks and higher ground if the season will be wet,
but in the hollows if dry. No doubt their choice is
influenced only by prevailing weather, and the position of suitable cover. In a cold, late spring, grass-
fields offer poor shelter, and so the birds choose the

hedges and dikes, where the wild, weedy growth finds moisture for its roots and protection for its top-growth. When birds are sitting, the less they have to do with water the better for their hopes.

Perhaps it is better for birds to be drowned than to suffer from drought. A long spell of hot weather is not in itself harmful to the broods, for sunshine is the essence of life in their early days; but while drought does not cause suffering through lack of water, it means lack of juicy food, and that is fatal. Succulent weed-seeds and grubs and insects are not to be found; the milkiness is dried out of the seeds, and grubs and worms go deeply into the soil, beyond scratching distance. But food enough of sorts could be found during the severest drought if a little water were also available. Ponds are useful only to a small proportion of the broods, and become waterless when drought is long enough to threaten serious loss. Heavy thunder-rain after drought completes the work of destruction. If it comes within a fortnight of Midsummer Day, it means calamity to hosts of young partridges, who mày be overwhelmed before they can reach their parents, or, gaining that shelter, are drowned when the ground is swamped.

Many keepers never give their young pheasants water until they have been removed from the rearing-field to covert—but their food is made dry or moist according to the weather. This plan answers well enough until there comes a hot, dry spell which ends suddenly in rain, and then the chicks drink immoderately, and suffer the penalty. That chicks take the first chance to drink the raindrops from the herbage shows that water is good for them ; and the best plan is to provide them with a continuous supply of clean water from the beginning, so that they never become thirsty and drink themselves to death.

❦   ❦   ❦

A continuous supply prevents the straying of pheasants as they grow up, and feel inclined to see the world, especially when they have been weaned from food more or less pappy to a diet of hard corn. Another benefit is felt by the gamekeeper : where there is no constant supply, he must trudge many weary miles carrying heavy buckets of water, and he knows all the time that his labour is almost in vain—so much of the precious water is wasted by evaporation, and fouled by the birds washing themselves, and by the drifting of leaves. If artificial supplies are relied upon, it is always difficult to supply enough ; if rain is relied upon, there is usually far too much. For game-birds, the ideal covert is one with never-failing brooks, and the ideal weather is the ideal weather of April —days of warm sunshine with occasional light, warm showers by day to supplement the dews of night.

Nothing keeps down rabbits more thoroughly than a
soaking wet summer ; while heavy rains drown the
partridge and pheasant broods above ground,
they also drown the little rabbits in their
furry nests below.   Yet in times of drought,
when herbage is parched and sapless, the
keeper who supplies water for the rabbits to drink
in arid, sandy warrens does much for the prosperity
of the does and their young. Rabbits eat their
young when in want of water, and a dry summer puts
a check on the increase of rats, since the old ones
kill the young for their blood. With rabbits, a
favourite place is always a dry spot by the side of
water, although the ground is likely to be favoured by
stoats. Rabbits found in such places are always extra
fine and fat.

" Please drive cautiously. Hound puppies are at
walk in the village." We came upon this notice
nailed to the trunk of an ash on the road
outside a village in Hampshire. The inference suggested itself that so long as those
who might drive furiously through the
village touched no hair of a hound puppy's head
nothing else mattered.   Usually, it is the old-fashioned
notices that bring a smile to the passer-by's face :
" Beware of Man-traps," " Spring Guns," " Dog-
spears set here." Walking along the River Stort
we have been startled by a notice beside some of the

K

locks, " The Punishment for Tampering with these
Works is TRANSPORTATION." " Trespassers will be
Punished by Transportation " would be a suitable
legend for a board in a strictly preserved wood,
hinting that if you do not go quietly on request the
keeper will carry you.   Reading the new caution to
drivers outside the Hampshire village, we were tempted
to simplify it thus : " Beware of hound puppies."
It is pleasant to see young hounds basking in the sun
in the farmyard ; but when they are at walk in the
charge of the village butcher they may be more than
a general nuisance ; they may terrorise the place.
People who walk hounds do not always undertake
the honour because they like it, but because they
cannot well refuse.   The hounds are turned out into
the streets to prowl at large—they slaughter poultry,
spread havoc in many a garden plot, knock down
children, and roam in through open cottage doors,
to steal the labourer's dinner from off his very table.
A pack of hounds under the control of a firm huntsman and his whips is one thing—but hounds at walk,
allowed to wander at their will, are a peril to the
community.   " Beware of hound puppies "—when
they come up treacherously behind you.

❧   ❧   ❧

Retriever pups born about the end of January are
old enough, by August or September, to begin their
careers of usefulness.   If given light work, during
the second half of their first year they may be ready

to take an important part in the next shooting season, when eighteen months old. Spring puppies

are certainly easier to rear than autumn puppies—they grow faster, and are likely to become finer specimens than the others, which must endure long months of trying weather during puppyhood. But there is this in favour of autumn puppies—they come to their first shooting season at a more mature age, and intellectually are readier to learn than the six months old puppies of spring. At the age of twelve months a puppy begins to put away puppyish things.

It is only possible to gain perfection in the education of a puppy by beginning so soon as it is weaned. From that time the puppy should be taken in hand by its future master, whom alone it should know and understand. One can hardly begin too early to teach the meaning of the word " No," which, to the puppy, is that it must not do something that it had thought desirable to do—whether to chase a cat or rabbit, to be excited at the rising of a lark, or to hunt a road-side hedge. Another important early lesson is teaching the puppy its name. For stud-book and show purposes the name may be, if you please, " Beelzebub of Babylon," or any other high-flown title, but for common use it should be distinct in sound, and preferably of not more than one syllable. Puppies may be taught their names and obedience at the same time ; in classes perhaps more quickly and more thoroughly than individually. It is a good plan at feeding-time to have the puppies together, and put food outside an opening in their kennel ; then to call out each puppy by name, and on no account allow any other to come than the one called.   In a surprisingly short time it will be possible to set open the door and call out each puppy by name, without forcibly keeping back the uninvited. In this way a good grounding might be given to the favourite fox-terriers in obedience, of which so many have not the slightest notion.

❦   ❦   ❦

The power of scent varies much with different dogs : usually a slow dog makes better use of its scenting nerves than the fast galloper.   It is pretty to watch a good retriever following a wounded bird over ground alive with unwounded game, yet never turning aside from the one trail. A dog could hardly distinguish one partridge from another—probably it is by the scent of blood that the one line can be followed so accurately.   Sportsmen do not always give the dogs fair chances ; they throw them cheese at lunch-time, or perhaps allow bagged game or themselves to taint the wind, so foiling other trails.   In one case a sportsman blamed a new retriever for not finding a bird which was actually lying beneath his own boots.   And even a first-rate retriever will sometimes tread on the very bird he is seeking, without finding it.

Dogs' Noses

❦   ❦   ❦

Gamekeepers, we know, have little love for foxes—
for the sufficient reason that they are at one with
foxes in their love of pheasants.   Keepers
have also some of that craftiness and worldly
wisdom so developed in foxes ; they know
it is not always policy to say with their
lips what they believe in their hearts.   There are
good people who tell keepers every now and again
that foxes do no harm to game.   Keepers have
heard stories in favour of foxes ; they know the rights
of them.   Dark and mysterious are the ways of the
fox ; but darker still and more mysterious are the
ways of the keeper with " the thief of the world."
This alone he will admit in favour of the fox : he adds
to the keeper's work an uncertainty which makes
success the sweeter.   The fox is a favourite of Fortune, his needs are fulfilled exactly ; all things seem
arranged in his favour to a nicety.   Other creatures
may die of starvation in time of snow ; but the fox
then finds his prey with greatest ease.   Cubs are
weaned about the middle of May, and must be fed
on flesh, when a majority of pheasants are sitting.
And when a sitting pheasant is scented or seen by a
vixen in search of food for her cubs, that pheasant,
you may say, is dead.   The keeper, though his blood
boils afresh at each nesting tragedy—at the sight
of the strewn feathers of the hen pheasant and at the
cold touch of the lifeless eggs—appreciates the deft-
ness of the marauder's work.   He reconstructs each
scene of the plundering—the silent passage of the

The Thief of the World

prowling fox, the pause of a moment to sniff and sniff again the scent that taints the air, the swift thrust of long jaws between bramble, brier, and bracken, the grab of gleaming teeth, the stifled cry of the dying bird, the floating of brown feathers on the wind of night, and the joy of the cubs at the sight of the dead bird and the scent of her welling blood. And then the carnival of feasting at the mouth of the earth, by the old tree of the cubs' playground, while the white owl screeches his protest as he passes overhead, and the mother fox, sitting on her haunches, licks her chops and watches. The work of a vixen among sitting birds differs from that of the dog fox. While she always carries her booty to her cubs, he kills in wanton waste, leaving the birds' bodies, often headless, near their nests. Some or all of the eggs may be eaten, or they may be left untouched, still as neatly arranged in the nest as the mother bird left them when she stole off to feed and take a bath in dust. The keeper may recognise the excuse of the mother fox's necessity, but for the wanton slaughter by her idle mate he sees no reason, and finds no forgiveness.

Only those who have seen the remains of game scattered round the earth of a litter of cubs—the cubs of an experienced mother—can realise what it costs in game to entertain foxes. Where rabbits are plentiful, pheasants and partridges suffer less from foxes than where rabbits are scarce, and the keeper may help a vixen to cater for her cubs by shooting

and snaring rabbits in her favour.   He leaves their
bodies, but scattered at a fair distance from the
earth, so that the vixen must spend some time in
fetching and carrying, and has the less time for
making a mixed bag of her own selection.

Unseeing eyes pass blindly over the home of a litter
of cubs ; but the keeper's never overpass the place.
        Long furrows through the dog's-mercury and
The Cubs' grasses tell their tale.   Primroses are torn
Play-
ground   and crushed, the great leaves of the burdock
        are bruised and broken, the moss is rubbed
from the underwood stumps and from the boles of
trees where the cubs have been gambolling and rubbing
their coats, the excavated soil near the earth is smooth
from the pattering of their feet, beaten hard and
polished—and in all directions there are scattered
wings, feathers and bones.   If the keeper calls, and
sees signs of recent rollicking play and fresh-killed
food, and fresh-drawn soil where the cubs amuse
themselves at earth-making and enlarging the burrows
of rabbits, he knows the family to be in residence.
Should the soil near the entrance to the earth have
a green look, he knows the family has gone away.

Who would believe that a full-grown fox could
pass through the mesh of ordinary sheep-netting ?—
four-inch mesh, if memory serves.   We know of one

case where a vixen was actually seen to accomplish this wonderful feat. With her cubs, she had been dug out from her earth, carried to a distant part of the country, and imprisoned. The four-inch mesh must have been a tight fit for her body ; but perhaps she had worried and fretted at her imprisonment, until she had worn herself to a shadow. Her cubs, which were unweaned, may have helped to weaken her strength, and reduce her waist until it could squeeze through the netting.

A Fox's Feat

The story has a sequel. A town doctor saw the vixen a few moments after her escape ; and happened to find himself sitting next to a M.F.H. at dinner. The doctor remarked, with a well-meant attempt at affability, " Foxes seem to be plentiful in your neighbourhood this year." " What makes you think so ? " asked the M.F.H., with encouraging eagerness. " Why, only the other day, passing your place about noon, I saw a vixen with cubs trotting across your lawn." The doctor swiftly perceived that he had let the fox out of the bag, so black was the look that came over the Master's face. But it was months before he solved the full riddle of the black look, when he learned that the fox he had seen on the lawn in broad daylight had only just escaped from her wire-net prison, so saving herself from the ignominy of being turned down with her cubs.

The keeper finds his game-nests with his eyes, the fox with his nose. The keeper who must preserve game and preserves foxes takes steps to overcome the scent of his birds. He sprinkles the neighbourhood of all the nests he can find with some strong-smelling fluid. But the foulest or strongest scent will not save a bird when a fox has once seen her. Fortunately he is not clever enough to know a new trap from an old one, nor a sound from a broken one, and the keeper finds at nesting-time a good use for his disused traps, placing them about birds sitting in dangerous spots. Anything in the shape of scrap-iron the fox suspects; anything unusual about a nest, such as a piece of newspaper on a bush near by, will arouse his fears, and possibly save a bird's life. But as rooks learn to treat scarecrows with contempt, so foxes learn to have no fear for harmless terrors, and the keeper rings the changes on all the fox-alarming devices which experience and ingenuity can suggest.

❧   ❧   ❧

Two or tree times a year, the gamekeeper gives all his dogs a grand washing; and his methods should be marked by other dog-owners, for there are few who understand dogs better. He

Dog-Washing Days

knows that a dog's coat, like a woman's hair, is spoiled by too much washing, which destroys the satiny gloss imparted by the natural oils. He knows, too, that a dip in a pond or a splash in a stream only wets the surface of a coat, and does not cleanse the skin. His method is thorough, and designed not only to cleanse the hair and skin, but to rid the dogs of all the unwelcome guests they may harbour. Choosing a warm, sunny day, the keeper gets to work betimes, so that he may have his dogs washed and out to dry by midday; they must be perfectly dry before nightfall. He sets up a wooden tub on an old box, for his own convenience, and brings forth his pails and cans of water—water of just that tepid temperature which a dog likes. He wants his dogs to enjoy their bath, and knows that if he scalds or otherwise frightens them they will be shy of the wash-tub for ever afterwards. To pitch a dog unawares into a tub of water is as foolish as to throw him into a pond. He must be coaxed to his bath with words of encouragement, so that he will see there is nothing to be frightened about. Properly treated, dogs soon learn to appreciate the wash-tub, and there may be trouble in making them come out.

Having brought the dog to the tub, the next work is to put him in and thoroughly wet his skin—not an easy matter with a retriever, who may lie in water for ten minutes and yet keep his skin dry. So the keeper works in the water by hand, rubbing the hair the wrong way, and gently persuading the dog to lie down. Once comfortably settled in the tub, a happy look comes over the dog's face. This, by the way, may not be true of the face of the keeper's wife, should she come to her door to watch proceedings, and find that her good man has borrowed her new wash-tub. To make the best of a bad business, she may decide to give her pet goose a good tubbing; and this will be one of the grandest treats in the goose's life.

One old keeper of our acquaintance has a curious recipe for a dog-wash, and swears that in more than fifty years he has not found its equal. You must uproot, he will tell you, an armful of foxglove plants, and boil them in a copper of water. When the infusion is cool enough, rub it well into your dog's coat, and lather him with a little soft soap. " And I'll lay," says the old chap, " that you don't see nothing about a dog after that, and his coat will look fit to go to a wedd'n." The keeper's plan is to leave the lather in his dogs' coats for some little time after they have left the tub. Every lathery dog is tied up in turn in a sunny spot, free from draughts; then all are rinsed in the order of washing, and are taken for a long gambol in a field of grass, the keeper taking care not to let a dog free in a dusty place, for his first act is to have a good roll, regardless of a clean coat.

❧   ❧   ❧

At harvest-time the old cock pheasants begin to show themselves in the woods again. In April one grew almost weary of the insistent, boasting crows of the vainglorious dandies. Then for months they seemed quite to drop out of woodland society. They like to take things easily through the summer, leaving all family cares to the members of their harems. And no doubt

Shame-faced Cocks

they feel out of sorts, and have no desire to be seen —for they have to pass through the strain of the moulting season.

As the last acre of the cornfield is cut, a hundred young pheasants rise, with self-important splutterings, before the binders, each bird clearly betraying its sex by the growing feathers of maturity. But the cunning old cocks seldom advertise their presence. They slink stealthily out of the field while the machines are making their first rounds, and in a couple of yards from the corn reach the shelter of the hedge. They steal away with lowered heads, as though to hide their faces behind each blade of stubble. A dissipated, dishevelled old ruffian the cock pheasant appears while moulting—with half a tail, many flight feathers missing from the wings (corresponding feathers drop out together from each wing, so that he is not deprived of power of flight), and lacking all the metallic gloss of plumage, burnished gold and bronze. To come suddenly on a moulting cock pheasant—as when he is enjoying a quiet dust-bath—is to pity him. And the way he blunders off suggests that he is heartily ashamed of himself.

In May the turtle-doves were skimming low across the fields, after their arrival in this country. During the last week of August we saw them gathering into little parties of dozens or scores against the hour of their departure. The doves leave before the end of harvest—the first chillness of autumn bids them go. The pigeons remain to continue their feasts of corn.

The Turtle-Dove's Summer Their cooing from the recesses of the beeches suggests a well-fed laziness. Great feeders as they are, they stuff their crops to bursting-point, and nothing vegetarian or fruitarian seems to come amiss to them—whether the greens of root-crops, acorns, beech-mast, clover, the sown peas, dandelion leaves, sainfoin, anemone roots, charlock, beech buds, the seeds of bluebells, wild strawberries, oak-galls, or corn in all its stages. Turtle-doves pay little attention to corn till harvest-time ; the seeds of charlock and of other noxious plants are a greater attraction. Though they fly with wood-pigeons a great deal, their diet is different, and they seem to come to ponds to drink more often than the pigeons, perhaps because some of their favourite foods, such as charlock seeds, are hot and thirst-producing. They are among the farmer's best friends.

Whenever we flush a landrail we wonder that so slovenly a bird should be able to cross seas in migration.

The Lagging Landrail One doubts its ability to cross a wide river. Those who for the first time see a landrail rise might be excused for supposing it to be wounded — the long legs trail at full length, hardly clearing the heads of the clover which forms its favourite

cover. Few birds are so slow in flight, certainly
no other game-birds—if it is entitled to be classed
with them, because, as for woodcock and snipe,
a game licence is required before it may be taken.
Beaters have surprised themselves by bagging
landrails with sticks and partridge carriers, and we
have known a clever retriever to catch a landrail
in the air. In spite of her wide experience, the
dog mistook the landrail for a wounded bird when
it rose, in its heavy way, some twenty yards before
her, while she quested for a partridge. As if in revenge
for having been fooled, she gave furious chase, and
retrieved it. Flushed in a gale of wind, a landrail will
make some progress, though its flight at first is rather
suggestive of a wind-driven leaf. But after a time the
flight grows stronger, as though the wings had worked
off some stiffness. No bird seems less willing to be
seen than the landrail. Yet it will make itself heard
almost continuously from the first streak of dawn
until darkness. Its harsh-toned " Crake, crake,
crake," seems close at hand at one moment, then
far away, suggesting that the bird is swift enough
on its legs, if slow in flight. It does not travel far,
having arrived from its over-sea journey, haunting,
as a rule, one chosen field, where it is seen only by
the mower, who may accidentally wound the close-
crouching bird with his scythe. Landrails seem to
become more scarce every year, and this is often put
down to the mowing machine, which it is claimed is
more fatal to sitting birds than the scythe. But birds

usually run from their nests before the approach of
the noisy, whirring machines, and, if they are caught,
seldom suffer more than a cut leg ; whereas the scythe
comes upon them almost unawares, and strikes fatally.
Probably some influences bearing upon the migration
of landrails have more to do with their scarcity than
unnatural destruction.   Hiding so closely in the grass
or the corn, landrails seem to have every chance of
long life in this country.

❧   ❧   ❧

The first day of August is the most important of the
gamekeeper's minor festivals, for the close time under
            the Wild Birds Protection Act has come to
The   an end ; duck-shooting begins to be a legal
Truce
Ends   if not a difficult pastime, and hares, which,
            unfortunately, may be harassed all the year
round, can now be sold openly.   The time has come
for the cutting of the first cornfields ; and this is ever
an important event to the keeper, for it allows him
to make a shrewd estimate of the quantity of game.

The opening of the duck-shooting season finds the
early broods of wild duck strong on the wing ; happily,
the old practice of shooting the immature birds is
dying out.   In the barley-fields where the wild duck
resort at dusk, the cool passing of an August day
makes requital for the heat of noon.   Sport, if an
object, will at least be unsullied by the modern taint
of wholesale slaughtering ; apart from shooting,

there is the quiet of the fields to be enjoyed, the cool breeze that sets the barley rippling, the perfumes of corn crops, charlock, clover, turnips, and swedes. In a duck country, barley-fields, left standing as they are until dead ripe and after wheat and oats have been harvested, may suffer severely from their nocturnal visitors.

⚘   ⚘   ⚘

At this time of year jays will make long excursions from their thickets in the heart of the woods to sample the wheat crops.   They go stealthily

The Thieving Jay

to their stolen feasts in the early morning, so soon as the ears show signs of turning, nipping off whole ears, and carrying them to some thick hedge for leisurely consumption. If there is a case against jays, there is much in favour of these handsome birds. They do far less harm to game than rooks and other egg-stealers ; they may be almost blameless in the matter of game eggs, although when a pair of jays acquire the egg-stealing habit they may clear off three or four hundred eggs in a few days. Their most useful work is the destruction of pigeons' eggs. Of course pigeons do no harm to game, except by clearing off beech-masts and acorns, and the corn sprinkled in the wood ; but the damage they sometimes do in the cornfields is enormous, going far to destroy perhaps two out of ten acres of wheat. Still, one must remember that charlock buds, served up with pigeon's milk, form the pigeons' favourite food for their nestlings.

☙   ☙   ☙

Day after day the keeper, going his rounds, reads stories of life and death. Here a bent leaf gives the clue : there a stray feather : the snout of a rat tells of a poaching cat that killed the rat, but left the head with its sharp front teeth and strong and long jaw-bone untouched. A shrew's body is seen, snapped up by a cat, but left uneaten on account of the bad taste. The remains of a feast are found, carelessly covered by only a few leaves ; another sign of cats' work. A determined cat will kill almost anything that a fox might take ; but whereas a cat leaves all the feathers of an old bird, and the skin and fur of old furred creatures, the fox swallows feathers, fur, skin, bones, and all but the wings of birds, and the stomach and clawed feet of ground game. Feathers in a circle by a field hedge tell of a hawk's killing. Feet of little pheasants, and bits of downy skin by the coops in the ride, speak of murdering rooks. A dead rabbit is seen, and four tiny holes are discovered beneath the damp, mouthed fur of the pole—a weasel has sucked the life-blood.

The Oldest Writing

☙   ☙   ☙

All through the long, anxious months of spring and early summer the keeper has been sifting and weighing

L

the points of evidence upon which he will be able to base a final judgment of the season's prospects. In

Prospects June there are many signs which go to make up a long story ; thus, nest after nest may be found to contain egg-shells, all broken in the same way—nearer the round than the pointed end—telling of the successful hatching of partridges. Then the keeper becomes so accustomed to encountering parent partridges who threaten to bar his way, while their downy chicks magically vanish, that he grows almost indifferent to their agitation. But in July, to judge the welfare of game is extremely difficult. Hedges and woodlands are in the prime of their growth ; and in midsummer days luxuriant vegetation hides nearly all birds on the ground. By chance a keeper may happen on a brood ; he notes that sixteen have dwindled to ten, and wonders whether the heavy shower three weeks ago come Sunday, or the old vixen he knows too well, or the widow's tortoiseshell cat, must bear the responsibility. But most game-birds seen are old ones—birds perhaps whose nests have been destroyed too late for a second nesting, or birds whose young ones have met with an untimely fate. Wary old birds with families are specially cautious to keep well out of sight. Distressing, then, as it is continually to see barren birds, there is con-solation in the knowledge that naturally they are more in evidence than parents with thriving young ones. With July the days pass that are most risky to young game—safe days lie ahead ; and with the cutting of the first harvest fields the most valuable of all evidence is gained as to the numbers of birds. Later on, as fields of standing corn become fewer, birds of all sorts flock to them, and estimates of quantity are likely to be misleading. But if it can be proved that three different coveys have been seen during the cutting of a piece of forward corn, it is to err on the moderate side to reckon that there are three others, though unseen. To all interested in the numbers of game-birds these are fateful days.

A dry summer is bad for swedes—among other things. Many grow disfigured by wart-like excrescences about the size of a pea. Therein lurk grubs, as partridges and pheasants know. They chip off the warts, and one may see the rusty-looking hole in the centre of each one whence the grub has been taken. All round the swedes these detached warts may be seen, lying face uppermost, and proving the usefulness of game-birds, particularly partridges.

Useful Work by Game-Birds

All through the year the cornfield gives food and shelter to a host unnumbered—from seed-time to harvest, in the days of stubble and of fallow. To all manner of creatures in fur and feather, insects as the grain in number, grubs below ground, butterflies above, to rank weeds and flowers, the cornfield gives

more freely than it yields bread to man. Seagulls
come from the coast. Peewits make the field their
home in the spring. There are congregations
of sparrows and finches. Hosts of starlings
that go to roost in the reeds. Wood-pigeons
stuff their crops to bursting; turtle-doves
come and go. Yellow-hammers sing in the hedges
through the midsummer days. The corn-crake runs
swiftly through the stems where the partridge has her
young brood. Rooks follow the plough, with wag-
tails that run and dart over the furrows as if gliding
on ice. Overhead are larks ; and the corn-bunting
flies heavily from field to field, his legs trailing as if
broken. And birds of prey take their toll of the
feeding multitudes. All through the year animal life
finds sanctuary in the cornfield. Underground are
the moles ; the harvest mouse weaves its nest in the
corn-stems ; the rabbit makes a stop in the field near
the hedge, and eats the green blades. To the ripening
corn the fox brings her cubs to play. In the ditches are
hedgehogs ; everywhere are rats, mice, and shrew-
mice. The hare follows secret paths, and there are
stoats and weasels seeking prey, and finding it on
every side. But nowadays there is little or no work
for our mills, as wheat-field after wheat-field is
turned into grass. The miller is only one among
ten thousand sufferers.

The days spent in the cornfield must pass pleasantly
for the little foxes in a fine summer. In cornfields,
unlike hayfields, there is room between the stems for

Life of the Cornfield

free movement, there is some chance to look about, there is air and light, cover and shade. Corn-stems are firm and dry, but grass-stems hold the soaking moisture of rain and dew, which saturates the skin even through fur and feather, and quite beyond the remedy of dog-like shakings. Wheat, as we have said, is the corn most favoured of all creatures—where not planted too thickly, and growing on ground not over clean, but dotted plentifully with bunches of knapweed, thistles, and bindweed, and intersected by furrows where the corn has grown poorly, and with open spaces bare to the wind and sun. Winged game, in case prompt flight is necessary, find it easier to start up into the air through the straight, stiff ears of wheat than through the ears of oats and barley. Barley that shares the ground with a rank plant of grass-seeds finds small favour among those many creatures that forsake the airless woods in summer.

☙   ☙   ☙

Numbers of hares live all the summer in the cornfields. But while many rabbits are born in the corn, when there is a wood at hand most of them retire by day, returning to the corn to feed at night. No rabbit, in sleekness of fur, is comparable to the rabbit that has lived for a few fine weeks among the corn-stems, for the constant brushing of the stems grooms his coat to a state of wonderful fineness. At any moment rabbits in the

The Keeper's Hopes

corn may meet death from the teeth of stoats or weasels; which in turn run a risk, if a slight one, from the fox's teeth; there are plenty of mole-runs into which they may dive in times of danger. In dry weather, the hedgehogs leave the ditches for the corn; and the cornfield, in real summer weather, when there are no foxes about, is a paradise for pheasants and partridges. The gamekeeper, whatever the weather, clings to the faith that the corn hides most of his birds from his sight. There is comfort in the thought that if the birds live he will see them, but if they are killed, nothing will ever tell him the story of his losses.

Man ploughs and sows, but for every man who eats the bread of the fields a million other mouths have been fed. There is no such perfect sanctuary to wild life as a field of corn. What the corn hides nobody knows; though many would gladly know, and seek eagerly to find. The gamekeeper guesses shrewdly what the corn may hide; later he will find what has been hidden, and it is as well for his peace of mind that he can only speculate, at this season, on the game in the field, for he is powerless to interfere. The community of the cornfield is almost safe from man, while the corn stands. If any creature moves in the corn, the stems, bowing to the breeze, cover its progress.

Many a fox family spends the entire summer in the cornfield, and no man is the wiser; but if any should

discover the secret, it will be the gamekeeper.
Only a giant could see, from the ground, the spot

Finding the Fox
where, in a level cornfield, a family of cubs is taking shelter; the keeper's plan is to climb into a tree, so that his eyes may

sweep over acre upon acre at a glance, and spy out the foxes. Even if the nearest tree be a mile or more distant from the playground and refectory of the cubs, his trusty " spy-glass " will reveal the secret—and while he keeps his place in the look-out tree he may signal to a companion, and point the way to the family's eviction. From the top of a tree on the edge of a wood we have found the secret place of a vixen in a field of rank rye ; and when we came to the spot, where a large patch of the rye had been rolled flat, we could have filled a wheelbarrow with the remains of partridges, pheasants, rabbits, and hares.

☙   ☙   ☙

With the harvest comes the great sporting festival of the countryman, in whom alone survives the

Harvest Sport
instinct to hunt for food—though the days have gone when every man killed his own game. This sport of the harvest-field is

the countryman's by custom, courtesy, tolerance, favour, and not by law. It is sport for the sake of food, and not for the sake of sport. The quarry is rabbit. Only two people have a real right to rabbits, and that a concurrent right—the farmer in occupation of the land, and the holder for the time

being of the sporting rights.   But during the cutting
of the corn few farmers or sportsmen deny their local
workers the privilege and pleasure of catching rabbits.
Where permission is withheld it is usually by a small
farmer, who looks to the rabbits to help with the
rent.   The keeper is the last to make objection to the
catching of the rabbits, provided that the hares and
the winged game are not only spared, but given a
chance to escape.   He even finds it a profitable policy
to help catch the rabbits, and hand over what he
catches to be shared out to those who have failed in
the scurry and scramble of the sport.   If there is
any rule or custom about possession of the spoil it is
that he who kills a rabbit keeps it.   This may be a
good rule for those who are lucky—those whose work
brings them into each field as it is cut, who excel with
stick and stone, or are better runners than their fellows.
But it is a bad rule for those who are unlucky ; while
a carter who sits on a binder from daylight to
dark for a month has perhaps the best chance,
another who must spend his time drilling turnips, or
ploughing a distant field, will never so much as see a
rabbit.

The self-binder has favoured the chance of escape for
those rabbits that camp out in the corn.   In these
days of neatly tied sheaves the rabbit that makes a
dash, with a little dodging and jumping, may find

a fair course, and can see ahead ; and it is almost
impossible to run down a rabbit that sets its face

The
Luck
of the
Game

from the corn to some other known shelter,
unless the distance is very great.   In olden
days, when the corn was not tied as it was
cut, but was thrown out loosely by the rakes

of the reaper, then the chances of escape
were all against the rabbit.   He could not run through
the corn, or jump over it, nor could he even see where
he was going.   All that the harvester had to do was
to hurl himself on the corn where he suspected the
rabbit to lurk, and pin it down.   Sometimes, while he
was feeling for the rabbit, it would bolt unseen through
his legs, to fall an easy prey to another harvester,
perhaps some fat old dame who had never been
known to run.   The sport is full of luck.   A man may
run until he and the rabbit are at the point of exhaustion ; the man falls, but the rabbit struggles
on for a yard or two farther, and another catches the
prize.   We have known a man, in falling exhausted,
to actually fall on the rabbit he was chasing.   Once
let a rabbit get clear away from the standing corn,
the speediest runner can do no more than keep an
eye on its bobbing tail during the first hundred yards
of its dash for freedom.   But by ruthlessly following
the tail, in a large field a man may walk it down ;
for a rabbit will soon run itself to a standstill, or in
despair will creep to hide beneath the cut corn.   The
rabbit is faint-hearted ; if he once loses his bearings,

he loses his senses also ; but it is surprising with what perseverance he will run when he can see a haven of safety ahead.

⚜   ⚜   ⚜

The man of experience, who knows his rabbits, does not unduly exert himself. Taking things calmly, he may catch more rabbits than others who **Rabbit-** are better runners but more excitable. He **Catchers'** **Craft** knows that the great thing is to stand still, rather waiting for the rabbits to come to him than going after them. As a binder works round a field, he moves quietly in the opposite way ; then, catching sight of a rabbit crouching beneath a piece of knapweed, some tangled bindweed, or a thistle, his upraised stick falls with certain aim, and instantly he puts into force the rustic law of possession. Or, moving quietly along, he will hold in his right hand a heavy stone, while several others are held in the other hand behind his back ; when he sees a rabbit far within the corn, his stones fly with crushing force, and the rabbit's day is done. Sometimes towards the finish of the cutting he will take up his position far from the frenzied throng around the binder, at some quiet spot at the edge of the haven wood ; here, watching the rabbits that have escaped the sticks and stones of the main body, he tries to turn them as they run the last few yards of their course. If he succeeds, the rabbit, already worn by a long run, makes a last desperate spurt, but can go no more

than a few score yards.   Should the rabbit run past
him, its course unchecked by his frantic yells and
flourishes, he troubles himself no further, and saves
his breath.

It is when the binder is going on its last few rounds
and only a small patch of corn is left standing in the
middle of the field that excitement reaches its height.
Hitherto no one has been allowed to enter the standing corn ; but now all sense of decency and restric-
tion is thrown to the winds, and the end is simply a
mad scramble for the rabbits that lurk to the last
moment.   Sharp eyes have followed the movements
of the rabbits by the slight swaying to and fro of the
ears of the corn ; but now the corn is alive with
rabbits, and among them are hurled the frenzied
bodies of men, women, and children, who hit wildly
and blindly with their sticks.   Sticks and stones rain
on rabbits, corn, and men.   And on the edge of the
fray stands the quiet figure of the man who will not
exert himself, who watches for the few rabbits who
come alive from the corn.   One other quiet and calm
figure is in the heart of the turmoil—the gamekeeper,
who bestirs himself only in the interests of game.
With ever-watchful eye and warning voice he sternly
represses those who, overcome by the lust of killing,
would recklessly slaughter, besides rabbits, the young
pheasants or the crouching leverets.   Great is the
relief of the keeper when the last corn is cut and the
harvest festival of the countryman is over for the
year.

This free and easy sport which the cutting of the corn provides for a mixed and excited crowd makes a scene very familiar in any English country-side. The driver of the binder, as he is carried round and round the cornfield, in ever-narrowing circles, gains a good view of the rabbits and the game, stealing about in their fear ; and now and again he may be observed to dismount to club a rabbit with his whip-handle. On farms where the rabbits are considered the natural rights of the harvesters, old hands grow very cunning at making the most of their chance when the last few yards of standing corn remain to be cut, and the rabbits, with which the little strip of cover is seething, at last bolt out, to be fallen upon by the men in waiting, and to be slain as fast as sticks can rain blows.   Rabbits remain in their sanctuary of corn long after the fox has stolen away, and the pheasants, rats, stoats, and weasels have followed after.

The Last to Leave

🏵   🏵   🏵

It is a matter of importance that the woodland rides shall be trimmed before harvest-time, so that the woods may be sanctuaries to the corn's evicted creatures. On many shoots this trimming is left to a woodman ; he may be responsible for all such work over a large estate let to various tenants. As a consequence, the rides of some of the woods are likely to remain untrimmed

In the Woods

until just before the time of covert-shooting, when the work will seriously disturb game. Keepers prefer to trim the rides on their beats themselves, at such odd moments as between the feeding of hand-reared pheasants, and with the help of labourers who are glad enough to earn a few extra shillings during the long evenings of July. The work in this way is done betimes, and all the better for shooting purposes. The harvest migration of game to the woods tells many a story to the keeper. Foxes who have spent a happy summer entirely in the game-stocked cornfields do not come in unnoticed. Fresh-made runs in the fences leading to the coverts tell of the passage of stoats. Hedgehogs work their way in from the fields ; they are more numerous than most people imagine, and the keeper holds them responsible for many a ruined game-nest.

✿   ✿   ✿

As the summer wanes, families of stoats and weasels break up, and parents cease to have any dealings with their offspring. This severance of the

Weasel Families family ties throws a light upon wild creatures and their young. Having given their young ones a good start in life, many seem to dismiss them from their minds. One grove will not nurture two robins, and the day comes when Cock Robin will drive his young hopeful into the world, and will attack him fiercely if he dare again approach his presence. The wild rabbit that on one day, in

defence of her young ones, faces and drives away
a stoat, her deadliest foe, on the next day leaves
them to the mercy of fate—a new family having
arrived. The mother stoat stays with her young
ones for a long while, sometimes until they are much
larger than herself; but sooner or later comes the
day of parting.

☙   ☙   ☙

She is an admirable mother. Her litters are large
ones—numbering as a rule from five to eight, though
occasionally as many as twelve are found—

**Mother
Stoat**

and the feeding of these hungry mouths
can only be a work of desperate energy in
the weaning days. It is a fine sight to see the mother
foraging at the head of her grown-up family. A
long time passes before the young stoats can cater
for themselves. The mother does not leave them
until they are perfectly qualified to hunt on their
own accord—which their innate blood-thirstiness at
last prompts them to do in preference to eating food
which their mother has captured. In the young
stoat's natural love of hunting lies the cause of the
final severance of family ties. With many animals
it appears that motherly solicitude continues relatively
to the relief obtained through the young taking their
mother's milk. Yet in the stoat there appears to be a
scrap of the human mother's reasoning love for her
children. We have known a stoat whose young
had been destroyed, when as large as herself, to seek

them out, and with diligent care and labour remove
their bodies to a distant resting-place, where she
stayed by them for days, though she appeared no
longer to bring them their former abundant supplies
of food. When a stoat, the mother of a family, is
killed, her young do not fail to come to her—but in
this case there is no disinterested love. The apparent
affection springs chiefly from desire of food. No
food forthcoming, the young stoats quickly begin
to devour their unfortunate mother. The gamekeeper knows that having once caught a mother
stoat, he will have little difficulty in catching her
family also ; but having captured the family, it is
by no means easy to secure the mother.

When June comes, litters of young stoats, each one
as big as the mother, are strong enough to travel
about, but for many weeks they remain together,
and depend for food on what their mother catches.
Like fox cubs, they spend their days eating, sleeping,
and playing. Without the aid of a trained dog the
keeper is unlikely to discover the lodging of a litter
unless he chances to see the mother going to her
young. He may see her entering a burrow, a bavin-
pile, a pile of hurdle-rods, or of hurdles, or he may
chance to see the young stoats out at play. Should
he come upon their playground his sharp eyes instantly note the runs and the signs of rollings in the
herbage—the playground is as the playground of fox
cubs in miniature. The comings and goings of a
mother stoat are cunning and silent. Once we found a

place where a litter had been lodging for weeks within
a few yards of a man who had been making hurdles
day after day, and his report was that he had not
seen " ne'er a sign of a stoo-at." The family had
gone when we found their lodging, and it was evident
that the old stoat had moved her young ones at night
just before they were old enough to proclaim their
presence by coming out from their wood-pile to play.

❧   ❧   ❧

The keeper's eyes are always open for stoats. They
are fond of prying about the base of a gate-post,
where a trap is often set to good purpose.
Lurking-places Then they delight in frisking along the
middle of a ride, especially after rain.
There the keeper sets a tunnel trap, covering it with
bundles of brushwood ; and every stoat that comes
along will explore so likely a lurking-place for a
rabbit, and each naturally enters by the fatal passage.
Those heaps of corn-rakings placed in the woods
for pheasants form a favourite stoat-haunt. Here
they find a warm, dry lair, and good hunting, for the
corn attracts a crowd of small birds. Chancing once
to right an overturned sheep-trough which had been
lying inverted for some weeks, we disturbed the
peace of a couple of stoats which had made the trough
their home. They were gone like flashes of lightning,
and though we overturned the trough again for their
benefit, they had the good sense not to be caught
napping a second time.

Not half the stoats that are caught are trapped by bait ; for the only bait which is a certain charm is something which the stoat has caught itself, from the enjoyment of which it has been newly disturbed. Many stoats are shot. They pursue young blackbirds and thrushes which hover about the sides of country lanes ; and when intent on dragging a blackbird up a bank they give the keeper the easiest of marks. Should his coming drive a feeding stoat to cover, he has only to wait within range for a few minutes for a chance to pull the avenging trigger. Stoats would soon be exterminated if they were attracted to baited traps for the sake of food. It would seem that they come chiefly from curiosity ; for though they live on warm flesh and blood, when they fall victims to traps it is usually in those with the bait stale and strong in scent.

꧁ ꧁ ꧁

We heard a gamekeeper say that he would be better pleased to harbour a litter of cubs on his beat than a litter of stoats. But this was too flattering a compliment to the stealthiest of the keeper's foes : foxes would smile at a comparison between the havoc they play with game interests and all the robber-work of stoats and weasels combined. No doubt the gamekeeper's idea was that while foxes may be found and dealt with according to their deserts without difficulty, stoats may be on the ground and do endless damage before

Studies in Stoat Ways

M

they are detected. With a litter of cubs on his ground the keeper, if minded, may promptly put an end to the nuisance. But he may never congratulate himself that there are no stoats. Where there is game, there stoats must be also. Just where they lurk the keeper may never know; and every art may fail to catch these sly thieves.

The keeper does not wait to see a stoat before he sets his traps; usually when a stoat is caught he sees it for the first time. During the mating season, in the early spring, stoats are trapped most easily. When one has been caught it serves as a lure to attract others. The body is suspended just out of the reach of curious relatives and friends, and a neatly hidden trap is set beneath it. Since rabbits supply the staple food of stoats, they serve as bait : anything that suggests newly done rabbit work is almost sure to attract the attention of any passing stoat. So after setting a trap just inside a hole in the track of stoats, the keeper with his stick scratches up a little fresh soil on each visit to the trap, to imitate what he calls the " ferricking " of a rabbit. A hollow underwood stump is always a likely place for a stoat. Rabbits love to sit in such stumps, and a stoat never misses a chance to investigate them, surprising the rabbit before he can scoot away, and then himself lodging in a recess of the stump, on a cosy couch made from the fur of his victim.

❦   ❦   ❦

Nowadays, the First on a large shoot passes much as other days, for October has usurped the prestige of September, and the big partridge drives are reserved until that month. But when the keeper goes home to his tea on the First, his wife, with ever-ready sympathy, is likely enough to notice " summat's up." There is a scowl on the tanned face, and a vindictive look in the keen eyes, and the way in which the thirsty throat is flushed with a pint or so of tea suggests a forlorn attempt to drown trouble. At last the murder is out : " They pot-hunters," growls the keeper, " they has bin and wiped out half my birds." Shots have been heard all day near his boundary ; on the neighbouring small shoot the First has not been allowed to go by un-honoured.

The
First

☙   ☙   ☙

With the First come poachers, anxious to win the big rewards paid for the earliest birds to reach the market. Netting is not so prevalent as of old, but more of it is done than most people imagine, since netting is practised in the dark, and in fields easily entered from public roads. The best preventive is to dress the fields in which the birds chiefly jug—stubbles, pastures, and fallows —with small pieces of tangled wire-netting, and small bushes, left lying on the ground, so that they may roll with the net, and entangle it the more hope-lessly. A sneaking method of poaching is to set

Early
Birds

gins in the partridges' dusting-places, such as ash-heaps, the remains of burnt couch—the keeper forms a habit of probing such dust-baths with his stick. As dawn breaks on September 1, the poacher conceals himself in a ditch commanding a fallow where the coveys jug. Then he sends his dog or his son to stroll casually and slowly to and fro across the field at the far end. The birds, not hard-pressed enough to take wing, make for a furrow, and run in a solid bunch towards the ambush, to be greeted by a heavy charge of shot, calculated to account for several brace. One shot—a rush for the fallen birds —and the poacher has flown.

❧   ❧   ❧

One hears a great deal of praise lavished on the old-fashioned style of walking-up partridges, to the detriment of driving. True, where birds

Walking-up

and cover are not abundant, a bag of fifteen brace or so made by two or three guns will often represent much clever sportsmanship—besides a hard day's tramping and some shots not to be despised. Yet there is a way of walking-up birds which is nothing more nor less than butchery. In September, the partridges are mobbed and worn out by men whose duty it is to drive them from the barer fields into thick roots, there to be walked up—and snuffed out like so many candles at short range. This may be magnificent for the bag, but it is not sport. Again, partridges on

occasion may even be walked up in standing corn.
That is a moral crime, and ought to be a legal one.

¥   ¥   ¥

With September, cubbing begins—and the young of
the thief of the world must justify their existence
by making sport.   Many sudden and be-
Thoughts wildering shocks the cubs receive.   Hitherto
on
Cubbing their lives have been peaceful enough.
No wolf has found them out in the cornfields where they have been learning to hunt their
own game ; no wild dog has dug a way into the
nursery earth.   To be hunted is quite a new experience.   The cubs are spared at least the dread of
anticipation as in the early hours of a September
morning they settle to sleep in their soft warm
kennel, canopied by bracken and brambles.   Dream-
ing, it may be, of their own night's sport, the cheerful voice of the huntsman, as he urges on his newly
entered puppies to draw with their elders, means no
more than a general alarm to the cubs' drowsy ears.
Again and again the hunt may come, yet a cub may
have no thought of a game, with life or death as the
stake.   Not until the attentions of the hounds become
pressing and particular can he awake fully to what
cub-hunting means.   Then perhaps it is too late.
But an old fox is quick enough to hear the first sound
of the hunt ; he breaks away at an unguarded corner,
and is allowed to go.

There is little chance for the cub when, fat from

long ease, he is pushed at last from the home-wood, with the pack in cry a few short chains behind his apology for a brush.   A fox-hound, if often cowardly, is a foe of terribly unequal size and strength, one carefully fed, thoroughly schooled to hunting, and trained to great staying power.   But a young hound is as indifferent to the business of hunting as is a cub when disturbed for the first time in its life.   Lacka-daisical is the word for the attitude of each.   It is an unfortunate cub that slinks aside to avoid a too-inquisitive puppy and walks into the jaws of an old hound.

A cub is to be known from an old fox by its lanki-ness and legginess.   Full growth is not attained until late November; from Christmas-time is the season when the amorous barking of the foxes of the year may be heard, as they run through the woods in the night, seeking their mates.   In early autumn the cub's brush is lacking in bushiness, and is obviously pointed at the tip.   By Christmas—if Christmas is to come for him—the brush will be in full-blown glory. A popular superstition among countrymen is that a white tip to a fox's brush denotes a dog-fox, while its absence is a sure sign of vixenhood.   Another old fallacy that dies hard is that a fox will fascinate a roosting pheasant by gazing steadfastly into its eyes—hypnotising it so completely that the bird drops at last into the waiting jaws.   But a fox's tricks need no bush.   He will hoax rabbits by rolling as if in inno-cent frolic, rolling his way nearer and nearer until,

with a perfectly calculated spring, he may make sure
of his supper. And he will feign death so well as
to deceive a wary old huntsman. Many a fox's
body has been dug out of a hole and thrown aside as a
carcass, only to come miraculously to life, and to fly
at the first chance.

✿   ✿   ✿

Country folk brew wine from numberless things—
and the marvel is how they survive the drinking. Yet
some of the simple wines are excellent—as
Wines of the Country parsnip wine and sloe gin. Beside all care
in the making, the secret of parsnip wine is
to brew it at the right time, which is just
after fresh top growth begins in roots left in the
ground, when the spine of the parsnips themselves
turns as tough as wood. A good recipe from a
keeper's note-book is this : Take three pounds of
parsnips, a quarter of an ounce of hops, three pounds
of lump sugar, and one gallon of water. Wash,
clean, slice and boil the parsnips until tender. Add
the hops, boil for five minutes, strain on to the sugar,
and stir until the sugar dissolves. When the liquor
is lukewarm add yeast, and when the working is
done, barrel, bung, bottle and drink in due season.

We would give a word of warning to the inexperienced : Do not sample home-brewed wines too
freely, however freely offered. Country folk put
quantity before quality, and seldom offer their wines
in anything but tumblers—and if you manage to

empty one tumbler, you will need will-power, if not willingness, to avoid taking another glassful. To leave a drop of home-brewed wine, when once you have tasted it, is an insult to the maker. We remember how the wife of a keeper was unjustly blamed for the power of her rhubarb wine, of which a caller had partaken freely. He went his way smacking his lips; lighting his pipe, he strolled happily along a path of rabbit-mown turf, through a fine old park. But in a little while he felt a desire to lie down, and soon his groans were spreading panic among the park deer. He cursed the gamekeeper's wife and her rhubarb wine ; but it turned out that he had borrowed from the keeper a little flowers of sulphur, which, escaping from its packet, had found a way into his pipe : hence his pain and sickness.

AUTUMN

To find out how the wild birds have fared is always difficult : one never sees them properly until the days of shooting are at hand—and not always then, when a sight of them rather under than over forty yards distant might be welcome. We may pass by a wood outside which many pheasants may be feeding, as a flock of fowls, or sitting lazily about on the fences, some perhaps indolently stretching a wing in the pleasant wallow of a dust-bath ; but this does not prove that pheasants have done well—merely that there are so many pheasants at a certain place ; it does not even prove that they will be there the next day. Such a spot may be a place where large numbers of pheasants are reared. One may count a hundred birds in the corner of a field—perhaps there should have been a hundred and fifty. Or perhaps the hundred to be seen means better luck than usual in the breeding season in that particular part. A man who sees pheasants where he does not know how many were bred may think a dozen a large number, or he may view with scorn the sight of several hundreds if he has been accustomed to see thousands. We know places where so many pheasants may be seen at any time as to suggest that they swarm there regardless of the season. But the birds seen casually may have been bought from a game-farm and turned down, to make up a supply that failed. However, it always delights the sportsman's eye to see many pheasants about a wood—especially if he has the shooting.

From a just standpoint, it is the comparison of what might have been with what is that settles the verdict on the pheasant season. The season cannot be judged by the birds of one preserve. Allowance must be made for many points. The number of wild broods to wild hens left to manage their own affairs, and the number of eggs set under fowls and how they hatched must be considered. Then the quality of the rearing-ground makes one district much better than another—whether heavy or light, low-lying or high, and rich or poor in natural food. The question of foxes must be weighed, and one would like to know before judging a season from any one case how many birds were turned into covert at five to seven weeks old, and how many fell victims to foxes—to say nothing of gapes.

The keeper may control the supply of hand-reared birds : he may make up for the spoiling of an egg, or the loss of a chick, which would otherwise mean a pheasant the less ; but he has no control over

the season as it affects wild birds. What he prays
for is a showery April, with a sun to shine between the
storms. And he wants fair weather after the
Weather middle of May, the longer the better.   A
to pray
for   bright warm summer is good for all pheasants, whether it be their fate to start life
beneath a fowl in a stuffy, if cosy, coop, or to be
gathered beneath the breast and wings of their real
mother in the wood, or among the corn. A fine
summer means more to birds than to man, for to
them it is a matter of life or death.

❦   ❦   ❦

Walking home through the woods on the evening
of an October First, we came to a standstill
before a low tree-branch on which an old
After   cock pheasant was going to roost. We were
the
Opening within a yard of him ; yet he sat stock-
still, and stared at us fearlessly with un-
blinking eyes. The minutes passed, and after we
had stood there for some little time, staring back
at the old pheasant, it really seemed that we had
established a bond of communication. And this
is what we understood the old cock to be saying :

" Here I am, you see, and not afraid of you ; and
none the worse for an opening day that has been, I
must admit, a trifle lively. And I may inform you
that before I went to roost I made careful inquiries
among my very numerous progeny, and not one is a
feather the worse for all the banging that has been

going on.   All are in good condition, in fine plumage, and strong on the wing as usual, and, I may add, on the leg.   By the way, I myself, in the course of the day, from a secure retreat, watched more than one sportsman critically examining the bodies of several unfortunate birds—needless to say, there was no son or daughter of mine among them.   *Good* night."

＊   ＊   ＊

Here is the gamekeeper's idea of what constitutes a pleasantly flavoured October 1 : The day should break with a misty dawn, grey dewy cobwebs every-
An Oc-
tober Day where, betokening a visible if tardy sun.
There should be a brace of spaniels whose occasional lapses after fur are atoned for by their untiring energy among the blind tangles of hedgerows and dells.   There should be three guns whose object is to enjoy sport and to make a mixed bag, including incidentally the first pheasants—without the formality of the so-called battue.   There should be a couple of experienced beaters, and a keeper whose soul is set on circumventing certain wary old cocks that are known to him as leaders astray of youthful birds.   The killing of pheasants should not be the main thing ; if the charm of the First of October lay only in this it would quickly fade.   Next to the potting of young rooks with a shot-gun as they sit stoically near their nests, few phases of shooting call for less skill than pheasant-shooting in early October.

＊   ＊   ＊

Grouse, partridges, and pheasants are low-flying birds, unlike wood-pigeons and rooks ; it is their habit to skim along near to earth. And **Low Flight and High** pheasants might be truly described as ground birds. Only on occasions do they fly high, and then usually for one of three definite causes. Flushed on high ground they may maintain a high elevation as they cross a valley. Rising on low ground, the direction of their flight may necessitate an upward line, as when trees or hills lie before them. Forced to rise suddenly, having lain low while danger has approached, on finding men in full sight between themselves and the place they have determined to reach they then rocket instinctively. Rooks and wood-pigeons naturally fly at a height well out of gun-shot ; and the cynical critic of British shooting methods might observe with truth that the bagging of a dozen ordinary wood-pigeons involves a higher order of sportsmanship than the bagging of fifty ordinary pheasants.

※   ※   ※

As with partridges, a great benefit has followed the fashion of driving grouse, instead of walking them up, with setters and pointers : for the **Wily Grouse Cocks** familiar reason that the old birds come first to the guns and are the first to be shot. If not shot, these old birds would not allow the young ones to nest near them, and would drive them far afield : and another advantage is that the young birds which are spared are the most productive. Moorland keepers at the end of the season are at pains to kill off old cocks, which are such enemies to the peaceful nesting of the young birds; and many are their devices for stalking and calling them to their doom. Except when feeding, the wary old birds like to be able to look all about them, and perch on walls and hillocks, whence, holding their heads high, their eyes may sweep afar for foes. Unlike partridges, they are not content with the grain in the stubble, but will perch on the stooks at harvest-time, to attack the sheaves.

❦   ❦   ❦

Until the last field of corn is cut, cubs are spared their introduction to the joys and sorrows of hunt-

Rewards for Cubs ing ; but at the end of harvest their time is at hand. Few keepers look forward to the coming of hounds for cubbing. When hounds do come there is nothing more disappointing to the keeper than that they should not find the cubs, of whose dark deeds he has been complaining all the summer. Not only does he lose the prospect of a sovereign reward, but the cubs are still at large to carry on their havoc, while he may appear to have been crying wolf where there were no wolves ; the loss of the sovereign is much less to him than the loss of his credit and the prospective loss of his birds. Different hunts have different methods of rewarding keepers whose cubs are found by hounds. One hunt works on the irrational plan of giving a keeper a sovereign for each litter found, and ten shillings extra if a cub is killed. This is almost as much as to ask the keeper to take steps towards handicapping the cubs when the pack presses. The keeper knows how important it is that the young entry shall taste blood at this time, and he knows that if scent fails, the best way to ensure a kill is to allow the cub to run to ground. Instead of completely stopping an earth, he arranges a slight barricade of twigs ; and then he may know, by whether the cub has broken the barricade or not, if it has run to ground. He takes care to have a spade and a pick-axe close at hand. The well-intentioned reward really ends in spoiling sport.

❧   ❧   ❧

In the bag of September partridge-shooting, the landrail is often the only bird booked under the heading " Various," save for an occasional
"Various"
—the
Landrail
wood-pigeon ; at any rate, many look to the landrail to fill the " Various " column, if they often look in vain. On a calm day, the landrail is a weird mark, with its heavy, laboured flight, and its dangling legs ; the bird hardly suggests a sporting shot. But few who have shot landrails have not also missed them. Landrails will even put to shame the sportsman who has been bagging his brace of partridges with wearisome monotony. So

slow, as a rule, is the landrail in heading away, after its silent rising from sainfoin or clover, that we have seen one bagged by a thrown stick, another knocked down by a keeper's partridge-carrier, as he held it in his hand, and another caught on the wing by a dog ; of course this is nothing uncommon. We have even seen a terrier point and pounce on a landrail that was crouching beneath its nose. But when a fair wind is blowing, the slow landrail becomes as difficult a mark to hit as a snipe or a woodcock. And a landrail has a disappointing habit of dropping when it comes to a hedge, for all the world like a dead bird, though very much alive.

☙   ☙   ☙

Sportsmen may find partridge-shooting among shocks of uncarried corn more interesting than shooting over a bare expanse of barren stubble.

Sport amid the Shocks The shocks or stooks help to mark the birds, alive or dead ; and they cause them to rise to a convenient height, so that they show sharp and clear against the sky, instead of skimming away low against the baffling tints of the autumn fields. And birds seem to lie better among stooks than on bare stubble. They cannot see well or far among the stooks, and they like to linger in the dusting-places that they make in sheltered, sunny spots. Another point worth mentioning is less obvious but none the less true—the stooks help the eye in aiming. It always seems easier to hit a pheasant flying high between the tops of trees, as down an avenue open to the sky, than in the open. So in the cornfields before the harvest is garnered. And there is still another point which adds to the charm found in shooting among the corn-sheaves : when a covey bustles up, the birds spread out and scatter, for they cannot see all the party at the same time ; and so they may give each gunner a mild taste of what the days of driving will bring.

❧   ❧   ❧

Some men have a special gift for marking a bird that is down, while others never know where the **"Mark"** bird fell within half an acre. But marking is only a matter of training the eyes, and anybody may learn the trick : in time the eyes accurately note what they see almost unconsciously. The sportsman cannot be too accurate in marking the fall of a bird. The great thing is to take a good line—an imaginary line drawn from the eye to the place where the bird fell : if at a far distance, the actual spot will be nearer in reality than it seems. The accustomed eye finds points which mark the line, if not the very spot, where the bird has fallen—a spray of charlock flower, a thistle-stem, or a tinted leaf. When a bird falls at a distance it is helpful to take some prominent object in front and behind to mark the line—such as a gap and a sapling in opposite hedges.

A sportsman who is a master of the art of marking knows where to come upon each bird he shoots

N

singly ; and when he scores a brace he knows all about the second bird. Often he knows much more about the first bird than those who have nothing else to do but to mark. The usual rule is for the attendant to mark the first bird that falls and the shooter the second. With two men to mark one bird it should be quite easy to find the place. The bird will be within a yard of where the two imaginary lines intersect. A common mistake made by sportsmen is to suppose that because they have fired at a bird coming towards them it must have fallen in front of them : more probably it has fallen several yards behind, especially if it be a bird brought down by the second barrel. It is not easy to mark the place where a covey pitches. On seeing the birds suddenly lower their line of flight, a sportsman may suppose they have alighted, unless he still keeps a watchful eye on them, for birds often lower their flight when they have crossed a hollow or a valley, and then skim on low over the crest of the hill. However, when birds lower their line of flight, after flying some distance, it is a sign that they contemplate settling.

       ❦   ❦   ❦

Among the many clever things that a gamekeeper's retriever learns is how to mark a partridge which flies a long way and then towers. When once he has grasped what is meant by the rising of a covey, the firing of a shot, and the sight of a bird soaring away from the rest and falling like a stone, he soon begins to watch for the bird that towers, even without

The Keeper's Dogs the exhortation, "Mark that bird!" A clever retriever will mark the distant fall of a bird seen by no one but himself, and either will dash off for the spot or show strong symptoms of wanting to go. The well-trained dog finds the bird that he has not seen fall. On being ordered to "go on" he gallops in the direction indicated by a wave of his master's hand, and when he hears the word "Halt," or sees a hand-signal, then he begins to cast, and seldom in vain. A retriever will retrace his steps for a couple of miles or more to bring home a dead rabbit or bird which his master has left behind in mistake. One fine retriever had been trained never to give up game except to her master; and it happened that as she was picking up a dead hare another was wounded and ran away before her. She set off in pursuit, carrying the dead hare, and though every man in a long line of beaters, keepers, and guns attempted to relieve her of her burden, she refused to give it up. On catching the wounded hare, she calmly held it down with one paw and waited until her master came to her assistance. Keepers, of all men, have least doubt about the reasoning powers of their dogs.

❧　　❧　　❧

Autumn brings with woodcock the woodcock owls —as the short-eared owls are called, because their flight is like a woodcock's, or because they come at the same time. We would make the strongest plea for the preservation of these most useful

Woodcock Owls

owls. When an unusual number appeared in parts of the South of England, they made themselves very busy among the rats that had taken lodgings in the root-fields. Yet a party of town shooters, out after partridges, gloated more over the bagging of one of these owls than over all the rest of their spoil. The owl was wounded only enough to be caught—and his wound had cost the party eleven cartridges. Perhaps if the short-eared owl bred here he might be tempted to prey on young game; but very few remain to breed in the north, and the young game is grown when the autumn migration begins. Rats and mice with occasional small birds and some beetles form the staple diet.

☙   ☙   ☙

The difference in the tastes of dogs is curious, and often strongly marked. Two terriers, boon companions at home, were taken to the

Dogs that Despise Woodcock

Hebrides; in their home haunts they hunted the same game together—rats, rabbits, hares, partridges, and pheasants—but in the north the chief sport was among woodcock, though there were thousands of rabbits. Yet neither dog flushed a single woodcock, save by accident, nor would take the slightest interest in any but rabbit sport. They showed that marked aversion to woodcock common to many dogs not used to them. Sometimes dogs will acquire a taste for hunting and retrieving woodcock, and then make this a speciality. A curious point in the case of the two terriers was that one suddenly became very fond of the remains of cooked woodcock, whether hungry or not, while the other refused ever to look at them, even when purposely kept on short commons by way of experiment. It was a strange sight to see the appreciative dog crunch up the frame of a woodcock, winding up the performance by stowing away the head, bill and all.

The best retrievers usually refuse to pick up and carry a woodcock, unless specially schooled to carry anything from puppyhood. To train puppies to fetch and carry things objectionable alike to their sense of smell and touch, perhaps the best plan is to teach them to retrieve well-filled tobacco-pouches. They may be thrown long distances, and a dog will never bite them—at least, twice—and so acquires a perfect mouth. A retriever not trained in this way will probably refuse to touch a woodcock, in spite of every coaxing—one, induced at last to pick up a woodcock, has been known to spit it out, turning up his lip in contempt, and otherwise showing his intense scorn. Now and again a young and obedient retriever may bring in woodcock at the first trial—but with a look of anything but relish.

One hardly thinks of pigs as possible pets ; yet those who have brought them up and acted the part of **Pets of Pigs** foster-mother, agree that they make charming pets, energetic and entertaining. They soon know the step of their master, and rush furiously to greet him with every sign of delight. If properly kept no pet could be more cleanly in habit.

We know a village pig-butcher who, by the irony of fate, made a pet of two little pigs, and was very proud of his black and white twins, as he called them. He reared them by hand, and nothing could be more entertaining than their way of taking their meals of milk and water ; they had been trained to rest their front trotters on a box, with the idea of saving their foster-parent's garments, and would greet the sight of their bottle with joyous grunts. These piglets, at weaning-time, had cost their master in food the sum of 7s. 9d. Had he cared to sell them they would have brought him in about £4 each ; or supposing he were to kill them himself and convert them into bacon, his bacon would cost him about $3\frac{1}{2}d.$ a pound. That this was his intention we gathered from his remark : " I'll see as I don't pay no more 'levenpences a pound for bacon." The pigs in the first place had cost him nothing ; they were the " darls " or last-born pigs of their litters, which are generally inferior to their numerous brothers and sisters, and are often given away. Clearly a darl may make a profitable pet.

The gamekeeper, as a rule, is an old hand at dog-dealing. All keepers have an eye for a dog, and are tempted to buy for a song any sort of sport-

Some Deals in Dogs ing dog, in the hope of making a few shillings or pounds by a quick sale. We knew a keeper who would buy almost anything that could be described as a dog, but his stock price was " A bob and a pot "—a shilling, that is to say, with a quart of beer. When a shoot is let, and the keeper's services go with it, he often has a good chance to make money over dog-deals. Outgoing tenants commonly make him a present of a useful, general-purpose retriever, or spaniel—a dog that has done a good deal of all-round work on the shoot. A dog may be a good dog only on one shoot, or he may obey only one keeper ; so when the tenant goes away he leaves his dog where it can do the most good in the world, kennel, chain, collar and all. Then a new tenant comes in, to whom the keeper offers the dog with its outfit—the whole being, as he declares, " honestly worth five pounds to the shoot." But he will take three pounds, and it is clear profit. And the new tenant makes a good bargain.

❧   ❧   ❧

A white or a pied bird, whether rook, blackbird, starling, finch, or sparrow, never fails to hold the eye, and may become a character of public interest in a neighbourhood. Its usual fate is to be shot—the fate of any rare wild creature. The sportsman sees no special reason for sparing a pied pheasant that has come to his coverts—he shoots it at the first chance

Marked Birds for the sake of the few seconds' pleasure given by the curious plumage before it is tossed with the rest on the game-cart. But the keeper silently mourns for the death of the pied bird. If he voices his lament, he receives a stock answer : " Well, it is too late now." Happy the keeper who succeeds in catching up a bird that he treasures, so that he may give it safe shelter until the rattle of guns is silenced.

☙   ☙   ☙

" Once a pied bird always a pied bird " is the expression of a common fallacy. A pheasant may be almost

Colour-Changes in Feathers white for months, then change colour, and become hardly different from other birds. A pied bird tends to become more pied as the time of moulting approaches. A homely illustration of this increasing lightness of colour is seen when a black cat is about to change its coat ; then the fur turns a rusty brown. When this is shed the new growth seems blacker than ever. A black cat or dog with white marks nearly always has young with similar markings. And if you have a white or pied hen pheasant, in spite of the fact that after a moult her new feathers may come of the ordinary brown shade, you may expect, perhaps, half the chicks from her eggs to wear their mother's

pretty white or pied dress. Birds that have been pied
in their youth, then have put on sober apparel, again
put on the showy shade of feathers in their old age,
though it is a lucky pheasant that reaches anything
like old age, whether pied or not.

❦ ❦ ❦

Nature is a kindly doctor—and though any accident
to the flying or running powers of a wild creature
probably means death, miraculous recoveries
Nature's Healing are to be noted. Rabbits commonly suffer
from broken legs, whether from gun-shot,
trap, or other cause; but limbs often heal and
become serviceable members again. Nor is a broken
wing always enough to cause the death of a game-bird.
Should the bird escape its foes while the broken
bone is setting, it may live to fly, if not quite as well
as ever. We noticed once that one bird in a covey of
partridges flew more slowly than the others; it was
shot, and when picked up we found that there had
been an old wing fracture, and that the broken ends
had crossed and overlapped in setting. A curious
case was that of a partridge which was shot in the
wing, and ran when followed through the turnips
by a retriever. Several times the bird sprang above
the turnips, attempting, but in vain, to fly; then,
when the dog seemed about to catch it, the bird gave
a final spring, and this time flew straight away.
But after fifty yards or so it dropped to earth, falling

almost perpendicularly. The explanation seemed to
be that the fractured bone-ends had joined, and
kept their place accidentally, for the few moments
of the flight.

❧   ❧   ❧

A sporting old gentleman, who was very deaf, always
took a small boy with him shooting, whose duty
seemed to be to stand behind his master and
do nothing. He never carried cartridges,
and looked incapable of loading a gun. One
day we asked the boy to explain his mission
in life. " 'Tis this way," said he. " In each hand I
holds a pin, and I gives the master a prick behind to
let him know when game be a-coming—if on this side
or on t'other."

A Little Story

❧   ❧   ❧

More than once, descending the steep face of the
Downs, we have set foot upon hares in their forms—
crouching so closely as to be unseen until
felt ; and once we have witnessed a curious
fatal accident which befell a half-grown hare
through the habit of lying low. Partridge-shooting
was going on in a field of sainfoin, and as the guns lined
out from the fence we saw this hare dancing, as it
were, on her head. It was a dance of death, and
before we could reach her puss was lying still. One
of the guns had actually trodden on her head, and had
passed on unknowingly. Half-grown and under-

Accidents to Hares

sized hares seen in autumn have small chance of
enduring through the winter; with the setting in of
cold weather their fate is sealed; they are unable to
thrive on the rough frosted food, and are claimed by
a lingering death.   In the wet days of autumn, when
showers of leaves and rain are falling, hares change
their quarters in the woods for the open fields, pre-
ferring of all places a stubble-field free of grasses
that hold the moisture.   The fall of rain and moist
leaves has an opposite effect upon the rabbits—
driving them to the shelter of their newly renovated
burrows, where they lie all day, snug, warm, and
dry.

☙   ☙   ☙

We have heard of terriers who have chased hares
and caught them after a burst of less than a field's-
breadth; but we have never seen a terrier
catch a sound hare in a fair run, though we
have known a clever little dog to flash up a
ditch and seize a loitering hare, and we
have often known a hare to be caught napping in her
seat.   The hares that terriers catch after short runs
have been in some trap or snare, or have been shot,
or otherwise wounded, or probably they are diseased.
The wonder is that hares can run so fast and long
as they do in a state of advanced disease.   Hares
suffer each year in some places from a disease of a
typhous nature, aggravated by feeding on frosted
clover.   Parting the white fur on the underside of

Hares no longer Speedy

such a hare the skin is found to be green.   There is
good cause to be suspicious of disease whenever a
thin hare is seen in autumn or winter.

❦   ❦   ❦

Too many starlings in a given place are likely to be a
serious trouble—in fact they make a place almost
impossible for other inhabitants.   Starlings
Starling haunt many kinds of roosting-places—the
Hosts
high reeds, the woods, and the shrubs about
a house.   The keeper finds small pleasure in the
thunderous noise of their wings in his coverts.   Towards the end of October the sales of underwood take
place; thereafter the underwood is cut, and this often
drives the starlings from an old roosting-haunt to
fresh woods, where their presence is far from desirable,
in view of the approaching covert-shooting.   Naturally, people hesitate to take preventive measures,
such as shooting or lighting fires of green wood, for
the shots or the smoke would drive away pheasants
as well as starlings.   Yet it is wiser thus to drive away
one season's pheasants than to have the wood made
impossible for many years—to all save starlings.

❦   ❦   ❦

While we have never met any one who actually hated
honeysuckle, if there is a man who curses it occasionally it is the copse-worker chopping underwood.   A
honeysuckle trail will turn a well-aimed blow from its
true direction, and so may cause the copser to cut

himself very badly—even a slight blow from his sharp bill-hook is a serious matter.   The copser's

Trials of a Copser

hand and arm have received the order to swing outwards to gather force for a quick stroke—honeysuckle arrests the bill-hook and turns its direction, while the hand and arm disastrously go on with the reflex part of the order. And though we do not suppose there is a copse-worker in the whole world who does not appreciate rabbits to eat, probably most of them speak at times as harshly of rabbits as of honeysuckle.   For rabbits gnaw the underwood, and when the butt of a stem has been gnawed by rabbits' teeth, part of the wood dies, and is far harder to cut than a clean stem.

We have heard from several people that owls are among the birds that cannot be tamed and kept as

Wild Birds in Cages

pets ; but this idea is a fallacy.   Barn-owls taken from the nest, and properly handled, will grow into attractive pets, and we know a pair of them, about four months old, who sit on their master's shoulders, and seem to return his affection.   We dislike the idea of rearing wild birds in captivity—especially such useful birds as barn-owls, who are better employed in catching mice than in doing tricks.   But nearly all birds are susceptible to a taming treatment, even such shy creatures as the redshanks of the marshes, the wariest of birds in their wild state.   There are people who seem to possess a

natural instinct for understanding birds, as others for
handling dogs, horses, or snakes.

❦   ❦   ❦

The truffle-hunter, roaming with his little dogs over
park lands and other pleasant places, seems to lead a
fine, independent life.   And he confesses
Truffles
to making money on no mean scale.   His
professional fee is a pound a day, with all expenses
to be paid.   The truffles are sold at 3s. the pound ;
but each truffle may cost the consumer fully half a
guinea, stewed, as it should be, in rich wine.   The
truffle-hunter may tell you that his dogs are of the
original truffle-hunting breed.   Yet we have no doubt
that any dog with a good nose could be trained to find
truffles as easily as a retriever can be broken to
hedgehogs.

❦   ❦   ❦

The gamekeeper's retriever will learn to discover the
whereabouts of every hedgehog in a ditch.   A clever
dog will find in a few hours as many hedge-
Retrie-
ver's Use-
hogs as a week of trapping will secure—
fulness   miles of hedges may be cleared in a day in
the summer.   The dog must be kept under
absolute control, lest he disturb sitting birds, thereby,
perhaps, doing as much damage as might the hedgehogs. Almost any dog may be trained to a particular
work, such as playing the bloodhound's part, and
following the trail of men, whether friends or stranger

—even terriers may become useful trackers. The night-dogs used by gamekeepers—crosses between mastiffs and bulldogs—will follow poachers through the woods during the blackest hours of night.

A retriever is wonderfully useful for many purposes besides recovering game. A dog, which had never seen a cricket ball, was with us when we chanced to be crossing a field, at dusk, where a ball had been lost in thick cow-parsley in the shade of trees. The cricketers appealed for our help; we cleared the course, and set on the dog. She took the wind, trotted along, turned suddenly, ran straight for a score of yards, and came back, the lost ball in her mouth. Perhaps she worked it out in her own mind that as no shot had been fired there was no game to follow, and the ball-scent must therefore be the one she was required to track. No doubt she would have left the line of the ball if the scent of anything in the shape of dead game had reached her sensitive nose.

❦　　❦　　❦

The gamekeeper classes the nutters among " the reg'lar plagues " of his life. Not that he begrudges

Nuts and Mice

them their nuts, but that they stand for an old, old story of innocent pleasures and game disturbance. As primrose-pickers are to the nesting pheasants of April, so are nutters to the young birds of October, and the final result is always an angry keeper. His young birds at this season are ever ready to avail themselves

of an excuse to stray to fresh woods.   The nutter who
would avoid the keeper should avoid paths, and lie
very low and still when the keeper comes his way.
This lesson in woodcraft had been mastered so
thoroughly by one young nutter of our acquaintance
that when a keeper chanced to pass along the ride
near which he was picking, he still lay low when the
keeper's words were almost in his ear : " Where be ye?
Ah, I sees ye.   Come out on it, then ! "   And he was
duly rewarded by the knowledge that these remarks
were merely an exhortation to pheasants to feed.

Dormice are the chief of all lovers of hazel-nuts.
They are found very often at work by human nutters ;
and their nest is seen sheltered by hazel leaves—
a neat round structure, built of dry grass, beautifully
woven.   One autumn we came upon a nest containing six young dormice, about half-grown and ready
to run, and three of them, wonderful to relate, were
wholly white.   Autumnal litters are common, and,
as though by a beautiful piece of foresight on the
part of Nature, the favourite nut food is most abundant just when the little mice are ready to give up a
milk diet.   Though called " the mouse of the hazel,"
he seems as partial to acorns as to hazel-nuts,
and he is insectivorous, and feeds heartily on nut-
weevil grubs.   With November he will be as fat
as nuts can make him, and before the month is out
he will have fallen into his long winter trance.   The
little reddish brown harvest-mouse seems to have
almost disappeared in the north of Hampshire and

other parts, and for years we have not seen a single
specimen. The nest of the harvest-mouse—cunningly
woven amid the corn-stalks—used to be one of the
prettiest of things seen in the cornfields, especially
when the mouse was seen also, nibbling in his dainty
way at the grain. To go round an oat-stack and
poke it with a stick was to disturb these gregarious
little creatures by the score. The common mouse
remains as plentiful as ever, and thousands are seen
during the threshing of a single stack; but the
harvest-mouse has gone. So much the better, no
doubt, for the stacks. Their population of furred
foes is always too large—as some idea may be gained
from the fact that in one season, and from a group
of three ricks, no fewer than 1300 rats were taken.
It is a proof of the barn-owls' value to farmers that
they are often caught in rat-traps set by holes at
the base of stacks. The stack is a favourite if sometimes a fatal hunting-place.

❦   ❦   ❦

The keeper looks his best in autumn. To many the
sight of him then is most welcome, especially if the
prospect of sport be fair, and the day of fine
promise. People who go to shoot season
after season on one estate are greeted year
by year by the same friendly faces, nearly
all of them a little the worse for time's passage.
The host is seen to have aged between this October
and last, with his butlers and his beaters and bailiffs.

The
Hand of
Time

o

The foreheads of the familiar old horses seem to have sunk a little above the eyes. The dogs are remembered as playful puppies; the headstrong creatures now grow grey about the muzzles. Boys employed of old as " stops," when their height was less than the length of the hares they dangled proudly over their backs, have now qualified for the army of beaters; they have long since learnt the wisdom of not leaving their " stopping " places to forage for hazel-nuts. All these have grown older, and perhaps the visitor himself heaves a sigh as he looks down on his own once trim and slender figure.

᯾   ᯾   ᯾

To the keeper alone of the time-honoured gathering seen on the lawn before the house on an early October morning have the years been kind. Over **The Keeper grows Old** his face the winds have swept lightly; hardly an impression has been made on his complexion by the sun, moon, and stars, and the hail, snow, frosts, and mists of the year. On his forehead half a century of life has ploughed no furrows. His cheeks are free of wrinkles; there are no crow's-feet about the outside corners of his eyes. He holds the secret of youth. His cheeks might be a girl's; there is a smoothness and suppleness about the skin of his face. Still the muscles of his arms stand out with proud fulness. And his eyes remain the keenest spy-glasses of the party. His limbs are supple and free; a gamekeeper hardly knows the meaning of stiffness. But you may notice now that he straddles mightily over the gate which of old he vaulted with the glide of the fallow bucks in the park. And if you were with him when, at the end of a long day, he goes home to his tea, by chance you might hear the remark made to his good-wife, " Well, mother, I bain't sorry to sit down."

He looks his best in autumn ; and he feels his best. He is ready for the test of his labours. He has had worries enough ; the rearing season has been a " shocking bad one," and he has had many late nights, watching his birds. Perhaps he has had toothache ; that is not unknown to keepers. Often he has been soaked by rain, and more often by the dews of night and morning. But he has lived all the year in the open and in the country, and there is the secret of his youth.

♣   ♣   ♣

In the cool autumn days rabbits grow in attraction to the poacher. They now have a habit of lying within their burrows by day, after the worryings, buffetings, and evictions of harvest-time, waiting for things to quieten down—until the sounds of binder and harvester are no more heard across the stubbles. Two people know this—the keeper and the poacher. Often it is a race as to who shall be first to take tribute from out-lying dells, with ferret and nets.

Rabbit Ways in Autumn

The ferreting season proper now sets in in earnest,

and at first the rabbits bolt freely, rumbling and
rushing along their subterranean passages, and with
blind force launching themselves into the nets.
A single ferret put into a burrow may send out a
dozen rabbits in quick succession ; or nothing may
happen when the ferrets disappear, hours of digging
follow, and then a bunch of ferrets and rabbits crowded
together are at last revealed.   In autumn days there is
exciting sport with the gun at the expense of rabbits if
open burrows can be found, or burrows in dells where
the bare-stemmed elder is the only undergrowth.

❧   ❧   ❧

In late autumn rabbits are very busy about their
burrows, making them fit for winter habitation.

Through the summer, while many of the
The   rabbits have been lying out, the burrows
Rabbits' have looked deserted and untidy.   Warned
House-
cleaning by the chilly nights that a subterranean
refuge will soon be useful, the rabbits do
up their premises, enlarging them, clearing away
the remains of old nests, and of relatives that have
died underground, and making fresh chambers where
they may lie snug and warm in place of those dug out
during last season's ferreting operations.   Judging
by the amount of soil excavated in a single night,
rabbits at this season seem to rival ants in energy
—one might think there had been a wholesale
invasion of new-comers.   At work, they kick the
soil sideways, forming a furrow perhaps six or ten

feet in length. Few have watched them while engaged in this toil, usually undertaken at night-time ; but we have seen them at work once or twice by day, and once caught a rabbit by the leg—so intent was he on his digging—while he was in the act of kicking the soil aside.

☙   ☙   ☙

The countryman is not always the guileless simpleton that he sometimes looks ; nor, as we can show, is the Cockney sportsman. A holiday-making Londoner was shooting one day in a field beyond the cottage of a labourer, who came out to watch the sport. Suddenly a cry broke from him : he leaped into the air ; then bellowed to the sportsman, waving a red handkerchief in signal. Up to the cottage rushed the sportsman, thinking that at the least the countryman had been stung by a hornet or bitten by a mad dog. "Look what ye've bin an' done," said the countryman, advancing. "'Tis a wonder I be alive; look what ye've bin an' done; look at my door, and look at these here shots." Saying which, he pointed to his newly painted door (the sportsman saw it was pitted with such holes as a rusty nail might make). He held out his hand and showed a good two ounces of shot (the sportsman saw they had never been fired from a gun). "These here shots," said the countryman, "they buzzed about me like a swarm of bees : 'tis a wonder I be alive." The

The Guileless Countryman

sportsman agreed in the marvel of the escape, adding to its wonder by pointing out that his shot had been fired at a distance of five hundred yards from the cottage—and in the opposite direction. "Allow me," he said, "to buy back these wonderful pellets at a fair market price"—and he handed the countryman twopence.

＊   ＊   ＊

In rural villages, keen sportsmen are often found beneath the uniforms of the policeman and the post-man.   No one knows better than the keeper

Sporting
Policemen

how useful it is to be on friendly terms with the policeman—and no one knows better how to manage it.   Often policeman and post-man may be found doing duty as beaters, especially during September partridge shooting, when the harvest is late and out-of-work labourers are few. If you see through his disguise of plain clothes, the policeman will remark how he just thought he would have a walk for an hour or two, just to oblige Mr. Keeper.   Upholding the law and delivering the post mean much walking : and country policemen and postmen, when passing along the roads early and late, find the haunt of many a fine covey.   Being good sportsmen, they take note of the customary line of flight ; and if you own some of the land of the covey's haunting they can tell you almost to a minute when the birds leave the turnips beyond the boundary for your stubble.

If a policeman is on duty during the early days of partridge shooting, he will manage to fall in with shooting parties ; then he makes it known that he heard shots, and was impelled to take a look round, " to see that there weren't nothing wrong." The policeman's favourite time for making known his presence is soon after the bagging of a good, broad-backed hare. Even policemen become spoiled with favours. On a sportsman telling his keeper to give a hare to a polite and zealous officer of the law, " Excuse me, sir," said he, " but the party over the hedge have just given me a hare, so might I have a brace of birds ? Thank ye kindly, I'm sure ; a hare will do nicely next time, sir." The sporting police-man can do much to help the luckless sportsman.

☙   ☙   ☙

Gipsies and gamekeepers have enough in common to make them deadly foes. They share an intimate knowledge of the ways of wild creatures.

The Wood-craft of Gipsies
They are skilled trackers and crafty trappers. They are hedgerow men ; born to the hedgerow, trained to know the meaning of every hole, and hollow, and run. Their eyes read the story of the hedge as the scholar's the printed page ; hedge-lore is their second nature, and it is as though an instinct tells them where the partridge has built, where the hedgehog has buried himself, or where the rabbits are crouching. In their know-ledge of the ways of rabbits and hares keepers and

gipsies stand alone ; and it often happens that all the knowledge and craft of the one class is pitted against the cunning and knowledge of the other. Between keepers and gipsies it is always war.

The keeper detests nothing more than a gipsies' camp. His eyes take no more pleasure in their red rags spread on the bushes than might the eyes of a bull. A gipsy camp means to the keeper so much dirt, so much thieving, so many lies, so much the more trouble, and so many the fewer rabbits in his preserves. The gipsies' cauldron, steaming at dusk over a fragrant fire of wood, brings only the bitter knowledge that some of the birds or beasts he is paid to preserve are stewing in the pot. Speak to him of gipsies, and scorn flashes in his eyes, anger flushes on his face. " They be always a-shirking about wi' a dog or two, perkin' into everything," an old keeper once said to us. " They can't let nothing bide."

A gipsy brought to trial for larceny made oath that his law allowed him to take as much from others every day as sufficed for his maintenance. That was more than three hundred years ago ; and gipsies still faithfully believe in and take advantage of that law. In our experience, we have known one gipsy who was honest ; he was famous for his honesty. His blameless character was so much appreciated that he was allowed to pitch his tent in an old ox-drove, where it ran past a sheltering wood. Within the wood the keeper had buried four-dozen traps ;

and it chanced that the leaves drifted over his traps, so that when he came to find them he hunted the ground in vain. One day the gipsy's boy came to the keeper's cottage. He said that while picking wood for his father's fire he had trodden on something hard, which turned out to be a heap of traps, and that his father, thinking they must belong to the keeper, had sent him to tell the story. Where is another gipsy in England who would throw away such a chance ?

❧   ❧   ❧

Gipsies are certainly good sportsmen, after their own fashion. But one seldom hears of a gipsy shooting with a gun ; the gun speaks too loudly. **Gipsy Lies** The gipsy makes sport with dogs, ferrets, and nets. He takes no open risks ; he holds it to be a disgraceful thing to be caught red-handed. And if caught he never makes confession. No matter how red his hands, there is always an excuse. His horse is found feeding, perhaps, on the farmer's crops. Then the horse must have broken loose unbeknown. Or his dog crosses the road, leveret in mouth. Then, "He picked un up dead, killed by a stoat what I seed a-sniffin' about." His dog has snapped up a sitting partridge. " It must be one as they beggarin' foxes 'ave killed." Or the gipsy himself, hunting a rabbit in a hedge, is taken in the act of knocking over the rabbit with his stick. All was done in mistake for a rat. The keeper remarks that he has lost a fine clutch of eggs—olive-brown eggs : he hints that the gipsy knows something about it.   Innocently comes the question : " They sart o' eggs be pison, bain't they ? "   If caught with nets and ferrets on a rabbit burrow, a fine tale he has to tell of poachers who ran away at his approach, leaving all their tackle.

A keeper, who had strict orders to allow no gipsies to stop on his ground, one day came across a strong swarm, and saw clearly that they intended to stay the night.   But in reply to his marching orders, they pleaded that they wished to stay only long enough to make some tea ; they promised they would be gone by the time the keeper returned, in a couple of hours. So he went away, but went no farther than behind the nearest hedge : whence he heard himself described in a picturesque and blood-curdling fashion, and heard the declaration also that the gipsies had no intention of budging an inch for such a blue-livered, red-nosed piece of pulp as he.   Thereupon the keeper took a run and a jump, and landed his eighteen stone self and his leaded stick in the gipsies' midst, sending their pots and pans far-flying.   The gipsies snatched burning sticks from the fire, and a desperate fight began, but they soon had enough of that eighteen stone of angry keeper.

♣   ♣   ♣

In autumn, rabbits receive special attention from the long-net poachers.   On a night not too dark

or windy, yet windy and dark enough, the long-
netters find all omens propitious. To begin with, the
rabbits are now in prime condition. Then
Long-
netters there is no fear of a hard frost to make the
fixing of net-pegs a difficulty, or to allow
the sound of footfalls to be carried far through the
silence of night. And rabbits are plentiful ; as yet
their ranks have been thinned by no serious covert
shooting. To crown all, the market is ready and expectant, for the chance of a sale of stolen rabbits has
not been spoilt by the large surplus bags of genuine
sportsmen. A warm night best suits the poachers'
object, with the wind blowing towards the side of
the selected wood—enough wind to prevent a panic
among the rabbits through sound or scent of danger
while the gear is fixed, yet not enough to deter them
from turning out in goodly numbers, and journeying
some distance from the wood to feed. The nets are
set up all along the side of the wood, then poachers
with dogs or drag-lines make a circuit and drive
the feeding rabbits home, and to their doom.

❦   ❦   ❦

Keepers have found it more or less possible to train
rabbits to a mode of life which shall baffle the long-
net poachers. By giving them regular
Training
Rabbits courses of driving-in at night they will take
to feeding chiefly by day, and will grow
very suspicious of the sound of a footfall after dark.
Where there are not enough rabbits to justify special

precautions and continual watching, long-netting may be made difficult by turning cattle at night into the grass fields bordering the woods. Not only will the cattle be sure to take an inquisitive interest in the long-netting, but they will have something to say to the dogs used for driving in, and will quite upset their work. In one place some poachers were baffled after a curious fashion. A local gang had set up some seven hundred yards of new netting, worth about ten guineas, and had gone off to round up the rabbits, when another gang from a distant part of the county arrived on the scene. The curses they heaped on their luck soon gave way to blessings— at any rate, they were quick to see the chance of poaching something more valuable than rabbits. They rolled up the new nets and fled. Then the men of the first gang returned in the wake of the rabbits, which had found nothing to impede their rush to cover. Curses were deeper and stronger than those breathed before. The men decided in the end to put their case and themselves unreservedly into the hands of the police, who telephoned to the nearest railway station, and captured the poachers with their poaching brethren's gear and their own rolled up in blankets.

Why birds and beasts flock, no doubt, is for mutual protection from natural foes. One has heard of swallows nesting on a cliff beneath an eagle's eyrie, yet having nothing to fear from the eagle's attack because of their combination ; and every one knows how a party of small birds will defy a hawk, or will **Why Birds Flock** mob and rout a cuckoo or a day-flying owl. Possibly the reason for the great congregation of sparrows in one chosen tree in a London square is mutual protection from cats. Food is a most important factor in flocking ; the keeper knows that the scarcer the food of partridges the greater is their tendency to pack. Birds may pack at night for mutual warmth—as when titmice snuggle on branches, and wrens, to the number of ten or twenty, crowd a hole in the thatch. Partridges gain something in warmth in snowy weather by their habit of jugging at night— a good covey on a yard of ground. But examination of the spot where they have passed the night shows that the main pack has been divided into compara- tively small parties, in the same way as there were small parties among the great herds of buffalo that travelled as one column across the plains of America. Sheltered hollows are naturally chosen for jugging, where the keen edge of the wind passes over the birds' heads. There is not always safety or benefit in numbers ; a flock may attract foes where in- dividuals would pass unnoticed, or may make short work of food which would keep an individual for many days. With insects, great congregations may be harmful, if an advantage to their bird enemies. Presumably, flocking is a matter of general con- venience.

During the first fortnight of October little parties
of fieldfares from Scandinavia drift over the fields,
chuckling in their throaty way, redwings are seen,
our wood-pigeons are reinforced by countless thousands from overseas, snipe come in, woodcock will
soon be here, parties of goldcrests, newly arrived,
cry their sharp notes among the larches, and the
winter flocks of tits, with goldcrests, tree-creepers,
and nuthatches busily move in the woods.   Everywhere birds are in flocks.   Chaffinches, greenfinches,
and sparrows move in vast congregations, plovers
circle in clouds above the fallows, flocks of rooks unite
in the evening and thousands upon thousands of
starlings rise, fall, and circle in perfect unison, filling
the air with the rushing noise of wings.

❦   ❦   ❦

Many animals snuggle together for warmth in bitter
weather—as the squirrels and the rats.   Those who
go ratting in hedges and dells in the winter
The Com- know they may try a dozen freshly used
panies of burrows without finding a rat—when sud-
Rats denly from a single hole the rats will come
pouring out in a stream of fur.   Twenty or more rats
will lie together in one hole.   They are clever enough
to block up a hole on the windward side to keep out
the draught—so that a rat-hole newly stopped with
soil, turnip leaves, or grass, is almost certain indication that rats are within.   They store food for
winter, and the keeper may find it more difficult to

secure his potatoes from frost than from the attack of the most numerous of his furred foes.

With the fall of the leaf we find the things we sought diligently in the summer in vain. Within a foot of the path we trod almost daily, we see, for the first time, where a pheasant brought off her brood; in the fork of a slender birch-pole is that jay's nest for which we long hunted —appearing now as a thick, deep wood-pigeon's nest; and where the bracken has died down are the whitening bones of a rabbit which, though his death-place was marked by the keeper's eyes, was not to be found. A single leaf of June may hide a bird's secret from prying eyes. By noting the things seen in the fall of the leaf we learn best how to find summer's treasuries.

The Fall

A man of grumbles, equal to the farmers, yet the gamekeeper is prepared to admit that a late autumn brings him one blessing. The leaves so screen his roosting pheasants that there is little fear of night-shooting in his coverts. Accordingly, he sleeps peacefully during many hours which he would have to devote to watching in a wet early season. Deep in his heart, all the same, he has a certain liking for the hours passed in watching over his birds at night.

Late and Early Autumns

They bring him rheumatism ; but also an excitement that adds much to the savour of existence. Not to know from moment to moment when his head may be smashed in is a stimulating change from dealing with small game whose worst powers of resistance are limited to a dig from the spurs of a winged cock, or a scratch from the claws of a netted rabbit.

❦   ❦   ❦

As winter sets in, hares and rabbits are tempted to pay casual nocturnal visits to the garden. To fence the garden securely may be inconvenient—

Hares in the Garden and unless the work is done thoroughly, not forgetting the bottoms of gates, it is almost useless. And possibly only a few plants are in danger, such as carnations or parsley, the special garden favourites of hares and rabbits. So the simplest plan may be to wire in the few plants or flower-beds that are threatened. Or a string may be fixed at about eight inches off the ground, after being saturated with one of the fluids used for tainting rabbits from their burrows. This is useful when isolated carnations are dotted about in herbaceous borders, or when there are several rows of Brussels sprouts in different parts of the garden ; hares are very fond of Brussels sprouts.

A mysterious affair occurred in a garden, which a gamekeeper was called in to investigate. It appeared that the inhabitants of the house had been awakened

in the night by a din as if the roof of a tin church
had fallen off, a din proved to be associated with a
piece of corrugated iron in the garden, used as a
stand for pots and pans. The mystery to be ex-
plained was what had upset the stand and the pots.
A tuft of the fur of a hare on the tin gave the clue,
with a nibbled patch of parsley a few yards away.
It was determined that a cat had come suddenly
round a corner on a hare enjoying an unlawful feast,
and that the hare in her fear had dashed headlong
into the corrugated iron, thus raising pandemonium ;
one effect was the hare came no more to that garden.

The cost of feeding pheasants is a question of some
interest at this season—to those who must foot the
bill. The keeper is commonly blamed for
Food for Pheasants running up too big a bill; a happy medium
between his maximum and his employer's
minimum is probably the correct amount of
money required for food. The object of supplying
corn to pheasants is not always understood. It is
less to feed the pheasants—for they can usually exist
on natural food, if not very thick on the ground—
than to keep them from straying, by giving them a
pleasing and profitable employment. That keeper
makes a mistake and is extravagant who strews
maize on a clean-swept ride. His pheasants in a few
minutes will swallow a cropful and will be free during
the rest of the day to seek and find mischief. They

P

explore foreign woods, and if they like them, stay away from home. But they may be kept where they should be if pleasantly engaged in feeding. Straw-corn—such as rough rakings and damaged sheaves from the tops of ricks which are being threshed—not only serves to feed pheasants, but forces them to spend the greater part of their time, which otherwise would be spare time, in searching for each mouthful. One plan is to tie bundles of straw-corn round the trunks of trees so that the pheasants must jump to peck the ears. The empty straw is piled up again and again for the birds to scratch down ; it is only neces-sary to throw in a little loose grain. Such a minia-ture stack will amuse the birds for hours at a time, and helps to keep them at home.

$$\clubsuit \qquad \clubsuit \qquad \clubsuit$$

Leaves may still cling to the newest growths of under-wood long after the older underwood is gaunt and bare. The sap, perhaps, is fresher and more vigorous in the younger wood—pro-longing the period of ripening—and the new buds have not pushed out far enough to dislodge the leaves. In coppices that have been thinned one sees how unusually big, and how strong and enduring, are the leaves on the shoots of tree-stumps—as though the whole energy of what was once a tree is concentrated in the few shoots and leaves. Where hedges are clipped, dead leaves re-main in place far into the winter, possibly because,

The Lingering Leaves

owing to injury, the growth is retarded of those layers of cork which form to assist the buds in dislodging the worn-out leaves. On the sides of rides trimmed annually the leaves form quite a screen in late autumn—to which one sportsman put down his many misses at rabbits, and ordered his keepers to walk along every ride and pick off all the leaves that remained. The shoots of underwood that has been cut always grow more luxuriantly in a hot, dry summer than in a rainy one ; every copse-worker will tell you this is the case, though we have not come across one who could solve the riddle.

❧   ❧   ❧

In early November many keepers are putting the perfecting-touches to plans that have been maturing all through the year. From the second **Planning** day of February the keeper whose work is **Big** not merely work, but the most absorbing **Shoots** interest the world has to offer, has been weighing continuously a thousand details—studying each in its relation to others—scheming to arrange all so that in combination they shall bring the best possible results when the big days of the shooting season come to pass. Few shooting men realise the immense importance of apparently trivial details. Let a single one—such as the exact placing of a " stop "—be forgotten or disregarded, and the whole of a day's sport by modern methods may be ruined. Many good beats, many good days, have been brought

to naught by a sportsman coolly and without permission despatching an important " stop " on an
errand.   And afterwards he will protest in all good
faith that he commandeered the " stop " only because
he seemed to be standing idly at a corner, as if waiting
for something to do.

❦   ❦   ❦

On the shoulders of the head keeper falls the
responsibility of all the mistakes that mar a day's
sport.   His   position   is   unfortunate,   for
Plots and though he may perfect every arrangement,
Counter-
Plots   the success of the day must depend on good
shooting and the perfect carrying out of
orders.   His plans must be set in motion amid every
kind of distraction—a general in command on a
battlefield is not more harassed by questions, plots,
and counter-plots than the commander of a shoot.
Guns are no sooner told where to go than they inquire
the way—one is asking querulously where he will
find his cartridges, another is sure his position is
hopeless, while the beaters require constant attention, for if they are left alone to move on to the next
beat they will lose themselves as a matter of course.
In partridge-driving the keeper's nerves are stretched
to breaking-point.   Half a drive is finished, and not
a bird has shown itself; the suspense grows almost
unendurable before the swirling clouds of birds at last
suddenly rise, and go on beautifully in twos and tens
and twenties—in a stream that no man can count.   The

great art is to give even shooting through the day, and to distribute sport evenly among the guns, without favouritism—unless, indeed, orders are that the cream of the sport must pass the way of an important personage. If a keeper, for reasons of his own, should wish the bulk of the game to go to one quarter, he can manage this by retarding one end of the line of beaters, or by ordering certain beaters to tap with their staves more vigorously than the others—and by this stratagem his partiality is hidden completely from the sportsmen.

A late spell of midsummer heat makes it seem as though summer indeed has lingered in the woods.
Indian Summer With the oak-trees still heavily canopied with green leaves, the season of pheasant-shooting seems an anomaly. A varied bunch of wild flowers may be picked, many belonging to June rather than to the months of nuts and berries. Primroses bloom freely. Flowers are to be found everywhere, and cottage gardens are ablaze with Michaelmas and tall yellow daisies and dahlias; the coming of the first keen frost will mean a floral massacre. On hedges laden with blackberries and the red bryony berries there are sprays of honeysuckle, and there are many bright blooms of scabious, knapweed, corn-poppy, daisy, harebell, violet, and scarlet pimpernel. Even some of the old cock pheasants seem to imagine that April has come, judging by

their spring-like crowing, and some of the hens nest
who should have done with nests by the end of July.
One very late nest we saw with eleven eggs, on
which the hen was only beginning to sit, as shown
by a broken egg. She had been cut out by the
mowing of seed-clover heads, but returned to her
mistaken duties, and was sitting on the evening of
September 30.

❦　　❦　　❦

On a perfect summer-like day of autumn, it is strange
to think that hedgehogs are going to their winter
quarters, and that sleep is overtaking so
many creatures—bats that hang amid the
dark rafters of the barn roofs ; toads in the
mud of the ponds ; field-mice, water-voles, lizards,
badgers, squirrels, hedgehogs curled in the ditches,
snugly rolled up in a great ball of dry grass and leaves ;
and the dormouse, " seven sleeper," as it is called
locally, or " dorymouse," " sleeper," or " sleeping-
mouse." Much country weather-lore, in all parts of
the world, is based on the storing of nuts by squirrels,
the building of winter houses by musk-rats, the early
or late cutting of winter supplies of wood by beavers,
the working of moles, who are supposed before winter
comes to prepare basins for the storage of worms,
and the laying up of food on the part of bears.
" The hedgehog," said the writer of " Husbandman's
Practice," " commonly hath two holes or vents in
his den or cave, the one toward the south and the

Winter Sleep

other toward the north, and look which of them he
stops; thence will come great storms and winds
follow." The badger in his winter retreat certainly
will block up holes from which draughts blow.

❦   ❦   ❦

Though hibernating hedgehogs will remain above
ground all the winter, in the hollows where leaves
to cover them have accumulated, most retire
A Dish to the rabbit-burrows. They are seldom
of Hedge- found when ferreting operations are going
hog forward, because the ferrets do not care to
have dealings with them—though when hedgehogs
are skinned or opened, ferrets relish their flesh as
food. Keepers do not care to carry hedgehogs
home, on account of the many unpleasant things
that they distribute between himself and his ferrets.
It is true that gipsies and others eat hedgehogs, and
this is the time when they are in season for those
who appreciate them, being at their fattest, as are
all creatures about to retire for the winter. Gipsies
caught trespassing at this time of year are always
ready with the excuse that they are searching merely
for hedgehogs—even if dogs and nets and ferrets
happen to be in their possession. That they prefer
hedgehog to rabbit is a tale for a grandmother. Yet
they know well how to make a tasty dish of hedgehog. They burn off the bristles, split the prickly
beast down his back, and broil him on a forked stick
over a fire of wood. That is the quickest and cleanest

way of cooking out of doors; and, for those who appreciate things grilled, the best. But for those whose taste is toward cooking with all the natural juices conserved, the elephant's-foot process is recommended. Take not merely your hedgehog's feet, but his whole body, " prickliwigs " and all, and encase in a jacket of clay, and bury in hot ashes. Before serving, peel off the clay and the prickles at the same time. Of hedgehog also may be made a stew of savoury brown. So that the stew's beginning may be in keeping with the traditions of the immortal cooks, take an onion stuck with cloves, then, having browned your neatly jointed hedgehog in a frying-pan, by means of a few ounces of butter (together with the clove-stuck onion), immerse it in good stock, to which add a few chopped truffles, and any other such appetising things you can lay hands on—a glass or so of champagne or other good white wine will not be amiss, while a squeeze of lemon-juice is held to effect a decided improvement. By simmering, reduce the liquid contents of the cooking-pan by one-half: and serve hot, garnished with little sippets of toast. Should you tire of hedgehog cooked in these ways, any of the numerous rabbit recipes may be applied. It is to be presumed that most people would soon have enough of the hedgehog dishes.

WINTER

Countrymen often display a dry humour all their own.
At a shooting party we fell in with a beater, into
whose charge one of the guns had given a
well-filled cartridge-bag. Every now and
again we noticed that the beater thrust his
hand into the bag, and regarded the cartridges which
he pulled out with a puzzled look. We inquired the
reason, and it transpired that some of the cartridges
were loaded with No. 5 shot, and some with No. 5½,
and that the beater had been asked to sort them by
their owner, a gun of indifferent merits. He said,
in continuation of his story : " He did tell I he can't
get on nohow wi' sich mixed tackle. *I* reckon if
there weren't no shots in 'em at all 'twouldn't make
ne'er a marsel o' difference."

Rustic Wit

❦　❦　❦

Every oak-tree teems with life. Of insects alone five
hundred species look mainly to the oak for support.
When the tree grows to the age of fruitful-
ness—when sixty or seventy years have
passed over its head—then its population is
increased tenfold. Here is a reason for the incredible

The Oak City

supplies of fruit—the great majority of the acorns go to support the pensioners, and thousands must be sown if one is to have a chance to develop into a seedling. Squirrels come to feast and hide the acorns as they hide nuts ; the dormice come ; human children come with sacks for the sake of the pigs at home ; pheasants feast on the ground ; rooks, more wary, amid the branches ; hungry jays warn hungry wood-pigeons when the keeper approaches. To the animals, birds, and insects are added the parasite plants, fungi flourishing where a broken branch rots, lichens covering the bark, on the topmost bough the mistletoe.

❦   ❦   ❦

Were it not for the oaks there would be scanty winter faring and feasting for many wild creatures. When **Acorns** acorns and hazel-nuts are scarce, and full beech-masts are not plentiful, birds and beasts have an unusually hard struggle to tide over the winter, even should it be mild, as a paucity of nuts is supposed to foretell. Different creatures like their nut food in different conditions and at different times. The rooks in their greed pull the acorns from their cups where they grow, others do not relish them in their fresh green state, and wait until they are ripe and mellow. Pheasants, who are very partial to acorns in autumn and winter, when more delicate faring is not available, prefer to eat them just as they begin to sprout. Like corn and other seeds, acorns when sprouting possess a peculiarly attractive sweetness.

Some of the trees seem to produce fruit of extra sweetness or extra fine flavour—at least, the game-keeper finds that his pheasants seem to prefer to feed beneath certain trees. Perhaps it is that those trees which are most sun-drenched produce the sweetest acorns, just as the most exposed hazel-nuts on the topmost twigs are so much better than the pale ones of the lowest branches.

The keeper welcomes a generous supply of acorns—provided that the trees which yield them grow in his woods, and not exclusively near the boundary of his beat. Wood-pigeons, as soon as they have cleared the beech-mast, their specially favoured food, will stuff their crops with acorns to the bursting-point—and so grow fat. Acorns also form an important item in the winter fare of rabbits and deer. It is true that they draw rats to the coverts, and even when the last acorn has gone it is not easy to clear the rats away completely. Whether or not there are plentiful acorns, the keeper is much indebted to the oak for food for pheasants, because they are so fond of the spangle-galls, to be found in plenty on the backs of the leaves, that they prefer them even to the maize which is freely scattered. All the galls of the oak, whether oak-apples, or bullet, artichoke, spangle, or root galls, are the outcome of eggs laid by the various gall-wasps, and the pheasants know that within the spangle-galls are the grubs, feeding on the galls' flesh. Left to themselves, the grubs will in due time reach the chrysalis stage of existence, to be hatched in June as winged insects, and to lay in turn the eggs which cause the pretty vermilion-spotted galls. So the wheel of life turns again and would turn for ever if unspoked by the pheasant's beak.

In mid-November rabbits are at their fattest. Grass has been green, sweet, lush, and growing ; under the autumn sun, winter oats and wheat have sprung inches high, and rabbits have been enjoying rare feasts. The stoats, in turn, have found benefit in the autumn. It is on full-grown rabbits that they now depend chiefly for food. No longer can they feed on young birds ; nor are small rabbits often to be met. Rats show fight when attacked, and stoats prefer to tackle game without power of resistance. Full-grown hares have too much staying power to be hunted down, and they are too fond of making for the open fields to be worth hunting. There are mice and field-voles, but the fat rabbits of the woods are the most obvious of possible meals. No hunt is more determined, ferocious, or relentless than when a stoat hounds a big rabbit to its death.

Plump Rabbits

By scent alone the stoat runs down the rabbit chosen for its dinner. No matter how devious the rabbit's course, or how many other rabbits cross the trail, the one line of scent is followed to the end, and sooner or later the death-scream of the rabbit is inevitable. We

have often seen the last act of the tragedy. One
hunted rabbit made for the shelter of young underwood, cleverly twisting amid the jungle
of fern, grass, and bramble, so that
the leaping stoat could have been guided
only by scent ; the rabbit seemed to
understand that the hollowness of the bottom of old
wood offered few chances of dodging. At last the
rabbit grew exhausted ; and, at a loss to know where
to run to shake off its pursuer, but a few yards behind,
took to turning and twisting with redoubled energy,
now rounding a leafy stump, then dashing into a
clump of brambles, doubling, again rounding the
stump, again flashing through the brambles—then
sitting up for a second, listening to hear if the stoat
were still following. The stoat, thus baulked again
and again, grew ever more furious. Coming up on
the hot scent to the leafy stump, round which the
rabbit had slipped in the nick of time, it would dash in
so furiously as to make the brown leaves rattle off,
as a terrier leaps at a rabbit's seat from which the
owner has just fled. The burning scent throws the
pursuer into a frenzy. But the stoat, with a chatter
of rage, lost little time in following on into the bramble
clump ; and the sight of man near by was not enough
to turn it from its object. At last, in the brambles,
it came upon the rabbit dead-beat—charged in a blind
fury, sank its teeth into the head, worrying home the
grip. Then, having disabled the rabbit, it retired
a yard or two and charged again, retiring and charging

*The
Stoat's
Hunting*

at intervals, as if to gain fresh power for driving in the needle-sharp teeth. . . . At such a moment the keeper feels more than ever justified in shooting a stoat.

Waiting for the end of such a rabbit hunt, for a moment we lost sight of the chase ; then felt certain we could hear the hoarse breathing of the captured rabbit in a thick spot, on the opposite side of the 20-foot ride near where we were standing. Yet we felt certain that neither stoat nor rabbit had crossed from our side. We waited, and sure enough the stoat caught the rabbit almost at our feet, where we had thought them to be. The mystery of the heavy breathing remained—the sound was exactly that of a rabbit being mauled by a ferret within a burrow. We crossed the ride, made search, and discovered a large hedgehog curled up in its nest. While the bloodthirsty business had been going forward six or seven yards away, the hedgehog had lain snugly wrapped in winter sleep—actually snoring !

❦   ❦   ❦

A stoat, if accidentally deprived of its power of scent, would soon come to starvation. All animals depend on scent not only for their food but for their protection, their power of recognition, and for nearly all the interests of their lives.

Mysteries of Scent

The scent given off varies with occasion. In a state of rest it is modified. Thus a game-bird who has been on its nest for some time is in less danger

of discovery than one that has just come to the nest,
leaving a fresh trail. So the scent given off by
foxes varies with their own condition—as, of course,
with the weather. The greatest scent is left behind
by the fox when he is warm with running ; the least
is given off at the beginning of a run, or at the end,
when he is exhausted. The hunted fox well knows
that his life may depend on the strength or weakness
of his scent—this is made clear when he runs purposely through a herd of cattle or a flock of sheep.

Deluges of rain, burning sun, or extreme cold
obliterate fox-scent, but slight heat combined with
moisture, as when the sun shines after a warm shower,
is in favour of a strong and enduring trail. But there
is little certainty in the matter ; as Mr. Jorrocks truly
said, " Nothing so queer as scent 'cept a woman."
On a promising day hounds may be at fault when
within a score of yards of a fox ; but on a day so
apparently hopeless that few sportsmen trouble to
attend a meet, as when a thin crust of hard-frozen
snow covers the ground, the scent may be red-hot.
One day may yield a perfect scent ; on the next,
apparently with the same weather conditions, the
scent is elusive, and the hounds no sooner give tongue
than they fall silent. Much depends on the nature of
the country, or of the substance on which the volatile
scent particles fall. Crossing the meadows, the
hounds speak the line with certain voice ; but when
they come to dry, crumbling fallow-fields, the chorus
dies away into a few doubtful whimpers. The time

of the day has its effect on scent ; in midsummer the woods may have no perfume in particular at midday, but are filled with sweet smells in the evening. Every one knows how a warm autumnal shower brings out the savour of dead leaves and the smell of earth.

To the fox, as to the stoat, the sense of smelling is the most important of all. With his nose the fox discovers nearly all his food. If the sitting game-bird has flown to her nest, and herself gives off the least per-ceptible scent, the fox easily finds her by that strong scent given off by chipping eggs. By scent he picks up the young leverets, after quartering the ground to gather the greatest advantage of the wind. He scents young rabbits in the stop when a foot beneath the surface of the earth, and when he starts digging them out he goes directly to their nest. So a good ratting terrier will point through a couple of feet of soil to the exact spot where a rat is lying. We have sometimes thought that an invention to magnify scents would prove of great benefit to the gamekeeper. But there might be fatal effects if a keeper, scent-improver on nose, came suddenly on that mushroom of the fetid odour commonly known as the Stinkhorn.

❦   ❦   ❦

One of the many thorns that pierce the keeper's side is driven home at the time of the cutting of the under-wood. Once in every span of ten or twelve years this time must come. Now and again the felling of part of a covert before shooting improves matters from a sportsman's view—the beats are simplified, or are more easily commanded with the regulation number of from five to nine guns. But the keeper The Axe in the Coverts knows to his cost that more often than not cutting the underwood is ruination to sport.

Birds and rabbits are alarmed by the sound of the woodman's chopping, and half the hares fly before the smoke of the greenwood fires. Many complications arise through wood-cutting, as when the shooting is in other than the landlord's hands. When he wishes to cut certain portions of his woods, and the cutting may interfere seriously with sport or the showing of game, unpleasantness must arise among all parties—landlord, gamekeepers, shooting men, and copse-workers. Those responsible for the shooting should find out as early as possible which parts are to be cut, and arrange in good time with the landlord to make it a condition of sale that no cutting takes place before a convenient date. When several acres of underwood are felled, and the wood is left lying in long rows called drifts, a good deal of inconvenience may arise, unless the underwood is worked up as cut down. On shooting days half the pheasants in the place may skulk in the drifts, whence it will be impossible to dislodge them by ordinary beating methods of the most energetic type. Besides, drifts provide a safe refuge for rabbits. They increase incredibly, and in the following year they will be by far too plentiful for the welfare of the young shoots that spring from the shorn stumps.

Q

Thirty years ago the price of underwood as it stood growing, at twelve years old, was about twenty pounds an acre ; but to-day five pounds an acre is considered a good price for first-class underwood, so hard has the industry been hit by substitutes for ash and hazel. Though we have known underwood to fetch only half a crown an acre, we have seldom seen it described by auctioneers as other than " prime and ripe." The most useful kind is hazel. All sorts of sticks and stakes for the garden are cut of hazel. Wattle-fences are made of it, neatly woven, and the " hethers " which bind the tops of live fences. Closely woven hazel hurdles form a splendid protection for sheep from wind and rain ; they cost, to buy, about eight shillings a dozen, and the hurdler is paid about half that sum. Hazel is now largely used in making the crates in which the product of the Potteries is packed. The cleanest growths were formerly made into the hoops of barrels, and one might see thousands of bundles stacked in a clearing. But iron is killing the hoop-makers' industry. One use of hazel has been unaffected by time—the use to which the country blacksmith puts it, when he winds handles of the shoots for his chisels and wedges—being pliant, they allow his tools to adjust themselves to the blow of the hammer. And the hazel-wand remains the favourite divining-rod of the water-finders.

The Uses of Under-wood

❦   ❦   ❦

Gamekeepers are much associated with tipping. If tips are to be reckoned as part wages, the element of chance is great and unfair. There are cases when tipping amounts to bribery, as when a rich man buys the best place in a shoot.

The Tipping System

For the system, it may be said that a tip is the most convenient token of appreciation of skill in producing good sport. And we agree that if any servant of pleasure deserves a tip it is the game-keeper. But among the fallacies of the system is the fact that the scale of tips is seldom in proportion to skill and energy. Thus, a tip of a certain amount is given for a day's covert shooting of, say, under a hundred head, half pheasants, calling for a certain amount of energy and skill on the keeper's part. But a tip of only half the amount will be given after a thirty-brace day at driven partridges, which has afforded five times the amount of shooting, and called for ten times more skill and energy from the keeper. There is a saying among keepers that tips may be looked upon to provide three useful things—beer, 'baccy, and boots. In old times a five-pound note was the order of the day—this is represented now by half a sovereign or five shillings. A few keepers are lucky enough to serve where wealthy sportsmen shoot regularly, who willingly give the keeper a ten-pound note. But most keepers praise heaven for £10 received in tips in a season. Where the scale of tips most fails is when a tip covers compensation for injuries. But the beater who received a note on

account of a stray pellet in his person was more than
satisfied. "Bless you, sir," he said, "you may give
me the other barrel for another of 'em." But beaters
always find contentment in a tip, whatever its
size. We recall how three beaters were more or
less bagged successively during a three days' covert
shoot. One, at the time, appeared to have had his
right eye destroyed, but saw his way to accept twenty-
five shillings. Another buried a shot in his little
finger, and on receiving seven shillings was eager to
undergo the same treatment for six days a week. A
third was peppered behind, and awarded eighteen-
pence, which satisfied him, being, as he lamented,
"only a boy, like." By the way, there seems no
place in the sportsman's scale of tips for awards for
narrow escapes. We have known a keeper mention
the fact quite unavailingly that his cap had been shot
from his head by a careless gunner, who had brought
down an easy bird with his first barrel, then, swinging
round, had blazed at a second bird just as it topped
the keeper's head. "Aw," he drawled, by way of
answer, when the keeper respectfully intimated that
he had escaped death by a miracle, "I certainly ought
to have killed both of those birds."

❧   ❧   ❧

How many foxes have owed their deaths indirectly to
covert shooting ? It is a nice question for hunting
men. The fox is one of the craftiest creatures in the
world. A very short experience is enough to make

him associate the particular squeal of a rabbit when
caught in a snare with a cheap supper. And he

discovers quickly that luxurious banquets
await him after a day's covert shooting.
The discovery has a certain result ; after
covert shooting foxes gorge themselves,
and become totally unfit to stand before
hounds. To keepers this is well known, of course ;
and there are those who are not slow to take advantage of the fox's gluttony. Suppose a keeper thinks
that a fox or two the less would not be amiss, and
knows that on the morrow hounds are to be expected.
There is, suppose also, no covert shooting at the
moment in his immediate vicinity. Though unwilling
to take more direct steps, he is fully prepared to
handicap foxes before hounds so far as he may, and in
the night before hounds come he provides free suppers
for his foes. He is hardly to be blamed, and if blamed
by the hunt one keeper at least has a ready answer.
In view of a visit from so fine a pack, he says, he
wished to show that he had forgiven the doomed foxes
their sins, by spreading a final feast.

There are keepers who, not making the best of necessity, harbour in their breasts an undying grievance
against foxes and take every chance to malign the
foe. After a beat, during which the guns had stood
in a hollow where pheasants had come at a good
height, a sportsman was collecting birds that had
fallen behind him, and to his surprise found a
pheasant with its head apparently torn off. He

suggested to the keeper that there must be foxes in the wood—foxes near at hand, and very bold. The keeper had reason to know better—but on picking up another headless pheasant, remarked sadly, " If they treats 'em like this 'ere when they be dead, it be cruel to think how they'd serve 'em when they ketched 'em alive." The sportsman was impressed by the keeper's melancholy tone, and began to share his fox-enmity. But the keeper's sharp eyes had seen what fate really had befallen the pheasants' heads—a fate strange enough, for as the birds fell their heads were torn off by the forks of ash-stems, in which they caught.

❦   ❦   ❦

By many signs keepers read the story of the presence and work of foxes. A fox makes a half-hearted attempt to bury game that he has partly eaten, and wishes otherwise to dispose of—and the buried game is so impregnated with his scent that no other creature will touch it. He barks at night in mid-winter days—and spreads uneasiness among sheep, as betrayed by the bleating of ewes. He digs in a way all his own, throwing out the soil behind him in a slovenly heap ; he noses about mole-heaps and ant-hills, and his visit is easily detected. On soft spots he leaves his footmarks—and he always leaves his scent behind him. Pheasants without tails tell a story of a young fox's spring that failed to bring him a

Clues to the Thief

supper. Heads of rabbits, and nothing else, in snares, rejected maws lying near by—the disinterment of poaching cats which the keeper has buried— these show where hungry foxes have passed. By day their presence is revealed if a cock pheasant cries a sudden, uneasy, short alarm-note, by the screaming of jays, and by a particular blackbird note, which, if it does not mean stoat or cat, certainly bespeaks a fox. A crow may be seen suddenly swooping angrily as he passes over a field—a fox lurks there. The hidden cause for the continuous uneasy springing of partridges is often a fox, or at least a cub amusing himself by partridge hunting.

❦   ❦   ❦

A fox does not grow very old without learning how to take advantage of a snarer's catch. He learns to follow up runs and visit places where the **Muzzled by a Snare** snarer has set his snares. And he often pays the penalty, his feet falling foul of the noose. Hunting people commonly suppose that traps—steel gins—are the chief cause of fox-maiming, yet not once in a blue moon is a fox trapped. But if too clever to be caught in a trap, he is not clever enough to keep his feet out of the brass wire of the simple snare. We came across a curious instance showing how a fox may suffer from a snare. Hounds found a fox which ran to ground almost at once. Men were set to work to dig him out, and they found he was merely skin and bone, and round his

muzzle they found part of a brass snare. The wire
had fixed itself in such a way that he could scarcely
open his mouth, so that he was handicapped both in
catching food and eating it. From his appearance
it was thought that he had been in this miserable
plight for a month. It had been better for the fox
if hounds had found him a month earlier.

☙   ☙   ☙

A fox, in emergency, will sham death to perfection.
A Master of Hounds once noosed a fox in a whip
as he bolted before a terrier from an earth.
Cunning
Rascals The fox appeared to have been strangled—
when held up by the scruff of the neck his
eyes were seen to be closed, his jaws gaped, and the
body hung limply down from the hand. He was
placed tenderly on the ground—only to dash off
into covert. To be over-cunning is a common
fault. One fox entered a fowl-house, and amused
himself by killing every bird. In departing through
the hole by which he had entered, he stuck fast,
and was found hanging dead the next morning.
Another sought refuge from hounds by jumping on
to the low roof of a thatched cottage, and crawling
beneath the rafters until he could crawl no farther.
It was years before his skeleton was discovered.
Some of the foxes found dead on railway lines, by
the way, have been put there after death by vulpicides. In olden days the punishment for the crime
of fox-killing was a spell in the stocks. Vulpicides

remain, but the stocks—some would say alas !—
have gone from use for ever.

※　　※　　※

The hunting man has a hundred reasons why hunting
is a blessing to the community. He argues that
hunting circulates gold every year to the
tune of seven and a half million pounds—
and that this is good for the horse trade, the
forage trade, for the blacksmith, the harness-
maker, and for an army of grooms. Then hunting
tends to keep at their homes in the country wealthy
people, who might winter abroad if there were no
foxes to follow. This means that many large estab-
lishments are kept open, servants are kept in food
and wages, local tradesmen stand to benefit. Further,
it is claimed that there is little to be said against
hunting—we often hear how riders, horses, hounds,
and foxes all enjoy the sport ; on this point, however, we have no direct evidence from foxes. And
it is claimed that the amount of damage done to
agriculture is infinitesimal—though farmers who
have had hounds over young corn, or seeds, or fine
fields of turnips, might bring conflicting evidence to
bear on the point. Perhaps the favourite argument
in favour of hunting is that the sport is good for
horse-breeding, and that the hunting-field is the
finest training school for cavalry. Gamekeepers
would be among the first to lament the abolition of
fox-hunting, for if it were not for the existence of

A
Hunting
Argument

foxes and their preservation for the hounds, few
keepers would be required to protect game. Nor
would there be those useful little sums to the keeper's
credit on account of litters, finds, and stopping.

❦   ❦   ❦

Nobody can persuade a gamekeeper that dogs lack
reasoning powers. We were watching a terrier at
work, and she gave us a pretty example
The
Clever of something very like intelligence. A
Terrier pheasant was winged, fell on a bare field,
and ran for a thick dell—the terrier in
pursuit. She made one or two ineffectual attempts
to gather the bird, until within a score of yards of
the dell—then she raced ahead. She seemed to
realise that there was so much cover in the dell that
direct attempts to take the bird were risky—and she
proceeded to work the pheasant to a safe distance
from the cover before tackling it again, this time
effectively.

When this little terrier has marked a rabbit or a
rat in a patch of grass or brambles, her common sense
tells her that if she dives in after her quarry it may
dash out unseen by her, by reason of the grass or
brambles. So she stands by, and stamps, and otherwise tries to make her game bolt, in a way which
will allow her to see the direction ; and she is seldom
baffled. It is difficult to decide whether this terrier
is more or less reasonable than her kennel companion,
a retriever, when feeding-time comes. If at feeding-

time the retriever has a biscuit left over from the last meal, which she has lightly buried, on her master's approach she will promptly disinter the treasure, holding it out as much as to say : " Thank you, I need no biscuit." But experiments with the terrier show that she will ever refuse to give the slightest indication of a buried hoard. Whether she needs a biscuit or not, she always takes one when offered, as though she desired nothing better in the world.

A good story in proof of a retriever's reasoning powers is told by an old-time sportsman. He was shooting beside a frozen stream, and winged a mallard, which fell in mid-stream. His dog crashed on to the ice, broke through it, and fought her way to the middle, where the ice only skimmed the water. She swam round for a moment, then broke her way to the opposite bank, paused to give a knowing look at the thin ice, and went down stream at full speed for about eighty yards. Running down the bank, she broke a hole in the ice with her fore-paws, then crouched back, watching the hole. In a few moments she made a spring and plunged in, reappearing in mid-stream with the mallard in her mouth. There was no doubt, at least in her master's mind, that she had broken the hole for the purpose of catching the bird when he came up to breathe.

A keeper owned two retriever puppies who were given a curious start in life. Their mother was shut

up at home, while her master went to shoot some
rooks.   She was the proud mother of five new-born
puppies, but her litter was not complete.   A
Born
Retriev- few rooks had been shot, and the keeper was
ing waiting for others to appear, when up ran
the retriever carrying a rook in her mouth;
somehow she had managed to get out, and had followed
to see the sport.   She was sent back to her
puppies, and directly she reached home two new
puppies were born.   They were born, as one might
say, retrieving.

❦   ❦   ❦

The most common type of gunner is the man who
kills frequently, but is not a good shot because he
does not know how to take his birds.   He
Some would double his bag if he would put every
Sporting
Types shot a foot farther forward—that golden
foot forward—if he would not fire when in
the act of turning (which must depress the gun's
muzzle), and if he would remember that driven birds
on seeing a man rise immediately and instinctively,
even at right angles to their line of flight.   The keeper
detests the man who continually sends him to pick
up game which has never fallen.   For these knowing
gentlemen, he is a wise keeper who carries a special
bird or two in his pocket, against the time when they
say, in their haughty way, " Aw, my man, kindly
pick up my bird that fell tha-ar ! "

The luckiest shot we ever met was a colonel who,

one windy day, happened to be stationed by himself
on a road lined by telegraph-wires.   All the birds
came his way, and with ten shots he killed one.
Startled by his volleys, a bunch of passing birds
blundered into the telegraph-wires which, more deadly
than the gun, claimed nine victims.   The colonel
was a study in modesty when he remarked a little
later that in ten shots he had been lucky enough to
bag five brace.

Unfortunately the best stands for partridge-driving
are often behind hedges flanked by telegraph-wires.
This is specially unfortunate when the birds
Victims   see the guns just before they pass beneath
of
Wire   the wires.   Up they go, and a whole covey
may be cut to pieces at the moment when
fingers were pulling triggers.   Though a brace of
birds fall dead at the sportsman's feet, evidently
neatly taken in front, to the sportsman this is not the
same as a brace to his gun : he would prefer, indeed,
a good old-fashioned miss.

Many country people who ought to know better are
hazy on the distinction between stoats and weasels.
We can forgive the Cockney uncertainty of
Stoat or   this sort, as we forgive him for calling
Weasel?
rooks,   and   even   starlings,   crows.   The
countryman may well confuse crows and rooks ; his

safest plan when in doubt about a big black bird is to name him rook, for in most parts crows are now scarce to the point of extermination. But those who live in the country have as little excuse for speaking of stoats, when they should speak of weasels, as for mixing rabbits with hares. It is easier to tell a weasel from a stoat than a rabbit from a hare, if one is fairly close and has a clear view. A weasel is quite a third of the size of a stoat and a third of the weight : the males of both weasels and stoats are about twice the size of the females. But the outstanding distinction between stoat and weasel is the long, black-tufted tail of the stoat, and the short, unassuming tail of the weasel—no more conspicuous than a mole's tail.

We have come across many curious cases of ignorance on these points. A countryman who had dwelt with stoats and weasels all his life, and had killed hundreds by trap and gun, yet had no idea of the true difference. Whichever he saw, or killed and hung up by a twisted twig, he determined to be stoat or weasel according to its size. Then we remember a lady who kept chickens, and suffered the loss of half a brood. She called in a passing keeper to settle the question of the thief. After waiting a while the keeper shot a weasel in the act of returning for another chicken. The lady of the chickens was overjoyed at this retribution,

"The Horrid Badger"

and presented the keeper with half a crown. Her words in making the presentation have been treasured by the keeper : " This," said she, " is for shooting the horrid badger."

❧   ❧   ❧

To the old chalk-pit, where the sun is trapped and the winds are kept at bay, come all kinds of creatures for warmth and sanctuary. However de-

Chalk-Pit Haunts   serted the fields of winter seem to be— however silent and sullen—signs of life are never wanting in the chalk-pits ; they are as inns to wayfarers who search the country for a living and lodging. Creep silently, against the wind, to the chalk-pit's edge, and in summer or winter, sunshine or shower, on a still day or a windy, you will catch a glimpse of some wild creature, a visitor, or one of those who have made their home in the pit for the sake of sustenance or shelter.

❧   ❧   ❧

The sparrow-hawk may be caught napping on some favourite perch, as on a stunted tree, in a sheltered nook. The partridge covey may

When the Fox sleeps   be seen for a moment, as the birds revel in the powdery soil, roofed by an overhanging ledge—seeing you, they go whizzing off amid a little cloud of dust. In the dead herbage a wily old cock pheasant crouches, who long since denied himself the luxuries and the dangers of social

life in the big woodlands : he crouches as he sees
you, but not so quickly that you may not note the
sinking of his glossy neck. Two or three rabbits
scuttle off to the doors of their burrows. Through
the bushes a hare steals away. No chalk-pit is
complete without a rabbit-burrow, a blackbird, and a
robin. If hounds came more often to the chalk-
pits they would save themselves many a blank hour.
There is no peace for the fox in the coverts, but the
old chalk-pit is as quiet as a church.

An exciting moment for rabbiters comes if a fox
bolts from a burrow when only a rabbit is expected—

When Ferret meets Fox

so exciting a moment that if there is a
man with a gun the fox is lucky to escape
a shot—especially should he have in his
mouth the quivering body of a favourite
ferret. And the ferret is lucky to come
alive from a hole if he meets the fox in the only
passage by which he can leave the burrow. But
ferrets often escape if the burrow is not a proper fox-
earth, but has been used only as a temporary shelter.
Even if caught in the fox's jaws there may be hope
for the ferret ; we heard of one who was none the
worse for a long ride between a fox's teeth. Like
dogs and cats, foxes can be soft-mouthed if they will.
We have known a fox to deal so tenderly with a
captured rabbit that it ran about after the long
jaws had released their hold ; and for some time it

amused its captor as a mouse amuses a cat. A fox,
when he wishes, can carry an egg without breaking
the shell.

☙   ☙   ☙

Towards the end of January rabbits begin to fall
off in condition. As food becomes less nourishing
their reserve supplies of fat gradually
February dwindle. But with the end of the game
Rabbits season the price on their heads begins to
rise : and the keeper who has hard work to meet the
expenses of a shoot looks to the rabbit-catch of
February to swell the credit side of his accounts.
Most people know that a hen pheasant is more tender
and delicate to eat than a cock, though cock and hen
may be of the same age. So with rabbits—those
who sell rabbits might well charge a penny or two
more for the does than for bucks. The countryman
knows that the tenderest rabbits are those that he
may skin with the least difficulty.

☙   ☙   ☙

While the gamekeeper is seldom at fault in the
matter of a ready excuse, he meets many people who
are his superior in carrying ever-ready lies
The on their lips. From poachers and mouchers,
Moucher's
Excuse as the haunters of hedge-sides are called,
he might learn the lesson that no excuse
is better than a fine excuse that is shallow. One
Sunday morning a keeper, dressed in his go-to-meeting

R

clothes—a useful disguise—came sauntering silently
down a road bounded by unkempt hawthorn hedges.
His trained ear caught the sound of a dog careering
past him on the field-side of the road : then he saw
the dog's master, who, on seeing him, set up a
sudden and energetic whistling. Of this the dog
took no notice ; with his nose well down, he rushed
on to a rabbit-burrow and began digging furiously.
" These hedges are full of rats," remarked the dog's
master. " My dog killed five just now." Asked
what had happened to their bodies, Mr. Moucher
replied calmly, " He swallowed 'em whole." On the
keeper suggesting that there was not much chance
of finding a rat in the rabbit's burrow, the moucher
agreed, called off his dog, and went his way. In
the hedges there was no sign of a rat, but a few
rabbits managed to eke out an existence, though
heavily persecuted by gentlemen of the road.

❧   ❧   ❧

The opening of the hunting season proper brings
a new anxiety to the keeper. While it opens in
early November, no date is recognised. The
**When
Hounds
come**
keeper would like to see one fixed, and he
would make it after his coverts had been
shot at least once. Many shooting men
would also like to see the idea established that hounds
should not come to their woods until after the first
shoots, especially where there are many hares. Often
a landowner will refuse a master's request for per-

mission to come his way until he has done with his
coverts.   The keeper does not so much object to
the hounds merely passing through when in full
cry, for then the hounds run in a compact body, and
pay no attention to game.   They only disturb a
line about ten yards wide right through the woods.
What disturbs every game-bird and hare in the place
is drawing a covert, particularly when scent is bad
and foxes are in evidence, but not to be forced away.
Unhappy the keeper who must throw open his coverts
at all seasons while other neighbouring coverts are
closed.   The prohibition of one wood often leads to
the closing of many more ; and hunt officials are
well advised to break down, by every power of per-
suasion, all restrictions which favour one or two
keepers at the expense of brother keepers.   At any
rate, we think it would be an excellent idea that the
keeper whose coverts are always open to hounds
should have double the reward paid for a find to the
keeper whose coverts are open only after Christmas.

❦   ❦   ❦

Those who shoot in the wake of hounds are no sportsmen.   To state a case in illustration of this : A
sportsman has the shooting of a wood
When bounded on one side by another's fields.
Hounds In days gone by he was glad to keep a fox
are
gone for hounds, and gladly he would throw open
his wood to the hunt, in a reasonable way.
In the cause of sport, he was content that his pheasants

and hares should be driven out of his wood into his
neighbour's fields and hedgerows.   But when he found
that his neighbour was the sort of man to shoot
in the wake of hounds, so that the evicted creatures
were given no fair chance to return to their homewood,
but instead were shot in the afternoon following a
morning visit of hounds—he felt compelled to close
his wood to the hunt, with the natural sequence that
he was soon compelled to bar the covert to foxes
also.   No shooting days in the wake of hounds
should be a golden rule for all neighbourly neighbours.

☙   ☙   ☙

Of poachers there are many types ; and the worst
are the organised bands that hail chiefly from colliery
**Poachers'
Weapons**
and manufacturing districts. These men
are murderous ruffians, and the keeper who
interferes with them carries his life in his
hand.   Wives look anxiously indeed for their hus-
bands' return when such a band is about.   The
gangs chiefly practise night shooting, and pheasants
are their object.   But they are as ready to fire at a
keeper as at pheasants.   We were shown a single-
barrelled muzzle-loading gun which a keeper had
taken from such a poacher, who had shot a roosting
pheasant under his very eyes.   After the shot, the
keeper went up to the man, who pointed the gun
straight at his head, threatening to fire if he
advanced another yard.   But the keeper knew his
man—and his gun.   He knew there had been no time

for the ruffian to reload. He knocked up the barrel,
and caught his man, who in due time was sentenced
to nine months' imprisonment. Had his gun been
double-barrelled, it would have been another story,
and a tragic one. A favourite weapon, and a deadly,
in these poachers' hands is a heavy stone slung in a
stocking.

❦   ❦   ❦

For moles' skins the keeper has no sentiment. He
will not part with his skins of rare birds—but will
willingly barter the prospect of wearing a
Moles' Skins for Furs moles' skin waistcoat for the price of an ounce
of shag a skin. By catching moles he pleases
the farmers, who know no more than he
himself about any good work that moles do : he
frees his rides from unsightly heaps and raised
tunnellings ; and now and then his mole-traps catch a
weasel. Many keepers make a fair sum of money
each year by selling moles' skins ; furriers will as
readily give twopence for a skin as others threepence or
sixpence. The skins, cut close round the head, are
drawn from the moles' bodies as a man draws stock-
ings from his legs ; they are pegged out, fur down-
wards, on a board, to be dried and powdered with
alum, then are stuffed with meadow hay, and packed
by scores or hundreds. Perhaps no fur is quite so
soft and beautiful as the mole's ; and the keeper
is always well pleased to note how well the pelts of his
enemies become women-folk's faces.

To shoot while there are still many leaves on the underwood and trees, and while there is a full muster
of pheasants, or to wait until there are fewer
leaves and fewer pheasants—that often is
the question. For there are many coverts
in which pheasants will not stay after the
fall of the leaf. Then the shooting man who does not own the coverts to which his birds will betake themselves must make the best of things, and be content to bring down more leaves than pheasants, and often nothing but leaves. What with the showering of leaves and the crashing of shot-pruned boughs and dead wood, he may imagine that a pheasant must be an extra heavy bird—only to find that not a feather has been touched. To shoot pheasants among a crowd of leafy oaks is no simple matter—it is more difficult than to shoot a rocketer in the open valley. One thing may be said for this aggravating pastime ; it teaches the slow shooter to be quick.

Covert-shooting Problems

☙   ☙   ☙

There are good reasons for shooting coverts for the first time before the end of November, apart from the
fear of a leakage of pheasants. A sack of
corn a day will quickly swell a bill to uncomfortable proportions. Unshot coverts
also mean that the whole time of keepers
and watchers is taken up, with a string of
awkward consequences. Thus, little can be done to thin the rabbits, for fear of disturbing the other game in the

"Cocks only"— to compromise

coverts. Each night some of the hares go out, never
to return. Hunting must be curtailed in self-defence.
Then again, neighbours may be shooting, and it is
very certain that what goes into your neighbour's bag
cannot go into yours. The best compromise between
shooting in woods still leafy and waiting for the
sporting Christmas pheasant to soar far above the
tops of the bare trees, is to shoot " cocks only " at
the first covert shoots. This may be a perplexing
plan to those not accustomed to it—either they include a good many hens, or they let off a good many
cocks which they mistake for hens. It is a plan to
make the nervous man shoot his worst. And the
keeper, as a rule, will not be found to favour it, unless
the guns are discriminating and good, and appreciate
sport more than bag. But sooner or later the
day of " cocks only " must come—why should it not
come at the beginning and be done with ?

A strange confession was made by a cat-lover con-
cerning the cat of her fireside. The confession was
made publicly ; in fact, in the columns of an
obscure local paper. It was to the effect
that the cat had brought in to her kittens,
in one week, twenty-six field-mice, nineteen rabbits, ten moles, seven young birds, and
two squirrels—all of which passed through her
mistress's hands ; there may have been others not
taken account of. It never seemed to enter the head

What a
Cat may
kill

of the cat's mistress that any hurt was being done to
other people's interests by this poaching of rabbits,
nor that any neighbouring gamekeeper might read her
words. It would be unfair to argue that all cats,
with or without kittens, are as bad as this one ; we
have heard of cats a great deal worse. Naturally a
mother cat forages far and wide for food ; but she
hunts chiefly for small things, and knows that mice
and birds are more suitable for her weaning kittens
than sitting partridges and pheasants. It is that
arch old villain, Sir Thomas, who commits the crimes
for which mother cats are blamed. But the
keeper has no hesitation in bringing home to all cats
a reparation, sudden and effective, for Sir Thomas's
sins.

❦   ❦   ❦

A gamekeeper friend told us, with infinite delight,
this quaint little story. If we are to believe him,
he was sitting one fine September day behind
A Cockney Story the hedge of a cornfield, thinking about the
coveys hidden in the corn, when he became
aware that a lover and his lass were sitting
on the road side of the hedge, directly behind him.
They were Cockneys, and this was the first of their
days of country holiday-making. Presently the lover
speaks. " Emma," says he, " just look at this pretty
fly wot's settled on me 'and." " Lor' ! " says Emma,
" ain't he a daisy ? " A pause follows ; the lovers
are silently contemplating the beauties of the fly.

Emma suggests he is out for an airing in his racing colours—yellow and black. Then the lover calls out in a voice of mingled amusement and pain. " Crikey ! " he cries, " ain't 'is feet 'ot ? "

᳴   ᳴   ᳴

The hare that haunts a small holding has a slender chance of dying a natural death in ripe old age. But we have a little story of how a small-holder was converted from hare-shooting. He was a man who rented a meadow on the outskirts of a large village ; and it chanced that hares were much attracted to this pleasant spot. The gamekeeper of the shooting tenant was deeply troubled by the drain on his stock of hares caused by the small-holder ; but there was little he could do to stop the slaughter that went on at all times and seasons, and by all manner of means. He had the good sense to keep on friendly terms with the troublesome sportsman, and at last he thought that some improvement might be brought about by arranging a laugh at his expense. He stuffed a hare, and one night set up the skin in the meadow, at a fair range from a gap in the hedge. Early next morning the news reached the small-holder that there was a hare in his field. Off he started with gun and dog ; saw from the gap that the hare was sitting up, " jest about a pretty little shot," took steady aim, and fired both barrels to make sure of a kill. How his dog retrieved a hare-skin stuffed with hay was a story that soon

[margin note: Hares in Small Holdings]

became public property in the village and the neighbourhood, and from that day forward there has been no safer place for a hare than this man's meadow.

❦   ❦   ❦

The gamekeeper often picks up hints about poachers in unexpected ways. His wife, as a rule, takes no great interest in the affairs of game ; yet

The Sins of the Father every now and again she is able to tell her husband some news that may be at once bad and good. It happened that the wife of a highly respected gardener fell ill, and one afternoon the keeper's wife kindly offered to take charge of her children. The eldest child, a boy of about six, seemed to have little to say for himself ; but, as the party was walking silently along a lane, he suddenly said in a voice that promised well to be a bass some day : " Our muver, she do make we some good dinners." " Indeed," said the keeper's wife, " and what does she give you for dinner ? " The boy answered eagerly and proudly : " Bunny rabbits, m'm." " Indeed," said the keeper's wife again, " and where does mother get the bunny rabbits ? " " Please, m'm, faither buys 'em off a man as brings 'em." " Oh ! in-*deed !* " said the keeper's wife, and it was not long before one more receiver of stolen rabbits was brought to justice.

❦   ❦   ❦

When the oaks shed their leaves night has a new danger for the roosting pheasants. They become

easy targets for the gun of the night shooter. While
the leaves remain the pheasants are well screened—

The
Pheasants'
Roosting-
Trees

and they often owe their lives to their habit
of roosting in oaks, where the leaves give
shelter long after beeches are bare. On
a night of bright moonshine beeches
scarcely provide any cover for the bulky
form of a roosting pheasant. No doubt it is rather for
comfort than through cunning that pheasants choose
a roosting-place in oaks. They show no cunning in
choosing their oak-tree, for they will roost night after
night on some low branch overhanging a road. They
seem naturally to prefer oaks to beeches for a lodging.
Unlike most trees, oaks throw out their branches
horizontally, but beeches' branches tend to rise
vertically. Their bark is smooth and cold, but oak
bark is rough, easily gripped, and warm.

When oaks have lost all their leaves the beeches
provide the better cover ; for their vertical lines
form some sort of screen. Even with a full moon
it is not always easy to see sleeping pheasants which
go to roost in the lower branches. It may be more
difficult to see a roosting pheasant than to shoot it—
though the hardest shot a pheasant can give is when
it flies by night. Fir-trees in a pheasant covert have
a special value to the roosting birds. While unsuitable as sleeping-places, for the birds cannot fly up
through the thick twiggy branches, nor can they see
where they are going, the firs make the more suitable
roosting-trees warm and cosy, and against their dark

background it is difficult to see the pheasants, and to shoot them. The poacher has no liking for sporting shots.

☙   ☙   ☙

Wet weather is often a benefit to the fox. Like all accomplished night thieves he is more venturesome in attacking hand-reared birds when the wind howls and rain beats heavily down. The storm drowns what little noise there may be from his stealthy feet ; and the scent of the birds is stronger by reason of their steaming bodies. In wet autumns foxes take their heaviest toll of the young birds that have grown to a fair size —the dripping trees incline the birds to sleep on the ground long after they are able to fly, and should be flying nightly to roost. Grave risks are run by birds that sit on their nests through wet June nights.

The Fox in the Storm

☙   ☙   ☙

Foxes are sometimes found among pheasants where wire, or string netting, has been set up at the flushing-places, to prevent the birds running instead of flying, and to cause them to rise and fly at a sporting height and pace. When it is too late, and the beaters have come to the flushing-place, the indignant " cock-ups " of the pheasants are heard, and then they rise in a great rush, too thick and fast for the convenience of sport. We remember one case where a stampede of pheasants

Foxes at Pheasant Shoots

so enraged a sportsman that he ordered his loader to bowl over the old sinner of a fox.   Should a fox show himself during the beating of a wood, it would be wise to give him every chance to escape.   What usually happens is that the beaters force him forward with sticks and curses, and the guns drive him back with cries of " Tally-ho ! "

But the fox's appearance is disconcerting ; and there is a touch of irony in the thought that a crafty old fox, who in his time has slain more than his share of pheasants, should yet be in at the death of those that escaped him.

The careful gamekeeper will stop all the rabbit-holes round about the place where he hopes that many pheasants will fall—perhaps for fifty yards
Pheasants that go to Ground before and behind the stands of the sportsmen.   Many a pheasant is lost through going to ground in a rabbit-burrow, and there is seldom a spade and a grub-axe at hand. The pheasant may be winged or otherwise wounded, and if it cannot be dug out may die a lingering death. But many a crafty old cock has revealed his hiding-place because, while he has taken the precaution of drawing his body into a burrow, he has forgotten his tail.   Only one partridge, in our experience, has run to ground after being winged.

A wise pheasant would go abroad before the middle of November.   He would leave the fallen beechmast for the pigeons, and turn a deaf ear to the per-suasive whistling of the maize-laden keeper. Since the issue of his death-warrant on October 1, the pheasant has fared well— he has never known the want of a hearty breakfast. But sooner or later comes a morning when he must breakfast on the remnants of a last good supper.   If he wonders why, he never thinks he has been denied his food because a big breakfast is not good to fly on, because a full crop will lessen his value in the eyes of the game-dealer, and because it is intended that he shall fly high, and give a sporting shot.   So he is kept short, like a pig whose time has come to be made into pork.   But no doubt even his short life has been worth the living.

Phea-sants' Doomsday

❦   ❦   ❦

We have a story of a retriever who was forced to fore-go breakfast on the morning of a shoot.   Retrievers, as they grow old, often grow cunning, and we saw this one getting the better of his master in a novel and drastic way.   The old dog had grown fat, and somebody com-plained that he was inclined to be lazy in his work.   It was decided that he had too much to eat, and it was to improve his activity during a day's partridge driving that his master kept him without breakfast, usually a heavy meal.   There was a cold

The Hungry Retriever

partridge that came within range of the dog's nose—
but his longings were not gratified. Out in the fields
the dog was sent for the first bird his master shot,
a runner. Away went the dog with unusual speed ;
he picked up the bird, and then quietly sat down and
made a meal of it. Having had his breakfast, he did
his work handsomely for the rest of the day.

* * *

The first covert shoot has a peculiar charm for the
sportsman—especially when the shoot is in familiar
woods. There has grown a feeling of friend-
The Old ship for the old rides and trees, and they
Wood seem to offer a warmer welcome every year.
He comes to the historic corner where he failed miser-
ably to do justice to a rush of pheasants. Here is
the opening through which his first woodcock tried to
glide—in vain. He remembers, perhaps, that even now
he has that woodcock's two pen-feathers in the depths
of some ancient purse. Here was where he scored a
double at partridges hurtling through the tree-tops
—only to be beaten a moment later by a hare, slowly
cantering. Nothing has changed in the woods.
They wear the same old look of nakedness ; save for
a hurrying pigeon, there is the same desolate lifeless-
ness. Nothing stirs, but the leaf fluttering to earth ;
all is dead quiet. Then in the distance is heard the
prelude of the beaters' sticks—tap, tap, tapping.
The sportsman dreams, musing of past days and their
great deeds. Then a lithe moving form catches his

eye—a hare has slipped out of sight. A shot rings out, echoes and re-echoes; another, and doubles, and clusters of shots. The old wood is the old wood still.

❦   ❦   ❦

Perhaps not many shooting men remember much about the old days of the muzzle-loader, or could recall all the items of the paraphernalia **Memories** necessary for a fair day's sport. In spite of **of** **Muzzle-** all their drawbacks, wonderful feats were **loaders** performed by the old guns; and certainly there was a truer ring about the word sport in the good old times. A fancy-dress shooting party, with the sportsmen in the old-time shooting-suits, armed with muzzle-loaders, would be entertaining —if dangerous. How many members of the party would arrive on the scene of action with all the appliances necessary for the firing of a fowling-piece —powder, shot, wads, and caps? And who would know how to load his weapon, even with powder, shot, wads, and caps at hand? The man who did not know how to load would be in a bad way, for, of course, no valets could be allowed on the scene, even supposing they might know more than their masters. Short-tempered men would be exploding perpetually in wrath at the delays caused by the process of loading, while birds were rising and going away—we have heard powerful language addressed even to the modern weapon when it has been responsible for a

hitch in shooting. It is shocking even to think
of what a short-tempered man might say if he
flung away an open box full of copper caps in mistake
for an empty case, or if he applied his powder-flask
to his lips and swallowed a few drachms of treble
strong black powder instead of a few drops of sloe-gin.
No doubt some of the party would suffer the misfortune of upsetting their whole supply of shot for the
day's sport.   Then the short-tempered man sooner or
later would break his ramrod—others would shoot
ramrods, like arrows, into the air.   At the end of the
day there would be headaches and black-and-blue
shoulders.   And what would be the bag ?

The old-time gunner went out in the morning with
all manner of contrivances and implements stowed
about his person.   He wore a shot-belt for
Relics distributing the weight of his lead, he carried
of the neat little magazines, so that he might the
Great
Days more easily handle his copper percussion-
caps, and he wore a wallet of leather containing such tools as a nipple-wrench and spare parts
—the nipples in the gun might break or blow out.
The careful man carried a wad-punch, and in emergency would punch wads for his muzzle-loader out of
his felt hat or his neighbour's—what could be a more
neighbourly act than to sacrifice a pair of leather
gaiters in the cause of wads ? A keeper friend
treasures many relics of the great days of the old

s

squire—among them a curious little mirror, the glass about the size of your little-finger nail, set at the top of a tiny brass box, small enough to slip into the barrel of a twenty-bore. The old squire would draw this mirror from his waistcoat pocket before the first charge was poured into the muzzle of his gun, dropping it glass upwards down each barrel in turn, so that he could see by the reflected light if they were well cleaned and polished.

❧   ❧   ❧

The cleaning of a muzzle-loader was an immense undertaking. First, the barrels were removed from the stocks, then bucketfuls of hot water were forced through them; out would pour a stream of black, liquid filth, having no respect for clothes or person, and smelling abominably. Heated water was used because it cleaned away all the foulness of the black powder, and quickly dried off. After washing, the barrels were fixed in vices carefully padded to prevent injury, and then they were given a hearty polishing inside with a tow-topped rod. Great attention was paid to the locks, which were not so well protected from water as they are to-day—they were removed every now and then, and taken apart by means of a neat little clamp for holding the mainspring. In those days people spoke of how many pounds of shot they had fired—not of how many cartridges. The old-time bags were not to be despised. One keeper,

Cleaning a Muzzle-loader

who has been in his present place for forty odd years, told us that he can always remember his last day's shooting with muzzle-loaders, because they bagged the same number of hares as pheasants—218—to say nothing of 324 rabbits.   They must have performed some wonderful feats of loading as well as shooting.

At covert shoots beaters often behave in unaccountable ways; but it is not every day a beater is seen

The Knowing Beater

crawling about on hands and knees.   A guest at a covert shoot, surprised at such a sight, inquired about the beater's object. "Beg pardon, sir; I thought as 'ow you was the guv'ner," said the beater, rising.   A further question as to why the guv'ner should be met on all fours brought this answer: "Well, you see, sir, 'tis this way like—the guv'ner, 'e don't allow no game to git up 'igh, not if 'e can anyways 'elp it.   Not 'e, for 'e wops it into any birds as rises 'ardly afore they be got on their wings like.   So you see, sir, soon as I thinks I be gittin' dangerous near 'im, I allus reckons to be a bit careful."

The shepherd and the gamekeeper are men in sympathy, for one is dependent to some extent on the other. In the eyes of the keeper, the shepherd is one of the most important persons on a farm.   And where there is not a good understanding between the two men the keeper will suffer loss in game, and the shepherd not only in sheep, but in rabbits. With rabbits to spare, the keeper's first thought is of his friend **Old Friends** the shepherd. The shepherd is vigilant by night as well as by day, and may watch the interests of game without detriment to his own charge. And it is a pleasure to the keeper to run his eye over the fold when he passes that way to see if all is well. He comes to the rescue of many a sheep on its back that would have remained on its back until dead without his timely aid ; and he saves the shepherd many possible disasters through the flock breaking from the fold, when the sheep might come to destruction by over-feeding on greenstuffs. Through the long nights of the lambing-time the keeper may give the shepherd his company over pipes of fragrant shag, and pots of heart-cheering ale—hands, hearts, and ale alike made warm by the little stove in the shepherd's movable house on wheels. Look well at a shepherd's back, and you are likely to see a keeper's old coat.

❧   ❧   ❧

Shepherds like their pot of beer—and some of them are wondrously fond of a fight, and so may become useful allies to the keeper when poachers are to be dealt with. We knew a shepherd who would always be especially retained to help the keepers of an estate at times when pheasants were liable to be shot at night. His appointment came about in this way:

the head keeper, during the absence of an assistant,
had employed the shepherd to watch, and had dosed
him with half a gallon of beer to keep the
cold out before sending him off on duty.   The
**What
Shep-
herds
enjoy**
beer and the night air were not without
effect; and when presently a human form
came stealthily along in the shadow of a moon-
lit ride, the shepherd was in grand fighting trim and
spirit.   He waited his chance, then sprang like a lion
on the intruder, gripped his throat, bore him to the
earth, and belaboured him in hearty fashion.   He was
about to tie him hand and foot when he saw that he was
tackling his own master from the mansion, who, having
been dining with a neighbour, had chosen to walk
home by way of his woods.   So impressed was the
master with the shepherd's valour on behalf of his
pheasants that he gave him a sovereign, and retained
him on the night staff at five shillings a night—*and* half
a gallon of beer.

⚘   ⚘   ⚘

Like most country workers, shepherds and gamekeepers may go through a long life of labour without
ever taking a holiday, possibly without
**Lives
of
Labour**
thinking of one.   We hear of eight-hour
days for factory workers and discussions
of an ideal work-day of six or even of four
hours ; but seldom a word is spoken for those country
labourers, the length of whose toil is limited only by
daylight—when it is not carried on as a matter of

course into the night. Farm hands may work
through all the days of the year ; for where there is
stock to be fed work is never-ceasing. Yet it is
reasonable to suppose that holidays are as needful
to the countryman as to the townsman, and that if
the farm labourer or the shepherd were sent away
to the sea every year for a fortnight's rest and
change, he would work with a new energy that
would more than compensate for the work lost. It
would be something at least to break the deadly
monotony of the daily round, even if the labourer
had no ideas for profitably spending a holiday.

    ❦   ❦   ❦

For the shepherd the days and nights of January
are heavy with responsibility—he counts himself
In the lucky if he can find time for an hour's sleep.
Folds   It is wonderful how the shepherd of a large
flock knows all the ewes and the lambs
over which he now watches. In his lambs he has a
personal interest, for there may be a sixpence in his
purse for each lamb that lives to be deprived of its
tail. The shepherd's knowledge of the lambs sur-
passes that of the ewes, whom sometimes he deceives;
for it is by scent rather than sight that the mother
recognises her offspring, while the shepherd believes
only what he sees. By fastening the skin of a dead
lamb on to an orphan he will induce a bereaved ewe
to adopt the orphan, and she will accept, guard, and
love it as if it were her own.

January is to the shepherd what June is to the gamekeeper. There is more than common meaning

Shep-
herds'
Care

to the shepherd in the greeting, " A happy and a prosperous New Year." Be luck good or bad, the bleat of the lamb is the sweetest sound of the year to shepherd ears : it means as much as the pee-peep of the pheasant chick to the gamekeeper. Keepers and shepherds are deeply attached to their respective " coops "— a word used by the shepherd for the enclosures, one hurdle square, made for the lambs. The experience of coop life is briefer for the lamb than for the young pheasant. After enjoying a few hours of privacy, the ewe and her lambs are turned into the large general nursery, to fend for themselves among the baa-ing crowd.

❧   ❧   ❧

Weather makes more difference to partridge-driving than to most forms of shooting. The ideal day

Winter
Partridge-
driving

comes when the weather is mild, and the air still. Then only can the movements of partridges be controlled with some certainty—not that partridges ever can be driven against their will. In high wind their speed is tremendous, and a hundred birds do not give the chances of ten too tired to swerve. In hard, frosty weather, when the fields are like rough paving-stones, though the day is still, the birds are up and off before the advancing driving-line can shape itself to influence their flight. But in mild, still weather, the soft soil clogs the birds' feet, they are slow to rise, and packs and coveys become split up and their ranks disorganised—to the advantage of the sportsmen.

A mild day may open hopefully enough, but if driving rain comes with blustering wind the sport is spoiled.

On a frosty day, when things have been going badly, the guns may be congratulating themselves as they reach some big turnip-fields for which the birds have been making. A turnip-field may be expected to steady and control the departure and the direction of birds ; but in the grip of frost turnips are only a little better than the bare, frozen field. For the leaves, that yesterday made luxuriant cover, to-day are flattened to the ground by the frost. Even the charlock, which may have done so much to make up for the thinness of the turnips, has been shrivelled to a few brown stems. Why the farmer leaves the late-grown charlock untouched is because he knows that before it reaches seed-time the frost will have killed every plant. On a small shoot, frost-flattened turnips may ruin the hope of a full day's partridge-driving. On big shoots frost counts for less, for long drives can be taken. Short drives in winter partridge-driving are seldom profitable— whether a shoot be small or big.

❦   ❦   ❦

By the very poor snow is regarded as among the most terrible calamities of life. Many types of countrymen, rural publicans, postmen, out-door labourers, and small traders, speak of snow as the worst of all possible weather, leaving the most serious after-effects. And snow means calamity to many wild things. Lucky are the robins of a garden who have a friend to stir the old hot-bed, and turn up the worms from beneath the frozen top-soil; happy the grain-feeding birds who find a rick that has been threshed. Thousands flock to the corn-ricks, and there is food for all—pheasants, partridges, rooks, jackdaws, starlings, sparrows, greenfinches, chaffinches, yellow-hammers, and the bramble-finches, orange, white, and black in plumage. To the holly-trees come the starving thrushes, and in hard weather even the fieldfares will lose their extreme shyness to besiege a holly-tree beside a door. The more delicate redwings die in thousands, though the dying and dead are seldom seen.

To a few the snow means profit—for the hawks there is a carnival of feasting, and the fox finds weak and hungry hares and rabbits an easy prey, if ill-nourished on a diet of tree-bark and withered herbage. As to the pheasants, they are well cared for—and the keeper, in snowy weather, scatters his maize with a liberal hand.

☙   ☙   ☙

By many signs wild creatures inform the game-keeper of the approach of hard weather. The wood-pigeons give him useful warning. In most

Hard-
Weather
Prophets

parts of the country flocks of pigeons take toll of the greens and root-crops—a thousand pigeons may be seen rising from a single field of roots. In mild weather they may return once or twice during a day. When they are seen constantly streaming to the root-fields, those disturbed returning again and again, it is a certain sign that hard weather is near.

      ⚘   ⚘   ⚘

Animals have a reputation as weather prophets—if their prophecies strike the human observer as some-what obvious. The cat washes her face,

Weather-
wise
Beasts
and
Birds

and this is commonly held to be a sign of coming rain ; in summer it is thought to be a sign of a thunder-storm when cats are remarkably lively. Dogs sometimes bury their bones when rain is in the air—perhaps an inherited instinct to save food against days of bad hunting. Horses by stretching their necks and sniffing the air seem to be scenting distant rain ; and donkeys have a way of braying before the storm. Shepherds hold that if sheep turn their tails wind-ward rain will come ; and cowherds read the same prophecy when a herd of cows gathers at one end of a pasture, their tails to the wind. Changes in weather mean much to wild life, and we are prepared to believe they are forewarned. A storm may mean the loss of a meal to a fox, a ruined nest to a bird, an end of all things to an insect. The fox has done well that has eaten heartily before the storm. Yet it appears that a change of weather must be near at hand before wild creatures take notice. The pheasant crows before the thunderstorm because he hears distant thunder. The wheatear, a bird nervous of clouds, flies to shelter as the cloud drives up. It is the first touch of cold weather that sets squirrels hiding nuts.

Weather has a marked effect on the moods of wild creatures. There are days when hares or partridges seem overcome by oppression; they move listlessly if disturbed, and lie or sit about as though all energy had gone from them. Thunder in the air may be the cause, or perhaps snow is coming; when the storm has blown over, liveliness is restored, and new life inspires all things. Before a storm, partridges in the stubble-fields set up their feathers, and in cold weather the feathers of many birds have the appearance of being puffed out, so that they look almost twice their usual size. Many creatures feed at an unusually early hour if storms are coming. It is a bad sign when rabbits are out feeding in the fields early on a bright sunshiny afternoon. The birds of the open fields— rooks, starlings, pigeons, or fieldfares—feed hungrily and hastily while rain-clouds overshadow the sky; but it is a sign of good weather when rooks fly to feed far from their roosting-trees, and fly high. Cock pheasants will go to roost early before the storm, choosing low branches, and trees that afford good protection. In bitter weather, even the warm feathers of birds may become ice-bound.

❦   ❦   ❦

Between a green and a white winter in England there is a world of difference to wild creatures. There may

Green Winters come day upon day, week upon week, of mist, rain, fog, and blustering winds, of hail, sleet, and furious snow-blizzards—to birds and beasts these are days of prosperity and fatness. Peewits, snipe, woodcock, blackbirds, and thrushes then find food far more plentiful than in the hot dusty days of late summer. Often, in late summer, their breasts are narrowed by leanness to the shape of a boat's keel. But in moist, warm winter days the flesh rises roundly as if it would burst the skin—the breast-bone, no longer up-standing like a bare ridge, is buried almost out of sight in a valley of fat, on the thighs are little hillocks of fat, and the bones of the back cannot be seen or felt for their thick warm covering. But should there come two or three days of frost, which hold through the day and increase their grip on the land by night, then this loaded store of fat vanishes as mist before the sun.

❦   ❦   ❦

A mild open autumn and a green winter also mean much to the farmers and to the gamekeepers ; a blessing on many accounts, a curse on others. The farmer groans because his land is so wet and heavy that he cannot sow his winter seeds ; the keeper sees the ruination of many a promising day's sport. The keeper gains when there are no frost and snow by having the pleasure of showing bills for corn reduced to a minimum—in a mild winter he will not need half the amount of corn that must be distributed to his birds in hard weather, when they are actually in need of food. What little he gives them in open weather is to keep them together, as natural food is abundant. But a low bill for corn hardly compensates the keeper for rain-spoiled sport, or for day after day of outdoor work in the wet. The work cannot be done in a way to satisfy the keeper—or possibly others. And the rain means that he falls behind with that everlasting tax on his time entailed by keeping rabbits within bounds. After a mild, open winter, by the time the game-shooting season is ended, and coverts are available for rabbit-killing, young rabbits have already made their appearance. The keeper welcomes a short spell of really hard weather in February, so that he may the more easily catch up all the pheasants he needs for penning. Otherwise the kind of winter that best suits him is a dry one—without hard frost.

What Rainy Days bring

We met a gamekeeper who had been blessed with a litter of fox cubs born about the middle of December— just before the usual mating-time of the foxes.

Cubs at Christmas When most of the season's cubs would be born these Christmas cubs would be three months old, and well grounded in the elements of a fox's education. And when the pheasants and partridges began to sit they could save their mother a deal of laborious work—as our friend the keeper found out. In cub-hunting days, there must have been some rude shocks for the puppies of the pack, and even the old stagers of hounds must have been taken aback when they came to close quarters with one of these forward cubs. The keeper caught one, and by a strange chance. He had been expecting a visit from hounds. He knew an earth where he thought that possibly a vixen later on might have a family ; not willing to disturb the place by spade-work when stopping it, he stuffed the entrance with sacks. Hounds came and went—and afterwards the keeper visited the earth to recover his sacks. What was his surprise when he found that inside one of the sacks a cub had curled itself comfortably for sleep. Well knowing that if he were to say there was a litter of cubs on his ground at Christmas none would believe him, he put the cub into a capacious pocket. Then when he told the story of his early litter, and was laughed at for his pains, he confounded sceptics by drawing the little fox, alive and uninjured, from his coat-tails.

The keeper always has a supply of odd jobs on hand to occupy his time on a soaking wet day, or when a snow-storm rages. He has always plenty to **Work for** do—but much of his work cannot be done **Rainy** properly in bad weather, and to work out of **Days** doors on a wet day may be as much a waste of time as to work indoors on a fine day on matters of no moment. It would be foolish to go ferreting in heavy rain—nets become soaked, rabbits will not bolt, and digging for ferrets in soft mud is heart-breaking work ; at the end of the day, while there may be a few rabbits that look as if they have been bathing in mud, there is all the tackle to be dried for the next day. Then again, it would be sheer waste of time to stop rabbit-burrows when snow has freshly fallen, for half the holes would be hidden, and the work would have to be done over again. It pays to wait until the next day, when rabbits have been out to feed and the holes are seen easily.

When he decides to stay under cover the keeper hardly knows where to begin, as he looks about his store-houses and sheds. Here are traps that should be cleaned and overhauled, broken chains to be mended, bent parts to be carefully straightened—a little judicious filing and a drop of oil are needed here and there to make all parts work together smoothly and swiftly. Snares must be overhauled and sorted, the sound ones to be neatly shaped so that the noose stays open ready for use, and each one must be fitted with its string, teeler, and plug. A supply of new snares may be made.   Plugs and pegs may be shaped, for holding snares and traps, from a length of solid ash which the keeper knows to be well seasoned, so that it will not crack when he drives it into stony ground with his heavy, steel-shod heel.   For months he has treasured that piece of ash—and terrible was the vengeance that he vowed on his wife when she dared to hint that it would serve nicely for her copper fire.

⚜   ⚜   ⚜

The wet day brings the chance for doing various little carpentering jobs, long neglected.   The keeper may have set himself the task of making a new **The Old Lumber** hand-barrow before the coming of another pheasant-rearing time—a barrow for carrying the coops, two at a time, with the hen and precious chicks within, where a horse and cart cannot pass through the coverts.   Perhaps he remembers a day when the crazy handle of the old barrow snapped off and upset two coops of his best birds. Then a wet day is a good day for sorting coops, and putting apart for professional treatment those beyond the keeper's makeshift craft.   He can set about painting the whole ones.   Now and again he must look to his ferret-hutches, and fit new wire-netting to the fronts if any meshes are rotten with rust— should the ferrets escape there is no telling what may happen.   And guns are never the worse for an extra special examination, and a thorough cleaning and

oiling. An all-round tidying-up of his varied assortment of tackle certainly makes for a temporary
improvement in the look of his work-places—but,
as it has been with every clearance, the same old
lumber is once more reprieved. " You see," says the
keeper, " it might come in useful some time."

           🦊   🦊   🦊

Soon after Christmas the gamekeeper hears the barking of foxes at night, and he well knows the reason.
The foxes are searching for mates. And
here is one of many reasons why hounds in
these days fail to find foxes in woods never
hitherto drawn blank. Hunting and shooting have disturbed the quiet of the coverts, the
underwood harvest is going forward, the supply of
fox-food is shorter than at any other time, and is most
hard to catch ; so foxes generally have forsaken their
haunts, finding lodging in out-of-the-way places
which offer some chance of peace and quietness.
Followers of hounds have much to learn about the
ways of the fox in January. They go from one blank
covert to another, cheerfully riding an intervening
couple of miles, while all the time the fox is lurking
in a dell or a hedgerow only two hundred yards from
the first covert drawn. Yet a suggestion that the
dell or the hedgerow should be tried meets with silent
scorn. This might be expected from people who hunt
to ride, or people new to the hunting-field ; but it does

When
Foxes
mate

T

not become the experienced to pin all their faith to the well-known coverts. In a southern county hounds have disturbed no fewer than twelve foxes together—probably a collection of suitors for the pad of one or two eligible vixens.

❧   ❧   ❧

On a Sunday after Christmas we paid a visit to an old keeper, who, on his own confession, had not dined wisely on the good fare provided by his wife on Christmas Day. Into our sympathetic ears he poured the strangest tale of the dreams that he had dreamed. The first began pleasantly enough, but ended in a nightmare. He was one of a party shooting in his best wood, and he was ever in the hottest part of the hottest corner, but each time he threw up his gun to shoot the crowds of pheasants, the gun fell all in pieces. Never, he said, had he known such a nightmare ; though some of the other dreams that succeeded were bad enough.

A Keeper's Dreams

One was to the effect that on an important occasion all the birds of his coverts utterly refused to rise and rocket, and when he pressed them with beaters he found that one and all had turned into foxes. This dream merged into one in which the foxes in his preserves were so numerous that they outnumbered and overpowered the hounds, and then attacked the Master, who was eaten. And there was a dream in which the old keeper found that he had changed places with his employer, whom he roundly abused for the mistakes he made in placing stops and managing the beaters. The climax of this was the unkindest cut of all. The gamekeeper dreamt that his employer, far from bearing him any ill-will for the abuse, sent to his cottage on Christmas Eve a large tin of tobacco, beneath the lid of which was a ten-pound note. This worthy old man has had many queer dreams in his time—if we are to believe him. He is ready to confess, for the sake of the story following the confession, that he has never really mastered the art of shooting driven partridges. But one night he dreamt that he had brought off the most masterly right and left, and from far and near congratulations on his brace poured upon him. Then he awoke to find himself in his own familiar chair by the fireside, in the chill dawn of a winter morning, and the local doctor, who was also a sportsman, was telling him how there had arrived safely in the room upstairs a brace of fine young keepers.

❦ ❦ ❦

We can vouch for the truth of this fox story : An old keeper—the keeper of a shoot where partridges were preferred to foxes—lay dying. It was **A Death-bed Vision** late in May, when the partridges were beginning to sit. Suddenly he called for his two sons and told them of a dream. In a certain burrow in a certain wood adjoining his partridge fields he had dreamt of a litter of cubs. And he refused to be comforted until his sons had gone forth to verify his dream. In due time they came home with enough evidence that the dream was of true things to allow the old man to give up the ghost with an untroubled mind.

❦   ❦   ❦

The partridge at Christmas is at his best—as a test of reputations. In this respect there is a world of difference between the slow, simple yellow-legged bird of September and the partridge of December. To bag a brace from a September covey is satisfactory to a sportsman. To get a bird with each barrel at an October drive is no mean thing. But to bring off a double event at Christmas partridges is to make a reputation. And it is to experience a feeling of goodwill towards the whole world. For Christmas and cold hands excuse a multitude of misses.

Christmas Sport

The birds whirl over the line of guns like brown clusters of bullets. And if the sportsman is tested, the gamekeeper's reputation hangs also in the balance; his highest art is called for if he is to drive birds in the desired direction. Whether or not his birds have been much harassed by previous driving makes a difference to his chances. Success will be appreciated, for sportsmen keenly relish a selected partridge drive as a foretaste to a pheasant shoot. When the drive is over and the pheasants' turn has come, they feel in slightly faster but certainly smoother water.

No bird is more artful than an old cock pheasant, or better able to take care of himself. At this season a

Cunning Cock Phea-sants solitary cock may be observed night after night roosting in some isolated tree, out in the wind-swept fields, and far from the sheltered coverts. Yet you may hunt this bird all day, high and low, in vain. When, on the way home, you pass his dark form on a lonely perch, you feel he deserves to rest in peace. Sometimes the old cock is over-cunning, or too confident in the safety of his retreat. He may allow one to approach within a few feet, although he certainly heard footsteps in time to make his escape. A certain keeper can tell many tales of the inglorious ends of his cunning cock pheasants, but most of these episodes are better forgotten.

☙   ☙   ☙

Winter flocks of pigeons are here to-day and gone to-morrow, travelling far in search of food. If they

A Dish of Greens find little or no beech-mast or acorns, they are forced early in winter to a diet of salad. It must be a relief to the wandering hosts when they come to a place where acorns are in plenty. In hard winters, turnips supply a great part of wood-pigeons' food ; and it used to be held that from this food their flesh acquired too pronounced a flavour, so that nice judges, who at other times thought them a delicate dish, would reject them. One old-

time sportsman held that the green leaves of turnips
gave a peculiar and very palatable flavour to the flesh
of larks and partridges.   In this connection we always
think of the story told by Gilbert White of a neighbour
who shot a ring-dove as it was returning from feed
and going to roost.   " When his wife had picked and
drawn it, she found its craw stuffed with the most nice
and tender tops of turnips.   These she washed and
boiled, and so sat down to a choice and delicate plate
of greens, culled and provided in this extraordinary
manner."

❧   ❧   ❧

Shooting parties in the week following Christmas have
a festive air.   As at the hall, so in the keeper's cottage,
the air is charged with the Christmas spirit.   Ten
o'clock on any morning soon after Christmas
Christ-   Day may find the keeper entertaining a
mas
Shoots   crowd of beaters at the expense of his own
private cellar, and the good things from the
cellar are served hot and spiced.   In hats and caps
are seasonable tokens—sprigs of mistletoe and holly.
The keeper himself does not wear button-holes, but
should his children make a garland of holly for the
collar of his old retriever, he will leave it for the
brambles to pull away.   The guns turn up late—
they have been dancing through the night ; when all
are met, in the brief greetings, in the distribution of
cartridge-bags, and in the inquiries about weather and
the possible bag, there is a note of unusual cheeriness.

At a Boxing Day shooting-lunch the talk among the guns was upon the ways and wiles of woodcock.

One spoke of his long bill, with its sensitive
Wood- nerves, which tell the bird what he has found
cock
Talk when the bill forages among the dead leaves ;
speculating as to whether he lived by his powers of suction only. Another wondered if the eating qualities of woodcock legs were really improved by pulling out the sinews. The question arose : Is the man who shoots a woodcock entitled to its pen-feathers, or is the man who first finds and secures those delicate trophies best entitled to stick them in the band of his hat? Woodcock provoked many controversies. Is there any secret in the proper roasting of them ? Would the law absolve a man who shot his fellow when shooting 'cock ?—and would the fact that he shot his bird as well as his man make any difference ? How many people could swear to have seen the mother woodcock carrying her young ; and exactly how does she carry them ? How many of the home-bred birds leave us in autumn ? What proportion of woodcock comes in from abroad, and what is the difference between the foreigners and the genuine Britishers ? In answer to the last question, a suggestion was made that the foreign birds were large and light in colour, but the British birds small and dark. Around this point arose a discussion, and the keeper was called in to give his opinion. " It ain't nothin' at all to do with Englishmen and foreigners," he said. " It be whether they be cocks or hens, and 'tis the large light uns that be the hens."

Most gamekeepers hold the killing of a hen pheasant after Christmas to be a moral crime.   And perhaps most genuine sportsmen feel a twinge of the conscience when they pull a trigger at a hen in New Year days—irrespective of the host's permission.   Of course, when the orders are to spare hens, the man who kills or even tries to kill one does something that the keeper will not forget— he loses caste for ever in the keeper's eyes; whereas the man who is not greedy to take advantage of an impromptu permission to shoot hens ensures for himself a niche in the keeper's good graces.

Spare the Hens

It is true, there are hens and hens.   Only a churlish keeper would not admire the man who stops one of those skyscraping hens, of the sort bagged by ordinary gunners about once in a lifetime.   But the order, " Shoot hens if they are real tall ones," alarms a keeper—unless he has full confidence in the guns of a party.   When the word has been given, it is wonderful how many hens are " real tall ones." There are excuses which must be accepted : for in certain conditions of light, when the golden moment for pressing the trigger is within grasp, it is almost impossible to distinguish hens from cocks—length of tail is then the most reliable evidence.

We remember a knowing old keeper who laid a plot to ensure at least a merry start to a Christmas shoot, when " Cocks only " was the order of the day.   This worthy, when catching up birds for his pens, had gathered together some twenty super-

fluous cocks. These, a dishevelled and more or less
tailless crew, he carried just before starting-time
to a dell thick with spruce, chosen doubtless for
decency's sake : and on a plausible pretext lined out
his guns between the dell and a wood. But he
forgot there was no natural inducement to the birds
to fly in the face of evident danger—and all the birds
broke away out of gunshot, and so suddenly as to
make their recent history all too evident.

❦   ❦   ❦

Boxing Day, in many parts, remains a regulation
fixture for rabbit-shooting by tenants, local tradesmen, keepers, and their friends. Nobody
could possibly appreciate the exciting nature
of these shoots unless present in person.
It is safer to be present only in spirit.

A Free-and-Easy

Otherwise, shot-proof cover becomes the
most desirable thing in the world : and it often
seems a wonder how more than one man can survive the day to count the bag. Talking to a tenant-
farmer on such an occasion, we noticed that his
hands were covered with warts, and suggested
remedies. "They b'aint woorts, bless ye—they be
only shots," came a proud answer—the honourable
wounds of many rabbit-shooting campaigns.

At another tenant-and-tradesman shoot we found
the guns unduly plentiful—there were twenty to
begin with, and the party grew as the day wore on.

But all of a sudden there was a magic disappearance of a large proportion of sportsmen, corresponding with the appearance of an important-looking individual, who calmly went to the man next to us, and relieved him of his piece and cartridges, which he began to use in a liberal fashion. Gradually, the original gunners reappeared—mostly from fir-trees. And it transpired that they were gunners without licences—who had taken courage when they saw the local officer of the law stretching a point himself. One, bolder than the others, made an appeal to the law for a ruling on the licensing question—and was informed that notice must be given of the imminent use of the gun, in order that the law's representative might have time to look the other way.

☙   ☙   ☙

The gamekeeper, perhaps, believes less in ghosts than other countrymen. He is not afraid to keep vigil in the loneliest wood, though well known to be haunted by a headless spectre. He carries a gun, and his dog is at heel, so it may be that the ghosts are afraid of the keeper. We know a house where great alarm was caused by the ghostly ringing of bells. Watches were set, and one watcher after another made report of a flitting figure, clad in white, that roamed the corridors. At last the keeper was called in to deal with the ghost. He took up his watch,

A Keeper's Ghost-Story

his trusty gun, loaded with buckshot, in his hand.
" There I bid," he relates, " till jest on twelve o'clock
—when all of a sudden the old baize door at the end
of the stone passage opens, of its own accord like,
and in slips the ghost. I ups wi' m' gun, and I sez,
' Be you the ghost ? ' sez I. ' And if ye moves,'
sez I, ' I shoots.' Three times I speaks, gruffer
and gruffer each time. And then I makes a rush for
the ghost—wot turns out arter all to be Mary the
'ouse-maid." " What did you do with Mary ? " we
asked the story-teller. " Lor' love ye, I took and
married 'er out o' the way."

This same keeper let us into the secret of his
shattered faith in ghosts. As a young man he and
a fellow under-keeper had been told off to watch
the carriage-drive for night poachers. In a jocular
moment the head-keeper warned them not to be
afraid if they should see the estate ghost—the headless body of an old coachman driving a pair of gallop-
ing horses harnessed to a hearse. Naturally, the
two young keepers, as the night wore on, fell to
talking about the headless apparition. Presently,
sure enough, hoofs were heard, and a hearse came
lumbering down the drive. The watchers crouched
low in the heap of dead bracken in which they were
hidden. Asked, an hour later, if they had seen the
poachers, " No," they said bravely ; " we only saw
the old fellow without a head, driving his hearse."
" Well," said the head-keeper, chuckling, " if you'd
looked inside his hearse you would have found it full

of corpses—rabbits' corpses! Me and Bill, we ketched the ghost, whiles he was drinking your 'ealth."

※   ※   ※

Many gamekeepers we have known. Looking back down the years we can summon to view a serried regiment of the servants of sport ; large men and small, rough and gentle, brown-clad men, some in velveteen, others in rough tweed, most of them in stout leggings, all with the keen eyes of watchmen, bronzed by the sun, beaten by the weather ; good men and true, every man of them. The best of them are strong, upright, fearless, full of confidence ; men who neither beg favours nor grant them ; set their own standards ; keep their own counsels ; take no false oaths, whatever the provocation of the poacher ; who, in preserving game, have no enmity against other living creatures ; who are all-round sportsmen and lovers of fair play. At the end of the long line, farthest from view yet most distinct, stands an old man with silver hair, with light blue eyes, and a face kindly, yet sharp as a hawk's, the keeper who was first to show us how to hold a gun.

Many fine stories this old man would tell, leaning over a gate, gun in hand, of Master this and Master that, uncles and such-like, even then old men to a boy's eyes, yet still called, by the older keeper, by their familiar names. " I mind the time," he would

Side note: Old Friends in Velveteen

begin, his eyes twinkling : and then he would ramble off into the history of some wild affray with gipsies or with poachers, enough to make a boy's hair stand on end.

One time that often came to his mind was when Master Charles plagued the life out of him to be taken, at night, through a bedroom window, by way of a ladder, on a hunt for poachers ; and how at last he yielded to entreaty, though it was as much as his place was worth if Master Charles's guardian got wind of the affair. So he chose a bright moon-lit night, when he was tolerably certain that no poachers would venture forth; whistled beneath Master Charles's window, upraised a ladder, and got the young gentleman safely to ground, in nothing more than nightshirt, greatcoat, and bedroom slippers. Off they went together, and it was the keeper's heart that beat fastest. Arrived in the Long Walk, what should they see but two poachers with bows and arrows, shooting the pheasants in their sleep. The keeper's first idea was to send the young master back to bed ; but he was not to be denied this grand adventure : and with a yell and a bound he was among the poachers before the keeper could say Jack Robinson. It was a desperate affair, not only for the poachers, but more particularly for the game-keeper ; but he still lives to tell the tale, with ever more wonderful variations.

❦   ❦   ❦

A favourite story of another old friend tells how he found the cure for a notorious poacher. It was

The Con- in the days before the Ground Game Act, **verted** and a farmer had complained, as well he **Shepherd** might, of rabbits that had cleared every blade of a field of oats, and were beginning to attack some wheat in the next field. The keeper set many traps and wires. His cottage was a long way from the wheatfield : but the cottage of the poacher, a shepherd, was near at hand. Knowing that the shepherd would in any case keep an eye on the captured rabbits, the keeper went to him, and frankly invited him to remove all those caught overnight, and keep them safe until he should come himself in the morning. The keeper, of course, could tell where a rabbit had been caught ; and no doubt the shepherd knew this, for he delivered up each night's catch to a rabbit. And he confessed, at the end of a week's campaign, that the confidence placed in him so unexpectedly had broken his heart of its love of poaching for ever.

☙   ☙   ☙

All keepers are shamed when sportsmen go home from their preserves with empty bags. To have

A Final in a party a shooter " who never shot **Story** noth'n' all day long " reacts on the keeper's fame. We noticed that a crafty keeper friend would always scheme to place an old colonel well forward of the line of guns; and as the colonel was never seen to add to the bag, we asked for an explanation. "Well, ye see, it be like this 'ere," came the answer. "I knows as 'e can't shoot, and 'e knows it; but I knows and 'e knows that if 'e be put forward 'e be likely to get a shot at a rabbit what's stopped to think. And 'e knows that I knows that 'e will pay somethink 'andsome when 'e can go 'ome an' tell 'is missus as 'ow 'e ain't bin an' disgraced 'isself agin. So I puts 'im forward; and every time 'e shoots a rabbit what's stopped to think, it reminds 'e of I."

With many gamekeepers we have known many game-keepers' wives. Strong-minded, capable women as they are, most keepers are wise enough to regard them as Ministers of Finance, religiously handing over all their gain in coins. A shilling a week, perhaps, is handed back again by way of pocket-money, besides an allowance of 'baccy, out of housekeeping funds. We have known more than one keeper who never would have had a shilling had it not been for his wife; and we have known more than one keeper's wife who would never fail to keep her hand on every shilling that her good-man brought home.

Careful Wives

One old friend, old Henry, made up his mind to revolt against his wife's cupidity. Coming home one winter night after a shoot, at which he had been so lucky as to pocket a couple of pounds, the temptation to conceal them from his good dame was irresistible. He buried the coins beside an old ash-stump in one of his woods—well beyond scenting distance from his cottage. He knew from many a past experience that if he left a farthing in his pockets overnight it would be gone before morning. That night no sleep came to him. His conscience was troubled. He turned and tossed; as his good-wife put it, "He carried on like, so as he couldn't sleep hisself, nor wouldn't let I." At last the good woman, who had drawn his pockets in vain, put a straight question: "'Enry," said she, "what *be* up with 'ee?" Then 'Enry confessed: he told how he had buried two pounds beside the ash-stump. And then the two of them rose, in the middle of that winter night, and walked out into the wood until they stumbled on the ash-stump, and they dug until they found the money. As poor Henry used to say, in days when no good-wife remained to take his gains, "That'll tell ye a little what her was like."

"What
Her
was
Like"

INDEX